ROUTLEDGE LIBRARY EDITIONS: PURITANISM

Volume 5

POETS AND PURITANS

POETS AND PURITANS

T. R. GLOVER

LONDON AND NEW YORK

First published in 1915 by Methuen & Co. Ltd.

This edition first published in 2021
by Routledge
2 Park Square, Milton Park, Abingdon, Oxon OX14 4RN

and by Routledge
52 Vanderbilt Avenue, New York, NY 10017

Routledge is an imprint of the Taylor & Francis Group, an informa business

© 1915 T. R. Glover

All rights reserved. No part of this book may be reprinted or reproduced or utilised in any form or by any electronic, mechanical, or other means, now known or hereafter invented, including photocopying and recording, or in any information storage or retrieval system, without permission in writing from the publishers.

Trademark notice: Product or corporate names may be trademarks or registered trademarks, and are used only for identification and explanation without intent to infringe.

British Library Cataloguing in Publication Data
A catalogue record for this book is available from the British Library

ISBN: 978-0-367-56981-5 (Set)
ISBN: 978-1-00-311164-1 (Set) (ebk)
ISBN: 978-0-367-62663-1 (Volume 5) (hbk)
ISBN: 978-1-00-311070-5 (Volume 5) (ebk)

Publisher's Note
The publisher has gone to great lengths to ensure the quality of this reprint but points out that some imperfections in the original copies may be apparent.

Disclaimer
The publisher has made every effort to trace copyright holders and would welcome correspondence from those they have been unable to trace.

POETS AND PURITANS

BY
T. R. GLOVER

METHUEN & CO. LTD.
36 ESSEX STREET W.C.
LONDON

First Published in 1915

TO
MARGARET GILCHRIST FINLAY
AND
HUNTER GILCHRIST FINLAY

PREFACE

WANDERING among books and enjoying them, I find in a certain sense that, the more I enjoy them, the harder becomes the task of criticism, the less sure one's faith in critical canons, and the fewer the canons themselves. Of one thing, though, I grow more and more sure,—that the real business of the critic is to find out what is right with a great work of art,— book, song, statue, or picture — not what is wrong. Plenty of things may be wrong, but it is what is right that really counts. If the critic's work is to be worth while, it is the great element in the thing that he has to seek and to find—to learn what it is that makes it live and gives it its appeal, so that, as Montaigne said about Plutarch, men "cannot do without" it; why it is that in a world, where everything that can be "scrapped" is "scrapped," is thrown aside and forgotten, this thing, this book or picture, refuses to be ignored, but captures and charms men generations after its maker has passed away.

With such a quest a man must not be in a hurry, and he does best to linger in company with the great men whose work he wishes to understand, and to postpone criticism to intimacy. This book comes in the end to be a record of personal acquaintances and of enjoyment. But one is never done with knowing the greatest men or the greatest works of art—they carry you on and on, and at the last you feel you are only beginning. That is my experience. I would not say that I know these men, of whom I have written, thoroughly—a man of sense would hardly say that, but I can say that I have enjoyed my work, and that, whatever other people may find it, to me it has been a delight and an illumination.

T. R. G.

St John's College,
Cambridge,
February 1915.

CONTENTS

	PAGE
SPENSER	1
MILTON	34
EVELYN	74
BUNYAN	104
COWPER	144
BOSWELL	175
CRABBE	211
WORDSWORTH	242
CARLYLE	279
INDEX	315

An acute young critic, who saw some of the proofs, has asked me, with a hint of irony, whether Evelyn and Boswell were Puritans or Poets. Any reader who has a conscience about the matter must omit these essays.

POETS AND PURITANS

SPENSER

SOME time ago I was reading the *Faerie Queene*, and one evening I laid aside the poem for a little. I was wishful to know what I ought to think of what I had read. I turned to the work of a biographer of Spenser,[1] and I happened upon the place in which he sets out the faults of the poem. I found that the allegory breaks down, that it is diffuse and inconsequent, that two or even three or four figures may stand for one thing; and again that the allegory is crossed by contemporary history hardly disguised at all, and is complicated with pagan mythology; that the poet is guilty of affectation of the antique in the structure of his scheme, the garbs and habits of his knights, and in his own language; in fact, that Ben Jonson was right in saying "Spenser writ no language"; that some of his passages, if innocent in intention, are hardly to be innocently read; and finally that the flattery of Queen Elizabeth, which pervades the whole, is excessive, and indeed a gross flaw upon the art and character of the poet.

The doubt came to my mind as to whether it were worth while to go on reading such a poem—a doubt that must often occur to those who read criticism. Happily this time I laid the critic down and took the poet up again, and read on till the Blatant Beast was captured by Sir Calidore, though to be sure, as the poet says and

---

[1] Dean Church. Mr J. W. Mackail, in his *Springs of Helicon*, adds several other counts to the indictment.

as I had perhaps reason to believe, it escaped, and goes barking and biting—

Ne spareth he the gentle Poets rime.

The poet, once accepted, had made his own impression despite the faults which the critic—it is true, an admiring critic—had found in him. But now I was thrown back on another question which I had to solve, for the unexamined life is after all, as Plato said, un-live-able for a human being. What was it that had triumphed over the defects of the *Faerie Queene*? Why had it been such a prolonged happiness to read it, and why did it leave so strong a sense of a permanent enrichment of one's life?

There can be no doubt that one great cause of this is the power of sheer beauty over the mind. It invades and it penetrates, and insensibly it brings peace.

> O! turne thy rudder hitherward awhile
> Here may thy storme-bett vessell safely ryde,
> This is the Port of rest from troublous toyle,
> The worldes sweet In from paine and wearisome turmoyle (ii. 12, 32).

Such a "sweet In" many a weary heart has found in the beauty of the *Faerie Queene*. But then a question may again be raised. These lines come from the song of the Mermaids. Is the peace that the great poem brings a vanity from which the Palmer with temperate advice would discounsel us? Can we trust it? In his *Hymne in Honour of Beautie* the poet suggests that we can.

> Therefore where-ever that thou doest behold
> A comely corpse, with beautie faire endewed,
> Know this for certaine, that the same doth hold
> A beauteous soule, with fair conditions thewed,
> Fit to receive the seede of vertue strewed;
> For all that faire is, is by nature good;
> That is a signe to know the gentle blood.
>
> (*H. Beautie*, 134.)

SPENSER

This is what the poets feel about their work. The pleasure which it produces is no trivial thing—it is, as Wordsworth said,[1] "an acknowledgment of the beauty of the universe," "a task light and easy to him who looks at the world in the spirit of love." Poetry depends on truth, on true feeling and true expression; its essence is not delusion but interpretation. It has well been called a "touchstone for insincerity."[2] No one, who read the *Faerie Queene* with an open heart, could think of Spenser as anything but one of the most deeply sincere of poets. For some his poetry lies too far away from the real. Yet if we watch our words, we have to own that there are two "reals," and that Spenser takes us from the accidental-real into the ideal-real—which he at least as a loyal Platonist and true mystic would call the true world.

But that true world of the ideal is rarely reached by those who have not made use of this common world, or if they do reach it they find it empty. They have travelled by the Negative Path and arrive with empty hands. But the poets take another way, and Spenser is as true a poet as he is a mystic. He has "looked at the world in the spirit of love." He has seen and fallen in love with "this worlds faire workemanship," and for him Atè has never managed (though it is evident that she tried)

> that great golden chaine quite to divide
> With which it blessed Concord hath together tide.
> (iv. 1, 30.)

So much is done for him by his gift of keen realization of beauty—the genuine experience of the world which none have but those who are in heart poets.

But such responsiveness to beauty carries with it a converse in a heightened sensibility to impressions of pain and ugliness. This is not however all loss. Fair and foul, foul-in-fair and fair-in-foul make this strange fabric

---

[1] Preface to *Lyrical Ballads*, 1800.
[2] Walter Raleigh, *Shakespeare*, p. 88.

and society we call the world. The great poets know them all, and better than the rest of us. Hence it is that Poetry is a thing (in the old definition) "of more high seriousness, of more intensity, than History." It is the interpretation of the world reached by a beautiful soul, greatly gifted for experience.

Spenser tells us that the Red Cross Knight, purified and strengthened by Truth, always does kill the dragon. Perhaps we shall not believe this at first hearing. Let us postpone decision, but let us keep in the company of the poet—this at least nothing can take away from us as we read—and as we move through scene after scene with this strong and serene spirit, so sensitive to all impressions of beauty, so happy in his knowledge of their meaning, so high and so pure, is it not possible that we too may look on the world at last in the spirit of love, and find that the golden Chain still holds it? This at least some of his friends found—

> For he hath taught hye drifts in shepeherdes weedes,
> And deepe conceites now singes in *Faeries* deedes.
> (Prefatory verses of R. S.)

Of Spenser's life the general course is well known; the detail not so well. He was born in London, he says—

> Mery London, my most kyndly Nurse,
> That to me gave this Lifes first native sourse.
> (*Prothm.* 129.)[1]

The date of his birth was 1552, or perhaps 1553—the latter the year in which Rabelais died and Queen Mary ascended the throne of England. The poet's parents must have been Protestants, and on the mind of a London child in a Protestant home the impressions of early years must have been indelible. When he was five or six years old Elizabeth succeeded Mary; and if, in years long after, the poet's praise of Elizabeth seems excessive, it is well to

[1] *Cf.* his references to Troynovant (London) in iii. 9, 38, 45 f.

reflect that the combination of the words Queen and Elizabeth had meant in his childhood that the fires of Smithfield were put out, and for long during his manhood the same combination was the surest guarantee that those fires would not be re-lit.

In 1561 the Merchant Taylors' School was founded in London,[1] and Edmund Spenser must have been one of its first scholars. The accounts of the expenditures at the funeral of Robert Nowell,[2] in February 156$\frac{8}{9}$, among very many items of less present interest, record gowns given to six scholars from the school, and among them is Edmund Spenser. In the same year the accounts of the same family contain the entry, under April 28, 1569;

"to Edmond Spensore, scholler of the m'chante tayler scholl, at his gowinge to penbrocke hall in chambridge, x^s."

A month later he was entered at Pembroke Hall,[3] and almost simultaneously a book appeared in which were printed without his name some lines that are certainly his —a pleasant conjunction of excitements. The lines were some blank verse translations of the French poet du Bellay, whose sonnets had appeared only the year before, and others in rhyme from Petrarch. Years after, Spenser re-issued them—the Visions of Petrarch little changed, the others rhymed as sonnets. One thought, to be met several times in Spenser's later works, is found already here in a rendering itself strangely prophetic of what he was to do with the English language—

>   Manie Muses, and the Nymphes withall,
>   That sweetly in accord did tune their voyce
>   To the soft sounding of the waters fall.

A curious letter survives of one of his College friends,

---

[1] It is perhaps of interest to note that the first English Algebra was published in 1557—Record's *Whetstone of Wit*. The author invented the sign =, and explained how to extract a square root; but Spenser may have escaped all this.

[2] R. W. Church, *Spenser*, p. 8.

[3] *Cf. Faerie Queene*, iv. 11, 34.

Gabriel Harvey, which tells of Cambridge in those days. A few lines may be picked from it. "*Xenophon* and *Plato* reckoned among discoursers, and conceited superficial fellows; . . . Petrarch and Boccace in every man's mouth . . . the *French* and *Italian* highly regarded; the *Latin* and *Greek* but lightly . . . *Turkish* affairs familiarly known: castles built in the air: much ado and little help: in no age so little so much made of; every one highly in his own favour . . . the Gospel taught, not learnt . . . *the Light, the Light* in every man's lips, but mark their eyes, and you will say that they are rather like owls than eagles . . . no more ado about caps and surplices: Mr *Cartwright* quite forgotten."[1] Here we have the Cambridge life of Spenser,—French and Italian poets, hardly prescribed perhaps by the dons; Greek and Latin; Puritan controversy; wars and rumours of wars—don John won his battle of Lepanto over the Turks in 1571;—and, the most abiding and perhaps most valuable feature of Cambridge architecture, castles in the air.

What use Spenser made of his time is plain to see in his poems. "Having," as his friend "E. K." put it in 1579, "the sound of those auncient Poetes still ringing in his eares, he mought needes, in singing, hit out some of theyr tunes." A close study of Plato, probably in Greek, certainly in the commentary of Ficino, left on him the deep impress that Plato must always make on sensitive natures.[2]

In 1576 Spenser graduated Master of Arts, and for the next two years he lived in "the North parts"—

---

[1] R. W. Church, *Spenser*, p. 25. Thomas Cartwright was appointed Lady Margaret Professor of Divinity in 1569. His lectures on Church Government drew great audiences. He was deprived of his chair in Dec. 1570, and of his Trinity Fellowship Sept. 1571—interesting episodes, all in Spenser's Cambridge days.

[2] See generally J. S. Harrison's interesting volume on *Platonism in English Poetry of the 16th and 17th Centuries* (New York, 1903), a book which every student of Spenser will be glad to have studied.

perhaps as a tutor. And there, and then, the story says, he fell in love with Rosalind, "the widdowes daughter of the glen." Colin Clout says so, and says she would have none of him. This may have been essential for Idyllic purposes. In 1578 he came South again. The following year saw the appearance of North's *Plutarch* and Spenser's own first volume *The Shepheard's Calendar*. Meanwhile the "Shepherd" went to Court and "saw good manners." He became the friend of Sir Philip Sidney and other heroic men. The splendour of the court lives in his verse, but not less its sordidness and ugliness. A great poet can be terribly clear-sighted for the actual.

In 1580 a great change came in Spenser's life. He went to Ireland with Lord Grey of Wilton, from whom he afterwards drew Sir Arthegall, the Knight of Justice with the Yron Man, Talus, for his squire. An iron man was needed. The Irish were in rebellion, and Spanish and Italian adventurers were holding Smerwick.[1] The rest of his life Spenser passed in Ireland, with only an occasional visit to England. He eventually received a grant of 3000 acres and Kilcolman Castle. There is in his fragmentary book on Mutabilitie abundant evidence of his sense of the beauty of the land, and he says as much in prose.

"And sure it is yet a most beautifull and sweet country as any is under heaven, seamed throughout with many goodly rivers, replenished with all sortes of fish, most abundantly sprinckled with many sweet Ilandes and goodly lakes . . . adorned with goodly woodes fitt for building of howses and shippes. . . . And lastly the heavens most milde and temperat, though somewhat more moyst then the part toward the West." But he has other things to tell of it—"nightly bordrags," wolves and "outlaws fell."[2]

In these Irish years much happened. Sir Philip

[1] The surrender was made 9 Nov. 1580. [2] *Colin Clout*, 314.

Sidney fell at Zutphen in 1586. The Armada came, but *flavit Deus et dissipati sunt*—many of the galleons being wrecked on the West of Ireland. Sir Walter Raleigh, the "Shepherd of the Ocean" came—

> And, when he heard the musicke which I made,
> He found himselfe full greatly pleasd at it.
> (*C. C. C.* 70.)

He told Spenser he was "alwaies idle"—like Virgil *studiis florentem ignobilis oti*—and bore him off to London to publish the first three books of the *Faerie Queene* in 1590. It was now that Spenser received his pension from the Queen, a poor one indeed—but "all this for a song," said Lord Burleigh.[1] He was brought into the next three books in one or two places for his saying.

Spenser went back to Ireland, sick of the Court. In 1594 he married a lady called Elizabeth and wrote his beautiful *Epithalamion* for her—the purest and most exquisite thing of the kind that bride ever had from lover. She too had "long loose yellow locks lyke golden wyre" (*Epithal.* 154). They had four years of married life and several little children. His two little boys he called Sylvanus and Peregrine, playful allusive names—like that of Hesperius which the poet Ausonius had given his son. Then in September 1598 the poet was promoted to be Sheriff of Cork but Ireland was again in rebellion. Arlo was a "chief fastness of the rebels," and in October they took and burnt Kilcolman Castle. Twenty years later Ben Jonson told the story to Drummond of Hawthornden—"that Spencer's goods were robbed by the Irish, and his house and a little child burnt, he and his wife escaped, and after died for want of bread in King Street; he refused 20 pieces sent him by my lord Essex, and said he was sure he had no time to spend them." His death (16 Jan. 1599) may

---

[1] So Edward Phillips, nephew of Milton, in his *Theatrum Poetarum Anglicorum* (1675).

not actually have been for want of bread, but his spirit was broken. He was buried in Westminster Abbey near the grave of Chaucer, "his hearse being attended by poets, and mournful elegies and poems with the pens that wrote them thrown into his tomb" (Camden).

Spenser, like every other poet and great man, is the child of his age. Whatever remains for such men in posterity, they inherit their own age as no others can. The large heart and the open mind absorb life in a wonderful way. Few periods of English history have been so interesting and so various. To begin with, there was the new sense for truth, and the new search for truth, together embodied in the great parallel movements (if they are not one) which we call the Renaissance and the Reformation. Old Learning, new Geography and eternal Religion—the elements came together; and Truth was carried alive into the heart of mankind by passion. The spiritual experience was the centre of it.

This was the atmosphere into which Spenser was born, which he breathed. It is wonderful to see how in his poetry the whole life of the day sooner or later is felt and finds expression in beauty. Let us begin at the circumference and work back to the centre.

In 1580, the year of Spenser's settlement in Ireland, Francis Drake came home after a voyage of nearly three years. Worm-eaten and heavy with weeds the *Golden Hind* entered Plymouth Sound on 26 September. She had been round the world, through seas no Englishman had sailed, strange oceans and archipelagoes. When men thought of where Drake had sailed and what he had seen, nor Drake only, there would be a quick response to such lines as these—

> Rich Oranochy, though but knowen late;
> And that huge River, which doth beare his name
> Of warlike Amazons, who doe possesse the same
> (iv. 11, 21).

When Spenser describes Fansy, like a lovely Boy, he goes to America for his garb—

> His garment nether was of silke nor say,
> But paynted plumes in goodly order dight,
> Like as the sunburnt Indians do aray
> Their tawney bodies in their proudest plight
> (iii. 12, 8).[1]

Drake had come home by the East Indies, and a year or so after Spenser's death the East India Company was formed in 1600. Hakluyt published in 1589 his book, "The Principall Navigations, Voiages and Discoveries of the English Nation made by Sea or over land to the most remote and farthest distant quarters of the earth." England was one in all this, and Spenser was her true-born son.

We may find another sign of the times in a strange little corner of his poem. When Belphœbe finds "the soveraine weede" to heal the wounds of Timias, the poet is not quite certain

> whether yt divine Tobacco were,
> Or Panachæa, or Polygony (iii. 5, 32).

King James had other adjectives for it. Raleigh, Spenser's friend, is famous in connexion with its introduction to English notice — and even if he learnt its use in France,[2] his name lives with that of Virginia, the great colony projected in 1585, for whose sake later on the growing of tobacco was forbidden in England.

The ships of England were not merely engaged in

---

[1] *Cf.* Milton, *P. L.*, ix. 1115.
>   Such of late
> Columbus found the American, so girt
> With feather'd cincture, naked else and wild
> Among the trees on isles and woody shores.

[2] Rennell Rodd, *Raleigh*, p. 67. See a very amusing letter of Howell's on Tobacco (1646), book iii. 7.

SPENSER

Spenser's day in discovery. The Red Cross Knight has to leave his bride to serve the Faerie Queene

> Gainst that proud Paynim king that workes her teene
> (i. 12, 18).

Whether the poet meant to tell the story or not (i. 11, 7), his sonnet to "the Lord Ch. Howard high Admiral of England" is full of the great victory of 1588—

> Sith those huge castles of Castilian King,
> That vainly threatned kingdomes to displace,
> Like flying doves ye did before you chace.

The whole poem is one of victory, of hope and triumph—clear proof of the poet's sympathy with his people. He was a Puritan of London; and the only party, according to a report drawn up in 1585 for the Pope by a distinguished Jesuit,[1] that would fight to death for the Queen were the Puritans of London and of the sea towns. Providentially, he held, they were few. The Jesuit was so far right in saying they would fight, but more than they fought for the Queen, for Howard was a Catholic. King Philip's wars in the Low Countries and the Inquisition are the theme of the tenth canto of book v. of the *Faerie Queene*. Spenser had been at College when the Saint Bartholomew Massacre took place,[2] and the Pope coined his medal to celebrate it. Englishmen then had no doubts as to the spirit and nature of the Roman Church, and here again Spenser stood with his countrymen.

Another characteristic feature of the time meets us when Sir Arthegall, the Knight of Justice, comes upon the "mighty Gyant" with "an huge great paire of ballance in his hand" (v. 2, 30). The Giant has his eye on the world around him and sees "realmes and nations run awry," and he undertakes to reduce them to equality again—

---

[1] Froude, *English Seamen*, p. 8.   [2] 18 August 1572.

Were it not good that wrong were then surceast,
And from the most that some were given to the least?

Therefore I will throw downe these mountains hie,
And make them levell with the lowly plaine;
These towring rocks, which reach unto the skie,
I will thrust downe into the deepest maine,
And, as they were, them equalize againe.
Tyrants, that make men subject to their law,
I will suppresse, that they no more may raine;
And Lordings curbe that commons over-aw,
And all the wealth of rich men to the poore will draw.

The Giant was perhaps an Anabaptist; and at any rate the vulgar clustered thick "unto his leasings vaine, like foolish flies about an hony-crocke." Sir Arthegall tests him; he claims he can weigh everything in his balances; can he weigh the wind, the light—

Or weigh the thought that from mans mind doth flow—

or even a single word? Can he weigh right against wrong, true against false? No, it proves that these cannot be weighed against each other. Talus, the iron squire, begins to suspect the Giant, and in his abrupt way, shoulders him off the cliff into the sea.

So was the high-aspyring with huge ruine humbled—

and the lawless multitude Talus scattered with his flail. The whole incident is full of suggestion. The giant has not proved so easy to deal with in history as in allegory.

But Spenser was himself a man of letters, a student and a poet, and while his friends fought on land and sea, his business lay elsewhere. It was a formative time, for the English language and literature took then directions they were not to leave. So far England had had one great poet, but two centuries had changed her speech and Chaucer was not wholly intelligible. Pronunciation in particular had shifted, and men, while they read him with enthusiasm, could never be sure of making his lines scan. His accents, his grammar, and his use of final *e* perplexed his readers, and his great gift of metre was obscured, as it remained till Tyrwhitt took him in hand in the 18th century. Few can have loved Chaucer in that day as Spenser did; indeed English taste, missing his secret, was looking to other models—" our maker, therefore, at these days shall not follow Piers Plowman, nor Gower, nor Lydgate, nor yet Chaucer, for their language is now out of use with us."[1] But to Spenser he is still "that renowned Poet"—

> Dan Chaucer, well of English undefyled,
> On Fames eternall beadroll worthie to be fyled
> (iv. 2, 32)—

and on Chaucer's English Spenser now and then modelled his own, archaizing, as a poet would, with an enthusiasm that owns no canons of philological science.

Milton, here as elsewhere in unity with Spenser, was also a student of Chaucer,

> him who left half-told
> The story of Cambuscan bold . . .
> And of the wonderous horse of brass—

that tale which Spenser tried to finish. With Chaucer Milton couples another poet—

> And if aught else great bards beside
> In sage and solemn tunes have sung,
> Of turneys, and of trophies hung,
> Of forests and enchantments drear
> Where more is meant than meets the ear.

What is more, they both thought of Chaucer as a sort of precursor of the Reformation. Foxe, the Martyrologist (whose book appeared in 1563), says of him that he " no doubt, saw in religion as much almost as ever we do now,

---

[1] Puttenham, cited by T. R. Lounsbury, *Studies in Chaucer*, iii. p. 60.

and uttereth in his works no less, and seemeth to be a right Wicklevian, or else there was never any." To Milton too it seemed that "our Chaucer" gives "a caution to *England*, to beware of her *Bishops* in time," and he cited the *Plowman's Tale* to prove it. Such judgments might have amused Chaucer, while he kept his own views whatever they were on bishops.[1]

To mend English verse men were looking abroad for models and to the great poets of classical antiquity. Before Spenser was born, Wyatt had tried translating Petrarch. Spenser himself tried it, as we have seen, just before he went to Cambridge. Other Italian models were the Idylls of Sannazaro and the epics of Ariosto and Tasso. It is interesting to note that some part—perhaps a book or more—of the *Faerie Queene* was written before the first complete edition of Tasso's *La Gerusalemme Liberata* appeared in 1581, but the last canto of the second book is closely modelled on Tasso—some of it is sheer translation. Meanwhile Edward Fairfax was doing the whole epic into English (published 1600). Tasso, if authors then exchanged books overseas, might have read himself again in Spenser, for he only died in 1595. France offered examples in du Bellay and Ronsard (died 1585).

Then there were the Classics, which were at the height of their fame. Rabelais and Montaigne before Spenser, and Burton after him, illustrate how much men read them, how much they could draw upon them and still be themselves. Spenser's knowledge is not quite so close, but perhaps he drew as much inspiration from what he read. Talus, the iron man, is not a conspicuous figure in the mythology, but that is where Spenser found him. Some of the later cantos of the sixth book are substantially a rendering, not literal but Spenserian, of the Greek romance of *Daphnis and Chloe*, and perhaps the intricacy or even confusion of books iii. and iv. owes something to the

---

[1] See Spenser's *Mother Hubberd's Tale*—a poem on Chaucerian lines, with passages on clergy.

influence of other Greek romances—an influence also to be clearly seen in Sidney's *Arcadia*.

Now was it possible that, as Rome had taken the dactylic hexameter from Greece and had produced an *Aeneid*, England in her turn might adapt it with as happy results? A few lines from two letters of Spenser to Gabriel Harvey may sum up the story. "As for the twoo worthy Gentlemen, Master *Sidney* and Master *Dyer*, they have me, I thanke them, in some use of familiarity. . . . And nowe they have proclaimed in their ἀρειωπάγῳ a generall surceasing and silence of bald Rymers, and also of the verie beste too: in steade whereof they haue, by authoritie of their whole Senate, prescribed certain Lawes and rules of Quantities of Englishe sillables for English Verse: having had thereof already great practise and drawen mee to their faction. . . . I am of late more in love wyth my Englishe Versifying than with Ryming: which I should have done long since, if I would then have followed your councell."[1] Harvey was of the Classical faction, and a letter is extant in which he dismisses the *Faerie Queene* as a mistake, which his friend will not however be brought to see. Spenser adds a specimen of his Versifying—which no one would ever read twice to advance his own happiness.

Some hold that Spenser has no humour. It is certainly not the first feature that impresses his readers, yet it is there in his work, quiet and grave almost, humour of the Virgilian kind.[2] But the English Hexameter tempts him into banter, and in bantering he touches its real weakness. "The onely, or chiefest hardnesse, whych seemeth, is in the Accente: whych sometime gapeth, and as it were yawneth ilfavouredly, comming shorte of that it should and sometime exceeding the measure of the Number,

---

[1] Letter dated "5 of October 1579"; published in 1580, "touching Artificiall Versifying."

[2] Compare Spenser's arming of Clarion the butterfly in *Muiopotmos* with Virgil's march of the ants—*it nigrum campis agmen*.

as in *Carpenter*, the middle sillable being used shorte in speache, when it shall be read longe in Verse, seemeth like a lame *Gosling that draweth one legge after hir*: and *Heaven* being used shorte as one sillable, when it is in verse stretched out with a Diastole, is like *a lame dogge that holdes up one legge*."[1]

There were other theorists in English letters. There was *Euphues*, and there were, as E. K. puts it, "the rakehellye route of our ragged rymers (for so themselves use to hunt the letter)." From them all Spenser learnt, but to none would he yield his judgment. He went his own way, trusting his own instinct and his own ear. English had its own harmonies; it was neither Latin, nor French, nor Italian; and he who would master its secrets must obey—neither pedant nor poet—but the language itself. Spenser listened to his own mother tongue while the rest theorized, and he learnt it—learnt its cadences, its suggestions, its variety and its music.

In 1579 he published his *Shepheards Calender*. It was a collection of idylls, grouped by the months of the year. The title was an old one borrowed from an old French book.[2] The idylls were frankly imitative, but there were new features. The shepherds were no longer all Damon and Melibœus. Cuddie and Hobbinol, Willye and Perigot appear, and they talk a rustic English— Lancashire English, some say, though others say they are Chaucer's words. Spenser himself is slightly disguised as Colin Clout—a name borrowed from Skelton. The shepherds, in the style familiar in Virgil and in *Lycidas*, discuss subjects not found in Theocritus—the church, for instance. For it is to be noted that, Grindal the Archbishop being now in disgrace for reluctance to put down Puritan prophesyings, Algrind the good shepherd is conspicuously praised by the young poet.[3] Two of the tales

---

[1] Letter published (not with the preceding one) 1580.
[2] See Sir Sidney Lee, *The French Renaissance in England*, pp. 184, 185.
[3] *Shepheards Calender*, Julye.

are full of gentle humour—the Oak and the Briar, and the Fox and the Kid. But the main thing is that here is real English poetry again—the native music of the language used by a poet, moving with freedom among beautiful words and beautiful thoughts. It was a book that reached Milton's heart and influenced his poetry in more ways than one. There were the bishops—" Those our admired *Spenser* inveighs against, not without some presage of these reforming times "; but the beauty of the rhythm and language is a more enduring service than the denunciation of prelates, and to this Milton was no less sensitive.

English readers were quick to recognize that they had a new poet among them. " The *Shepheards Calender* hath much poetry in his Eglogues," wrote Sidney. "Sorry I am," wrote another critic in 1586, "that I cannot find none other with whom I might couple him in his rare gift of poetry."

We come now to the *Faerie Queene*. In a prefatory letter addressed to Sir Walter Raleigh and calculated to "give great light to the reader," the poet says that "The generall end of all the booke is to fashion a gentleman or noble person in vertuous and gentle discipline: Which for that I conceived shoulde be most plausible and pleasing, being coloured with an historicall fiction, the which the most part of men delight to read, rather for variety of matter then for profite of the ensample, I chose the historye of King Arthure. . . . To some, I know, this Methode will seem displeasaunt, which had rather have good discipline delivered plainly in way of precepts, or sermoned at large, as they use, then thus cloudily enwrapped in Allegoricall devises. But such, me seeme, should be satisfide with the use of these dayes, seeing all things accounted by their showes, and nothing esteemed of, that is not delightfull and pleasing to commune sence. For this cause is Xenophon preferred before Plato, for that the one, in the exquisite depth of his judgement, formed a Commune welth, such as it should be; but the other in the person of Cyrus, and the Persians, fashioned a governement, such as might best be."

The apology is a pleasant one from a professed Platonist, who avows that he is following Xenophon to please his age. It has been suggested that the example of Plato's myths was a factor in his choice. He explains that in the Red Cross Knight he expresses Holiness, in Sir Guyon Temperance, and in Britomart Chastity. The Allegory is manifold; sometimes one forgets it is Allegory at all and at other times it is plainly nothing else. The House of the Lady Alma, which is the human body, with its wonderful structure, and the cook "cald Concoction," and the library where Prince Arthur stops for a whole canto to read Geoffrey of Monmouth,[1] and that other house of the three Aristotelian ladies (who represent the Mean and the Extremes), with their sadly incompatible tempers and their impossible lovers,[2] do not find favour with every reader.

The Legend of Arthur had long been associated with Fairyland. So to Fairyland the poet takes us. But here another objection occurs; there is no such place. But he is ready for this and meets it with a reply that should be studied by those who say he has no humour.

> Right well I wote, most mighty Soveraine,
> That all this famous antique history
> Of some th' aboundance of an ydle braine
> Will judged be, and painted forgery,
> Rather then matter of just memory;
> Sith none that breatheth living air does know
> Where is that happy land of Faery,
> Which I so much doe vaunt, yet no where show,
> But vouch antiquities, which no body can know.

[1] ii. 9, 31.   [2] ii. 2, 13.

But let that man with better sence advize,
That of the world least part to us is red;
And daily how through hardy enterprize
Many great Regions are discovered,
Which to late age were never mentioned.
Who ever heard of th' Indian Peru?
Or who in venturous vessell measured
The Amazon huge river, now found trew?
Or fruitfullest Virginia who did ever view?

Yet all these were, when no man did them know,
Yet have from wisest ages hidden beene;
And later times thinges more unknowne shall show.
Why then should witlesse man so much misweene,
That nothing is but that which he hath seene?
What if within the Moones fayre shining spheare,
What if in every other starre unseene
Of other worldes he happily should heare,
He wonder would much more: yet such to some appeare.

(ii., Introductory stanzas [1])

This is Spenser's *Multi pertransibunt et augebitur scientia*, and we must not let its seriousness be lost sight of in its application, nor the humour of the application in the gravity of the thought.

One might not have expected that the ways

In this delightfull land of Faery
Are so exceeding spacious and wyde;

but then no one could have foretold either

such sweet variety
Of all that pleasaunt is to eare or eye

(vi., intr.).

---

[1] *Cf.* Montaigne, *Essays*, i. ch. 30. This discoverie of so infinit and vast a countrie seemeth worthy great consideration. I wot not whether I can warrant my selfe, that some other be not discovered hereafter, sithence so many worthy men, and better learned than we are, have so many ages beene deceived in this. (Florio.)

We are in the same region where Sidney's Arcadia lies, a land where knight and shepherd meet as happily in the open air, and where Shakespeare's Forest of Arden and maritime Bohemia are not far away. It seems seldom to rain in Fairyland.[1] The forests are large and wild, where Satyrs dwell, creatures of the true Classical type, but yet very like the "Salvage men" of the explorers. There are strange monsters on land and in the sea, but perhaps no stranger than the seamen told of, who came back from the Eastern and Western seas—[2]

> Spring-headed Hydres; and sea-shouldring Whales;
> Great whirlpooles which all fishes make to flee;
> Bright Scolopendraes arm'd with silver scales;
> Mighty Monoceroses with immeasured tayles—
> (ii. 12, 23);

these and many more—a whole stanza full of them—some of them familiar to students of the literature of that day, and some known to zoologists.[3]

But Fairyland has not only forests and monsters and enchantments. It has castles and gardens. It is perhaps a mark of the times that the castles are turning into palaces, and less of the poet's mind is given to their defences than to their tapestries and pictures. Here his Classical reading was fruitful of suggestion. Catullus and the Greek romances have many such descriptions and Classical mythology lent itself to pictorial treatment. It is perhaps worth noting that most of these splendid palaces belong to the enemy, and the decoration is rather after his heart, as at Castle Joyeous (iii. 1, 34), and in the house of the enchanter Busirane (iii. 11, 28).

---

[1] It rains heavily in i. 1, 7.

[2] A song of the period reflects this pleasant habit of travellers and mariners—
> For many an honest Indian ass
> Goes for an unicorn.

[3] See Phipson, *Animal Lore of Shakespeare's Time*, pp. 95, 456-7. The Monoceros seems to be the narwhal, and its horn served to prove the existence of the unicorn too.

With the pictures we may group the pageants—Busirane's pageant of love, and the other of Pride in the first book. The latter is undisguised symbol. The lady, who is Pride, could never have driven forth with the Seven Deadly Sins as outriders, mounted on such appropriate animals as the poet describes (i. 4, 18-37)—nor would Duessa have ridden with her if she had.

The temples of Venus and Isis are more attractive. It is curious how the poet fluctuates among religions. The Red Cross Knight is frankly Christian; Britomart on the other hand has a vision in "Isis church," and Scudamour to win Amoret goes through great adventures in the Castle and shrine of Venus. But it is surprising how Christian Isis and Venus have become.

Then there are the gardens—that of Proserpine, which Sir Guyon sees (ii. 7, 51), and that of Adonis where Amoret grew up—the latter a beautiful allegory of the ideal world and the life before birth (iii. 6, 29).

> In that same Gardin all the goodly flowres,
> Wherewith dame Nature doth her beautify,
> And decks the girlonds of her Paramoures,
> Are fetcht: there is the first seminary
> Of all things that are born to live and dye.

"Old Genius" is its porter, thronged by souls asking for bodies.

> Infinite shapes of creatures there are bred.

Their substance is eternal though "chaunged and often altred to and froe." Time with his scythe is the one enemy to the happiness of flowers and lovers in that garden. Not Venus' self might

> find redresse for such despight:
> For all that lives is subject to that law;
> All things decay in time, and to their end doe draw—

a note often heard in Spenser's poetry and in the poetry

of all who feel. Plato's influence is to be read in this Garden.[1]

Such is the world of Fairyland. The people are brave and true knights and "faytour knights," fair ladies true or false, enchanters, faithful dwarfs and cruel giants. The promise of the prologue is redeemed.

Fierce warres and faithful loves shall moralize my song.

Malory and Geoffrey of Monmouth have been the poet's reading,—and perhaps other books, the fascination of which may be recalled by a few words from a contemporary writer.

"This gentleman, during the interval that he was idle, which was the greater part of the year, gave himself up to the reading of books of chivalries, with so much fervour and relish that he almost entirely neglected the exercise of the chase and even the management of his estate. And to such a pitch did his curiosity and infatuation reach that he sold many acres of arable land in order to buy romances of chivalry to read. . . . He filled himself with the imagination of all that he read in the books; with enchantments, with quarrels, battles, challenges, wounds, amorous plaints, loves, torments and follies impossible."[2]

A knight errant, he held, "must be chaste in thought, true in word, generous in works, valiant in deeds, patient in toils, charitable to the needy, and, in fine, a maintainer of the truth, though its defence may cost him his life."[3]

So said Don Quixote. The great book, which tells his story, belongs to the years 1605 to 1615. The chapter, in which the Licentiate and the Barber hold "the pleasant and famous Inquisition on the library of our Ingenious Gentleman," shows the interest of

[1] *Cf.* J. S. Harrison, *Platonism in English Poetry*, pp. 210-216.
[2] *Don Quixote*, Part I. ch. 1.
[3] *Don Quixote*, Part II. ch. 18. Cf. *F. Q.*, iii. 2, 13, 14. The old stories kept their charm and fascinated in a later age Samuel Johnson and Edmund Burke.—*Boswell*, i. p. 49.

Cervantes himself in romance; and his conception of the high-minded and chivalrous hero,—waiving the two unhappy facts of his madness and his living in modern Spain,—is not very far from Spenser's ideal. The different turn given to the same series of ideas will not conceal the kinship. Cervantes had been himself a sort of Red Cross Knight, a fighter and a captive, a great and earnest nature, as full of generous impulse as of genial humour.

Spenser's knights are men consecrated to honour and to high purpose, who live not for themselves but for duty and service. To Braggadochio, the comic figure of the poem, who plays at being a knight in virtue of "purloynd steed and speare"—

> avaunting in great bravery
> As Peacocke that his painted plumes doth pranck
> 							(ii. 3, 6)—

Belphœbe speaks of honour. He does not understand her, but her words represent the faith of all Gloriana's true knights—

> Abroad in armes, at home in studious kynd,
> Who seekes with painfull toile shall honor soonest
>   fynd;
>
> In woods, in waves, in warres, she wonts to dwell,
> And wil be found with perill and with paine;
> Ne can the man that moulds in ydle cell
> Unto her happy mansion attaine:
> Before her gate high God did Sweate ordaine,
> And wakefull watches ever to abide;
> But easy is the way and passage plaine
> To pleasures pallace: it may soon be spide,
> And day and night her dores to all stand open wide
> 							(ii. 3, 41).

In these lines there are at least two echoes of famous passages in the classics—τῆς ἀρετῆς ἰδρῶτα θεοὶ προπάροιθεν ἔθηκαν and *Noctes atque dies patet atri janua Ditis*; yet the stanza is Spenser's own in thought and word and music. The transference of the open doors is not without significance.

Each of his figures stands out distinct and clearly seen; the ladies are perhaps more individual than the knights. Una may be an allegory of Truth—a singularly beautiful one—but she is a tender and very human woman, "true as touch" (i. 3, 2), capable of tears and terrors and forgiveness. Britomart, again, is a sort of Jeanne d'Arc, dressed in knight's armour to protect her honour, as she rides the world seeking the lover, whose face she had seen in "the glassy globe that Merlin made" (iii. 2, 21). She meets the Red Cross Knight, who, in answer to her questions gives high praise to Arthegall, and she "waxes inly wondrous glad"; but, to lead him on to further speech of her hero, she feigns not to believe him. Later on, again, she has after her marriage a pang no allegory ever felt. Arthegall is a captive, under conditions she mistakes—

> Oft did she blame her selfe, and often rew,
> For yeelding to a straunger's love so light,
> Whose life and manners straunge she never knew
> (v. 6, 12).

But she learns the truth and buckles on her arms again and rescues him like the heroine she is. Carlyle once wrote of "Spenser's frosty allegories," but he cannot have been much out-of-doors in Fairyland, or he would have known its gentle airs better and perhaps found women after his own heart in Una and Britomart.

Little has been said so far of the music of the poem. The stanza Spenser adapted from the Italian, adding the ninth line, the Alexandrine, here no "wounded snake" of "slow length." The nine lines, with the interwoven rhymes, sometimes two, generally three, form a unity capable of remarkable variation. No stanza is wanting in music, but it is not till one has read some hundreds of them that the full value of the metre is felt. Spenser, like the great metrists — Virgil and Milton—has a wonderful instrument, and can use it so as to bring out all its powers of strength and sweetness. The poem is a very long one; the allegory, some say, is exhausted; but the reader is carried on and on. Milton's description of the "airs" in *L'Allegro* might be borrowed to express it—

> immortal verse,
> Such as the melting soul may pierce,
> In notes, with many a winding bout
> Of linked sweetness long drawn out.

Or better still, there is Wordsworth's true and sympathetic judgment on the book itself—

> Sweet Spenser, moving through his clouded heaven,
> With the moon's beauty and the moon's soft pace.[1]
> *(Prelude,* iii. 283).

The song in the Bower of Bliss is famous—it was a translation from Tasso,[2] but it is Spenser's own, and a critic has well spoken of it as "not lost, but still not salient among the profuse beauties of his inexhaustible treasures of poetry."[3] Nothing is salient in his verse, all is harmony. Sir Guyon moves on through the Garden,

> The whiles some one did chaunt this lovely lay:
> Ah! see, whoso fayre thing doest faine to see,
> In springing flowre the image of thy day.
> Ah! see the Virgin Rose, how sweetly shee
> Doth first peepe foorth with bashfull modestee,
> That fairer seemes the lesse ye see her may.

---

[1] The lines in *Prelude,* i. 170-185, also suggest Spenser. See Intr. to *White Doe.*
[2] *Gerus. Liber.,* xvi. 14.
[3] Barrett Wendell, *The Seventeenth Century in English Literature,* p. 151.

Lo! see soone after how more bold and free
Her bared bosome she doth broad display;
Lo! see soone after how she fades and falls away.

So passeth, in the passing of a day,
Of mortall life the leafe, the bud, the flowre;
Ne more doth florish after first decay,
That earst was sought to deck both bed and bowre
Of many a lady, and many a Paramowre.
Gather therefore the Rose whilest yet is prime,
For soone comes age that will her pride deflowre;
Gather the Rose of love whilest yet is time,
Whilest loving thou mayst loved be with equall crime.[1]

(ii. 12, 75.)

But now that we are with Sir Guyon in the Garden of Acrasia, we must ask what we are doing there. Why has the poet brought us here, where everything lies before us that can appeal to sense or set imagination on fire? And he seems to have lavished all his gifts on the description.[2] "The poet," in Wordsworth's phrase, "trusting to primary instincts, luxuriates among the felicities of love and wine." Is it safely? asked Dean Church, and concluded it was not. But the final comment is after all Milton's,—

"I cannot praise a fugitive and cloister'd vertue, unexercis'd and unbreath'd, that never sallies out and sees her adversary, but slinks out of the race, where that immortal Garland is to be run for, not without dust and heat. Assuredly we bring not innocence into the World, we bring impurity much rather: that which purifies us is trial, and trial is by what is contrary. That vertue therfore which is but a youngling in the contemplation of evil, and knows not the utmost that vice

---

[1] *Cf.* Herrick after him "Gather ye rosebuds while ye may," and the *Wisdom of Solomon*, ii. 8 (A.V.), "Let us crowne our selues with Rose buds, before they be withered." Milton, *Comus*, 742-3, two grave lines.

[2] It is curious to note how the wonderful beauty of the style seems, as one reflects, to show up the meanness of evil.

promises to her followers, and rejects it, is but a blank vertue, not a pure; her whiteness is but an excremental whiteness: which was the reason why our sage and serious Poet *Spenser*, whom I dare be known to think a better teacher than *Scotus* or *Aquinas*, describing true temperance under the person of *Guion*, brings him in with his palmer through the cave of Mammon, and the bower of earthly bliss, that he might see and know, and yet abstain."[1]

Guyon hesitates indeed, so near he comes to being

> Drawne with the powre of an heart-robbing eye,
> And wrapt in fetters of a golden tresse (v. 8, 1).

The Palmer, who is Reason, speaks, and he goes forward. He makes a prisoner of Acrasia, and her bowers and palace he "broke downe with rigour pitilesse" (ii. 12, 83); and all this, because he knew in himself the enchantment of beauty, "made but the bait of sinne." Plato's quarrel with the poets will never be understood till first one has realized what fascination Poetry had for him, and how like it seemed to lead him away from his proper work. Guyon and Plato have both been reproached for Puritanism. Perhaps this may help us to understand Puritanism also.

The power of beauty for good or evil is one of Spenser's deepest convictions.[2] When Britomart and Arthegall meet, it is as enemies. He thinks her a knight, and they fight. His sword cuts away a part of her helmet, and her face is bared—

> And round about the same her yellow heare,
> Having through stirring loosd their wonted band,
> Like to a golden border did appeare,
> Framed in goldsmithes forge with cunning hand . . .

---

[1] Milton, *Areopagitica*, Prose Works (1738), i. 147. Yet he also says (*P. L.*, iv. 222), "Knowledge of good, bought dear by knowing ill."

[2] See J. S. Harrison, *Platonism in English Poetry of the* 16*th and* 17*th Centuries*, ch. i. § 1, for a discussion of this, and Spenser's debt to Plato in his treatment of Una and § 3 Britomart, where he contrasts the passage in Ariosto on which it was modelled.

> And as his hand he up againe did reare,
> Thinking to worke on her his utmost wracke,
> His powrelesse arme, benumbd with secret feare,
> From his revengefull purpose shronke abacke,
> And cruell sword out of his fingers slacke
> Fell downe to ground ; as if the steel had sence
> And felt some ruth or sence his hand did lacke,
> Or both of them did thinke obedience
> To doe to so divine a beauties excellence (iv. 6, 20).

The battle is over; he loves her—"yet durst he not make love so suddenly"—a line which, I think, illumines the poet's character.

Beauty is a spiritual thing, and the apprehension of beauty may take us far into the spiritual region, the ideal world.

> How vainely then doe ydle wits invent,
> That beautie is nought else but mixture made
> Of colours faire, and goodly temp'rament
> Of pure complexions! (*H. Beautie*, 64-67.)

On the contrary the "wondrous powre" attributed to "white and red" comes from above, comes with the soul when it descends to human birth and the body.

> Therof it comes that these faire soules, which have
> The most resemblance of that heavenly light,
> Frame to themselves most beautifull and brave
> Their fleshly bowre, most fit for their delight,
> And the grosse matter by a soveraine might
> Tempers so trim, that it may well be seene
> A pallace fit for such a virgin Queene.
>
> So every spirit, as it is most pure,
> And hath in it the more of heavenly light,
> So it the fairer bodie doth procure
> To habit in, and it more fairely dight
> With chearefull grace and amiable sight ;

> For of the soule the bodie forme doth take;
> For soule is forme, and doth the bodie make.
> (*H. Beautie*, 120-133.)

Thus it is that Una has such power. She is Truth and her beauty, being spiritual, tames the lion and softens the "Salvage-men." Truth may seem an austere and abstract thing; but here Spenser's love of beauty gives him insight, for Una is the tenderest of all his women,—

> Her love is firme, her care continuall . . .
> Els should this Redcrosse knight in bands have dyde
> (i. 8, 1).

She finds the champion who frees him from the bondage of pride, and when he is set free, "to him she ran with hasty joy; to see him made her glad" (i. 8, 42). But he is weak and wan, all unfit for his task of slaying the dragon. So Una leads him away to the house of Caelia or Holiness, and there he goes through a spiritual experience, which few will understand who do not know— the sense of sin, remorse, repentance, distress. After that she takes him to Caelia's daughter Charissa, the mother of many babes, and asks her to instruct him, which she does, "right joyous"; and soon Mercy, "an auncieut matrone," brings him to the hill of the godly aged Sire, heavenly Contemplation. Mercy has to help him to climb it, and thence he has a vision of "a goodly Citty"—at once Apocalyptic and Platonic.

The tenderness and healing power of Truth have rarely been so well drawn. On through repentance and forgiveness to the heavenly vision Una has brought her knight, and now he can slay the dragon. The battle lasts three days, and he is hard pressed and overborne; but the "Well of Life" and the "Tree of Life" restore him, and he triumphs. And now, the dragon slain, at last he sees Una without her veil, and wonders at

> The blazing brightnesse of her beauties beame . . .
> Oft had he seene her faire, but never so faire dight
> (i. 12, 23).

Spenser has grasped the fact that, while Truth captures us in the first instance by its beauty, we never realize that beauty till we have had to fight for Truth and have found in suffering its inner meaning.

In 1596 Spenser published four hymns. Two had been made "in the greener times of my youth" in praise of Love and Beauty. He was dissatisfied with them, but they were beyond recall; so to mend them he made two more in praise of Heavenly Love and Heavenly Beauty. The "Hymne of Heavenlie Love" tells how the world began in God's love—

> Before this Worlds Great Frame, in which al things
> Are now containd, found any being-place,
> Ere flitting Time could wag his eyas wings
> About that mightie bound which doth embrace
> The rolling Spheres, and parts their houres by space,
> That High Eternall Powre, which now doth move
> In all these things, mov'd in it selfe by love.

Angels were begotten—"all glistring glorious in their Makers light." But the brightest of them rebelled in pride and drew millions more with him. The Almighty "with His onely breath them blew away." And then "seeing left a waste and emptie place in His wyde Pallace" cast "to enstall a new unknowen Colony therein," and made man of clay

> and breathd a living spright
> Into his face most beautifull and fayre,
> Endewd with wisedomes riches, heavenly, rare.

But man too fell, and "that great Lord of Love" cast to redeem him and pay the price.

> Out of the bosome of eternall blisse,
> In which he reigned with his glorious syre,

He downe descended, like a most demisse
And abject thrall, in fleshes fraile attyre,
That He for him might pay sinnes deadly hyre,
And him restore unto that happie state
In which he stood before his haplesse fate.

The poet calls on Earth to rouse itself and lift up its clouded eyes to behold His bounty:—

Beginne from first, where he encradled was
In simple cratch, wrapt in a wad of hay,
Betweene the toylefull Oxe and humble Asse,
And in what rags, and in how base aray,
The glory of our heavenly riches lay,
When him the silly Shepheards came to see,
Whom greatest Princes sought on lowest knee.

From thence reade on the storie of his life,
His humble carriage, his unfaulty wayes,
His cancred foes, his fights, his toyle, his strife,
His paines, his povertie, his sharpe assayes,
Through which he past his miserable dayes,
Offending none, and doing good to all,
Yet being malist both of great and small.

And looke at last, how of most wretched wights
He taken was, betrayd, and false accused;
How with most scornefull taunts and fell despights,
He was revyld, disgrast, and foule abused;
How scourgd, how crownd, how buffeted, how brused;
And lastly, how twixt robbers crucifyde,
With bitter wounds through hands, through feet, and
    syde! . . .

With sence whereof, whilest so thy softened spirit
Is inly toucht, and humbled with meek zeale
Through meditation of his endlesse merit,
Lift up thy mind to th' Author of thy weale,
And to his soveraine mercie doe appeale;

> Learne him to love that loved thee so deare,
> And in thy brest his blessed image beare. . . .
>
> Then shall thy ravisht soule inspired bee
> With heavenly thoughts farre above humane skil,
> And thy bright radiant eyes shall plainely see
> Th' Idee of his pure glorie present still
> Before thy face, that all thy spirits shall fill
> With sweete enragement of celestiall love
> Kindled through sight of those faire things above.

This is the secret of true beauty, of bright eyes and "sunshyny face."

It is here too that Spenser finds that fixity which a world of change cannot give him. England, Ireland, Europe, the sixteenth century at large—the life of man with love and hope, the fear of death, the chill of loss—the world itself—"the beauty and the wonder and the power"—

> Nothing is sure that growes on earthly grownd.
> (i. 9, 11.)

These are the words of Prince Arthur.

> This is the state of Keasars and of Kings!
> Let none therefore, that is in meaner place,
> Too greatly grieve at any his unlucky case
> (vi. 3, 5).

In two fine cantos, the sixth and seventh—all that he lived to write—of a seventh book, the poet describes the splendid Titaness Mutabilitie climbing to "the Circle of the Moone," with a mind to go higher still and assert her sovereignty over all the universe. The Gods—and even Jove—soften to her, "such sway doth beauty even in Heaven beare."

She is beautiful but she is terrible. Her very beauty, which the poet has felt so keenly, heightens the terror of her. The claim to rule even Gods is referred to Nature.

Can it be that all things are phænomena, that nothing is eternal? Nature shall say.

So before Nature Gods and Titaness appear. The Titaness brings before them the wonderful pageant of months, seasons and planets. Nothing is "firme and permanent," and she demands her due—which is the rule of all. But Nature finds that all the mutations to which the Titaness appeals are themselves ruled by law, and thus, so far from Change ruling over all things, they "raigne over Change," and the day is to come when Change shall cease to be. There is an eternal element.

Two stanzas alone survive of "The VIII Canto Unperfite"—the last word perhaps of Spenser, and with it we may leave him. In a world of change he has found rest, and that of no abstract or impersonal kind.

> When I bethinke me on that speech whyleare
> Of Mutabilitie, and well it way!
> Me seemes, that though she all unworthy were
> Of the Heav'ns Rule; yet, very sooth to say,
> In all things else she beares the greatest sway:
> Which makes me loath this state of life so tickle,
> And love of things so vaine to cast away;
> Whose flowring pride, so fading and so fickle,
> Short Time shall soon cut down with his consuming
>   sickle.
>
> Then gin I thinke on that which Nature sayd,
> Of that same time when no more Change shall be,
> But stedfast rest of all things, firmely stayd
> Upon the pillours of Eternity,
> That is contrayr to Mutabilitie;
> For all that moveth doth in Change delight;
> But thence-forth all shall rest eternally
> With Him that is the God of Sabaoth hight:
> O! that great Sabaoth God, grant me that Sabaoths
>   sight.

MILTON

HUMPHREY MOSELEY was a London bookseller in the seventeenth century who made up his mind to take a line of his own. It was the great age of pamphlets and sermons, but he was content to leave these to rival publishers: he would publish literature, and in the course of his life he brought out nearly all the best volumes of poetry of the time, buying old copyrights as he could and finding out undiscovered genius. In 1645 he published a small but neat little volume of "Poems of Mr John Milton, both English and Latin, compos'd at several times. Printed by his true Copies." He wrote a preface to the Reader, from which a sentence or two deserve to be remembered.

"I know not thy palate, how it relishes such dainties, nor how harmonious thy soul is: perhaps more trivial airs may please thee better. . . . Let the event guide itself which way it will, I shall deserve of the age by bringing into the light as true a birth as the Muses have brought forth since our famous SPENSER wrote; whose Poems in these English ones are as rarely imitated as sweetly excelled. Reader, if thou art eagle-eyed to censure their worth, I am not fearful to expose them to thy exactest perusal. Thine to command, Humph. Moseley."

"Perhaps more trivial airs may please thee better." There lies the secret of the comparative unpopularity of Milton. He is admired, of course, for Tradition says he should be admired, but perhaps he is not so often read as he is praised. In his famous sonnet Wordsworth says in his own way the same thing as Moseley.

Thy soul was like a Star, and dwelt apart :
Thou hadst a voice whose sound was like the sea :
Pure as the naked heavens, majestic, free,
So didst thou travel on life's common way.

He compares Milton to sea, star and sky, and does it with the fine insight that marks his judgments upon English poets. Sea, star and sky are not amusing things, as the practical people at watering-places know. To be amused we want something "more trivial." The solitary companionship of sea, star and sky has in it something awful. And there again they are like Milton, as Wordsworth saw—

> Soul awful—if the earth has ever lodged
> An awful soul.[1]

It is this likeness which makes him so easy to neglect, and yet so permanent. He moves like a planet, unhasting, unresting ; he sees his orbit ; he is to be a poet and he will write his great poem, not now, but when the time comes, "slow choosing and beginning late." (*P. L.* ix. 26.) Like Cervantes and Defoe he was well over fifty when he wrote the work on which his fame chiefly rests, and yet manuscript notes are still extant which show that the theme had been in his mind for many years.

Milton is serious. Inheritance and environment combined to make him serious. His father had been bred a Catholic and became Protestant for conscience sake, though it cut him off from father and home. We can imagine how he trained his eldest boy[2] (born 9 Dec. 1608), and how he spoke to him of what had come to England, and what had come to himself, in the new freedom of these times—what gladness and what know-

---

[1] *Prelude*, iii. 289.

[2] "God," says Milton, "can stir up rich fathers to bestow exquisite education upon their children, and so dedicate them to the service of the Gospel."—*Animadversions*, Prose i. 97.

ledge of God—and what was yet to break out of God's word. Or if we cannot imagine it, here is what Milton wrote of it years after.[1]

"When I recall to mind at last, after so many dark Ages, wherein the huge overshadowing Train of *Error* had almost swept all the Stars out of the firmament of the *Church;* how the bright and blissful *Reformation* (by Divine Power) strook through the black and settled Night of *Ignorance* and *Antichristian Tyranny*, methinks a sovereign and reviving Joy must needs rush into the Bosom of him that reads or hears; and the sweet Odour of the returning *Gospel* imbath his Soul with the fragrancy of Heaven. Then was the sacred BIBLE sought out of the dusty Corners where profane Falshood and Neglect had thrown it, the *Schools* opened, *Divine* and *Humane Learning* rak'd out of the *Embers* of *forgotten Tongues*, the *Princes* and *Cities* trooping apace to the new-erected Banner of *Salvation;* the *Martyrs*, with the unresistable *might* of *Weakness*, shaking the *Powers* of *Darkness*, and scorning the *fiery Rage* of the old *red Dragon*."[2]

It is a high seriousness—this spirit of Milton, on fire with joy. Take the nouns of this passage, and watch how he sees in turn the things and is thrilled. There is passion in his prose—enthusiasm and hero-worship. He lives in a great age, an age of freedom and of victory— and round about him are men for whom it is all commonplace. How can it be? How can they not feel the same "sovereign and reviving joy"? It was perhaps long before Milton realized that they felt nothing of it, and this was one of the problems of his life—a great question to be explained to himself if he is to "justify the ways of God to men." It is the inconceivable com-

---

[1] The quotations from Milton's prose works are uniformly taken from the folio edition in two volumes, printed for A. Millar, London, 1738. References will be made to them, as in the previous footnote, to the volume and page of this edition.

[2] *Of Reformation in England*, Prose i. 2. Compare *Defensio Secunda*, Prose ii. 315.

monplaceness of the men and women round them that makes tragedy of the lives of uncommon men.

In the meantime let us look at his country and let us do it with his eyes. Is it the England we know, of which he speaks? It is a familiar passage, but I do not apologize for transcribing it again.

"Lords and Commons of *England*, consider what Nation it is whereof ye are, and whereof ye are the Governours: a Nation not slow and dull, but of a quick, ingenious, and piercing spirit, acute to invent, suttle and sinewy to discourse, not beneath the reach of any point the highest that human capacity can soar to. . . . God is decreeing to begin some new and great period in his Church, even to the reforming of Reformation it self; what does he then but reveal Himself to his servants, and as his manner is, first to his *English-men*?[1] I say as his manner is, first to us, though we mark not the method of his counsels and are unworthy. Behold now this vast City; a City of refuge, the mansion-house of liberty, encompast and surrounded with his protection; the shop of War hath not there more anvils and hammers waking, to fashion out the plates and instruments of armed Justice in defence of beleaguer'd Truth, than there be pens and heads there, sitting by their studious lamps, musing, searching, revolving new notions and ideas wherewith to present as with their homage and their fealty the approaching Reformation: others as fast reading, trying all things, assenting to the force of reason and convincement. What could a man require more from a Nation so pliant and so prone to seek after knowledge? What wants there to such a towardly and pregnant soil, but wise and faithful Labourers, to make a knowing People, a Nation of Prophets, of Sages, and of Worthies? We reckon more than five months

---

[1] Cf. *Animadversions*, Prose i. 90, "For he being equally near to his whole Creation of Mankind . . . hath yet ever had this Island under the special indulgent eye of his Providence; and pitying us first of all other Nations. . . ." He refers to Wiclif.

yet to harvest; there need not be five weeks, had we but eyes to lift up, the fields are white already. Where there is much desire to learn, there of necessity will be much arguing, much writing, many opinions, for opinion in good men is but knowledge in the making. Under the fantastic terrours of sect and schism, we wrong the earnest and zealous thirst after knowledge and understanding which God hath stirr'd up in this City. What some lament of, we should rather rejoice at, should rather praise this pious forwardness among men, to reassume the ill deputed care of their Religion into their own hands again. A little generous prudence, a little forbearance of one another, and some grain of charity might win all these diligencies to join, and unite into one general and brotherly search after Truth." [1]

Can these bright and eager men, "revolving new notions and ideas," be after all our ancestors? Or were they all driven over seas by Archbishop Laud? Could we claim anything of this description for ourselves, but the sects? Yet it is true of the England of Milton's boyhood, youth and middle age, for England was never so full of "seekers" and idealists, of "notions and ideas," of men who believed so intensely in first hand experience of God,—nor ever perhaps so full of "sects and schisms," though not everybody saw into the heart of the matter as Milton did.

On the 12th of February 1624-5, John Milton was entered at Christ's College, Cambridge. In Cambridge he was nicknamed "the Lady of Christ's." His life was one of dignity, and study,—aloof, pure and high. Wordsworth, who used long after to visit a friend " in the very room honoured by Milton's name," pictures him:

> I seemed to see him here
> Familiarly, and in his scholar's dress
> Bounding before me, yet a stripling youth—

[1] *Areopagitica*, Prose i. 156-7.

A boy, no better, with his rosy cheeks
Angelical, keen eye, courageous look,
And conscious step of purity and pride.[1]

There is no doubt about the "keen eye." There he sits watching "the young Divines, and those in next aptitude to Divinity," acting plays upon the stage, "writhing and unboning their clergy limbs to all the antic and dishonest gestures of Trinculo's, Buffoons, and Bawds; prostituting the shame of that Ministry, which either they had, or were nigh having, to the eyes of Courtiers and Court-Ladies, with their Grooms and *Madamoisellaes*."[2] Milton himself was looking forward to that Ministry, but a change came over him.

It is to be noted that now begins that long series of developments in Milton's thought and mind that marks him through life. To many he stands as the exponent of a rigid and obsolete theory of Theology and Cosmogony. In reality he was a man steadily moving onward, with the gift rare (at least to-day) among his fellow-countrymen of being able to face new and unwelcome ideas, to come up to them and examine them without discomfort or nervousness. By and by, it might almost be said, from this faculty developed the sense that such examination of new ideas is not only inevitable but desirable.

But it was not at the moment the privilege of a priest of the English Church. Laud became Archbishop (1628), while Milton was still at Cambridge, and the set was the other way—toward authority, antiquity and the "beauty of holiness" and away from freedom and new thoughts and the search for truth. "Mistrusting to find the Authority of their Order in the immediate Institution of Christ, or his Apostles, by the clear evi-

---

[1] *Prelude*, iii. 290.
[2] *Smectymnuus*, Prose i. 110. Luther, it is interesting to note, recommended the use of such Comedies. See his Table Talk *Colloquia Mensalia* (translated by Capt. Henrie Bell, London, 1652), chapter 72.

dence of Scripture, they fly to the carnal supportment of tradition. . . . And do not shame to reject the Ordinance of him that is eternal, for the perverse iniquity of sixteen hundred years, chusing rather to think Truth itself a Lyar, than that sixteen Ages should be taxed with an error."[1] As for the "beauty of holiness," Milton will have nothing to do with "the dark overcasting of superstitious Copes and flaminical Vestures,"[2] and other "deformed and fantastick dresses, . . . Palls and Miters, Gold, and Guegaws fetcht from *Aaron's* old Wardrobe, or the *Flamins Vestry*."[3] So he wrote some years later, and he added his reason, which is characteristic. Ritual turns the soul away from the divine and ideal world. "The soul by this means of over-bodying herself, given up justly to fleshly delights, bated her Wing apace downward: And finding the ease she had from her visible and sensuous Collegue the Body, in performance of *religious* Duties, her Pinions now broken, and flagging, shifted off from herself the labour of high soaring any more, forgot her heavenly flight, and left the dull and droyling Carcase to plod on in the old Road, and drudging Trade of outward Conformity."[4]

Freedom was threatened. The soul was to soar no longer, at least not in England. For, "let the Astrologer be dismay'd at the portentous blaze of Comets, and impressions in the Air, as foretelling troubles and changes to States: I shall believe there cannot be a more ill-boding Sign to a Nation (*God* turn the Omen from us) than when the Inhabitants, to avoid insufferable Grievances at home, are inforc'd by heaps

---

[1] *The Reason of Church Government*, bk. ii. ch. ii.; Prose i. 63.

[2] Prose i. 63.

[3] *Of Reformation*, Prose i. 1; *cf.* Luther's *Table Talk*, c. 25. See also *Of Reformation*, Prose i. 6—the touch at that "fast Friend of Episcopacy, Camden, who cannot but love Bishops as well as old Coins, and his much-lamented Monasteries, for antiquity's sake."

[4] There is a Platonic tinge in this, cf. *Phaedrus*. The recurrence of the word and idea of "soaring" in Milton is noticeable.

to forsake their Native Country."[1] And this was now happening.

So for his own part, "perceiving what Tyranny had invaded the Church, that he who would take Orders must subscribe Slave, and take an Oath withal; which unless he took with a conscience that would retch, he must either strait perjure, or split his Faith; I thought it better to prefer a blameless silence before the sacred Office of speaking, bought and begun with servitude and forswearing."[2] So much had been done by "a Tympany of *Spanioliz'd Bishops* swaggering in the fore-top of the State."[3] With orders Milton abandoned all hope of a fellowship of his College, and had nothing to do but to leave Cambridge. He was not one of "those drossy spirits that need the lure and whistle of earthly preferment."[4]

But if he was clear that the Church was no place for him in these times, he was full of the sense of responsibility now as ever. "Were it the meanest under-service, if God by his secretary Conscience enjoin it, it were sad for me if I should draw back," he wrote in 1642.[5] "When God commands to take the Trumpet and blow a dolorous or a jarring blast, it lies not in Man's Will what he shall say, or what he shall conceal."[6] But we can go back to an earlier date and find the same thought in the Sonnet written "on his having arrived at the age of twenty-three"—he hopes to live and work

> As ever in my great Task-Master's eye.

It is curious to note how opinion has changed about these Sonnets. Hannah More was surprised, she told Dr Johnson, that the poet who had written *Paradise Lost* should write such poor sonnets:—"Milton, Madam was,

---

[1] *Of Reformation*, Prose i. 19.
[2] *Reason of Church Government*, ii. Prose i. 62.
[3] *Of Reformation*, Prose i. 19.
[4] *Animadversions*, Prose i. 97.
[5] *Reason of Church Government*, Prose i. 62.
[6] *Ibid.*, Prose i. 58.

a genius that could cut a Colossus from a rock, but could not carve heads on cherry-stones."[1] Wordsworth saw better, and using Milton's own phrase, perhaps unconsciously, wrote that

> in his hand
> The thing became a trumpet, whence he blew
> Soul-animating strains—alas, too few!

It is to Milton, indeed, that we owe the suggestion from which came Wordsworth's own sonnets.

Now comes the period of Milton's quiet life at Horton, spent in reading and writing, in realizing gradually what sort of trumpet it was that God meant him to take and what strain it was he had to blow upon it. It is of import to see what he conceived to be the function and the training of a poet. "It was found," he says, "that whether aught was impos'd me by them that had the over-looking, or betaken to of mine own choice in *English*, or other Tongue, prosing or versing, but chiefly this latter, the stile by certain vital Signs it had, was likely to live."[2] Let us look for a moment at these pieces. At fifteen he had done Psalm cxxxvi. into English verse familiar still to more readers than ever read *Paradise Lost*.

> Who, by his all-commanding might,
> Did fill the new-made world with light;
> And caused the golden-tressèd sun
> All the day long his course to run; . . .
> The ruddy wave he clave in twain
> Of the Erythraean main;
> The floods stood still, like walls of glass,
> While the Hebrew bands did pass;
> But full soon they did devour
> The tawny king with all his power.

---

[1] *Boswell* (ed. Birkbeck Hill), iv. p. 305.
[2] *Reason of Church Government*, bk. ii. Prose i. 59.

MILTON

There is something in this suggestive of verse written forty years later—

> When with fierce winds Orion armed
> Hath vexed the Red Sea coast, whose waves o'erthrew
> Busiris with his Memphian chivalry   (*P. L.*, i. 305.)—

the same feeling for the classical adjective with its fine colour, the same turn for allusion. The "gladsome mind," familiar in the psalm, runs through all the young poet's work. But more striking is the *Ode on the Morning of Christ's Nativity*, written by a sudden inspiration on Christmas day, 1629, when he was just turned twenty-one. The poem does not suggest his age, but after all that is not strange. Great poets somehow produce at quite incredible ages work that has every mark of maturity—"certain vital Signs" that it is "likely to live." The poem shows the influence of "our sage and serious poet, Spenser,"[1] who, he owned to Dryden, was "his original";[2] it has conceits Elizabethan in character; but it is Miltonic none the less in its sureness, its great simplicity, its nobility of thought—in its richness in classical learning easily carried, in its full and deep music "making up full consort to the angelic harmony"—and in its insight.

With such "vital Signs" in his work he might well feel that "these abilities, wheresoever they be found, are the inspired gift of God,"[3] and might hope that "by labour and intent study (which I take to be my portion in this Life) join'd with the strong propensity of Nature, I might perhaps leave something so written to after-times, as they should not willingly let it die."[4] So he begins to prepare for his life's work—"to fix all the Industry and Art I could unite to the adorning of my native Tongue; not to

---
[1] *Areopagitica*, Prose i. 147.
[2] This is interesting, as it was Spenser who first fired Keats with enthusiasm for poetry.
[3] *Reason of Church Government*, ii. Prose i. 60.
[4] *Ib.* Prose i. 59.

make verbal Curiosities the end, that were a toilsome Vanity, but to be an Interpreter and Relater of the best and sagest things among mine own Citizens throughout the Island in the mother dialect."[1] He saw, too, "that he who would not be frustrate of his hope to write well hereafter in laudable things, ought himself to be a true Poem ; that is, a composition and pattern of the best and honourablest things, not presuming to sing high praises of heroic Men, or famous Cities, unless he have in himself the experience and the practice of all that which is praiseworthy."[2] This high fitness he saw was only to be obtained "by devout Prayer to that eternal Spirit, who can enrich with all utterance and knowledge, and sends out his Seraphim, with the hallow'd Fire of his Altar, to touch and purify the Lips of whom he pleases ; to this," he continues, "must be added, industrious and select Reading, steady Observation, insight into all seemly and generous Arts and Affairs."[3] From a promise like this, as Johnson said, might be expected the *Paradise Lost*.

While he lived in this mind at Horton, he wrote *L'Allegro* and *Il Penseroso*, perhaps in the autumn of 1632, *Comus* in 1634, and *Lycidas* in 1637. Henry Lawes, who composed the music for *Comus*, printed it, but without Milton's name. *Lycidas* appeared in the volume commemorating Edward King. Milton did not yet collect or print his pieces, and when Moseley published them in 1645 the initiative came from the publisher not the poet, and apparently some pressure was needed.

These poems are better known than any of his works, and yet they may be known well and familiarly and still only partially. The two shorter pieces are perhaps the best liked of all his poems, so full they are of what is pleasant to us all and at once intelligible. It is "the

---

[1] *Ib.* Prose i. 60; cf. Bacon, first words of *Nov. Org.*, "Homo Naturæ minister et interpres."

[2] *Smectymnuus*, Prose i. 111.

[3] *Reason of Church Government*, bk. ii. Prose i. 61.

MILTON

Poet, singing a song in which all human beings join with him,"[1] and, as Keats said of Milton,

> Giving Delight new joys,
> And Pleasure nobler pinions.

We need not linger over them, but two points may be noted—first, how Milton is influenced by sound, and then how he has his eyes as ever on the stars. The greater poets do their work by stray touches which call to the reader the same glimpse or sound that has moved them, and it does for him the same work of opening the door and setting free the imagination. Here the thing is done by sound. The bright day dawns, and how does Milton bring it before us? He hears and we hear, and from the hearing comes realization. Listen!

> While the ploughman, near at hand,
> Whistles o'er the furrowed land,
> And the milkmaid singeth blithe,
> And the mower whets his scythe.

I shall never forget what the last line did for me one dull winter day in a London lecture-room. I picked up the book by accident, and my eye fell on

> And the mower whets his scythe—

only that, and I escaped,

> As one who, long in populous city pent,
> Where houses thick and sewers annoy the air,
> Forth issuing on a summer's morn, to breathe
> Among the pleasant villages and farms.
> (*P. L.*, ix. 445.)

I saw a tree and the mower under it whetting his scythe, and all the country scene lay open round about.

Or again, here is a passage, found after old acquaintance with a sense of surprise in a new-bought and quite needless copy of *Il Penseroso*. There is a great deal to

---
[1] Wordsworth, *Preface to Lyrical Ballads*, 1800.

be said for multiplying editions of great authors; they always open at different places, and thrust new passages on the reader. Here it is the coming of Night

> ushered with a shower still,
> When the gust hath blown his fill,
> Ending on the rustling leaves
> With minute-drops from off the eaves.

Further on he speaks of the stars—

> And may at last my weary age
> Find out the peaceful hermitage,
> The hairy gown and mossy cell,
> Where I may sit and rightly spell
> Of every star that heaven doth shew.

To this point we must shortly return.

In April 1638 Milton set out for Italy. The grand tour in those days took English youth to France and to Italy, and brought them back sometimes none the better for their new experiences—"transform'd into Mimics, Apes, and Kecshose."[1] There was a proverb—

> An Englishman Italianate
> Is the Devil Incarnate.

Howell's *Familiar Letters* and Coryat's *Crudities* are explicit enough on the company a young Englishman might find, but Milton moved in other circles, keen-eyed as ever in letters and politics. "Look into *Italy* and *Spain*," he wrote later on, "whether those places be one scruple the better, the honester, the wiser, the chaster, since all the inquisitional rigor that hath bin executed upon Books."[2] He came home a more convinced believer in liberty for what he saw—"indeed none can love freedom heartily, but good Men; the rest love not

---

[1] *Of Education*, Prose i, 140. There is an interesting book by E. S. Bates, *Touring in* 1600 (London, 1911), full of all sorts of curious information about European travel.

[2] *Areopagitica*, Prose i, 150.

MILTON

freedom but licence; which never hath more scope or more indulgence than under Tyrants."[1] Tyrants, monarchical and ecclesiastical, governed Italy, and with what results in conduct and in thought! "I have sat among their learned men . . . while themselves did nothing but bemoan the servil condition into which Learning amongst them was brought; that this was it which had dampt the glory of *Italian* wits; that nothing had been there written now these many years but flattery and fustian. There it was that I found and visited the famous *Galileo* grown old, a prisoner to the Inquisition, for thinking in Astronomy otherwise than the Franciscan and Dominican licensers thought."[2]

It is curious to remark the impression made on Milton by Galileo and the telescope. They come into *Paradise Lost* repeatedly. Milton speaks of Satan's Shield—

> The broad circumference
> Hung on his shoulders like the moon, whose orb
> Through optic glass the Tuscan artist views
> At evening from the top of Fesolè,
> Or in Valdarno, to descry new lands,
> Rivers, or mountains, in her spotty globe.
> *(P. L.*, i. 288.)

Satan lands in the Sun,

> a spot like which perhaps
> Astronomer in the Sun's lucent orb
> Through his glazed optic tube yet never saw.
> *(P. L.*, iii. 588.)

Raphael's first distant view of the Garden of God reminds Milton of the old astronomer again—

> as when by night the glass
> Of Galileo, less assured, observes
> Imagined lands and regions in the Moon.
> *(P. L.*, v. 261.)

[1] *Tenure of Kings*, Prose i, 309.   [2] *Areopagitica*, Prose i. 153.

Galileo is the only contemporary mentioned in the great poem. In *Paradise Regained* Milton drops periphrasis and boldly says "telescope" (iv. 42), and very soon adds the "microscope."[1]

The problem, too, for which, or for his solution of it, Galileo was persecuted by the Inquisition, haunts Milton. He can hardly keep away from it. There are a good many sunrises and sunsets in the great poem, and a great deal of traffic among the stars between earth and heaven, and the question comes up repeatedly—

> whether the Prime Orb,
> Incredible how swift, had thither rolled
> Diurnal, or this less volúbile Earth,
> By shorter flight to the East, had left him there
> Arraying with reflected purple and gold
> The clouds that on his western throne attend.
> (*P. L.*, iv. 592.)

Eve asks Adam about the stars (*P. L.*, iv. 657), and he hazards some account of them to her, with some hint of "various influence" and "stellar virtue." Later on, when he has the chance, Adam puts the question straight to Raphael (*P. L.*, viii. 32). The "affable Archangel" does not admit that Adam's statement as it stands is correct, nor does he definitely say it is wrong. The general opinion of Europe was not clear yet whether the Ptolemaic astronomy or the Copernican was to prevail, yet Raphael's reply, though not definite, is suggestive. It shows at any rate how Milton's mind works, moving onward among theories, wedded to none, but keen to be as close to the fact as he can. The Archangel will not pronounce, but his words on the Ptolemaic system, cumbered as it now was with theory upon theory to fit it to the knowledge of the facts which had really made it obsolete, are very like criticism.

---

[1] Mr Pepys bought a microscope in 1664 for £5, 10s.

MILTON

> The great Architect
> Did wisely to conceal, and not divulge
> His secrets, to be scanned by them who ought
> Rather admire. Or, if they list to try
> Conjecture, he his fabric of the Heavens
> Hath left to their disputes—perhaps to move
> His laughter at their quaint opinions wide
> Hereafter, when they come to model Heaven
> And calculate the stars; how they will wield
> The mighty frame; how build, unbuild, contrive
> To save appearances; how gird the Sphere
> With Centric and Eccentric scribbled o'er,
> Cycle and Epicycle, Orb in Orb. (*P. L.*, viii. 72.)

He suggests the Copernican theory with more sympathy—

> What if the Sun
> Be centre to the World, and other Stars,
> By his attractive virtue and their own
> Incited, dance about him various rounds?
> (*P. L.*, viii. 122).

We need not follow him over "the planet Earth's three different motions," and "other Suns, perhaps, with their attendant Moons," nor need we conclude that Milton would have taken too literally the injunction with which Raphael closes—

> Solicit not thy thoughts with matters hid:
> Leave them to God above—

for Adam's reasoning is approved by the Angel, as a promise of what will be the mark of mankind. (*P. L.*, viii. 85.)

After this it is interesting to find that Satan is definitely Ptolemaic. His astronomy is Geocentric and astrological. He addresses Earth

> danced round by other Heavens
> Light above light, for thee alone, as seems,
> In thee concentring all their precious beams
> Of sacred influence. (*P. L.*, ix. 103.)

So thought Satan, and so think the Inquisition and others

> who, to be sure of Paradise,
> Dying put on the weeds of Dominic,
> Or in Franciscan think to pass disguised.
> They pass the planets seven, and pass the fixed,
> And that crystalline sphere whose balance weighs
> The trepidation talked, and that first moved ;
> And now Saint Peter at Heaven's wicket seems
> To wait them with his keys,   (*P. L.*, iii. 478.)

but a violent cross wind blows them over the backside of the World to a Limbo, the Paradise of Fools, where they will find the builders of Babel, Empedocles,

> Embryos and idiots, eremites and friars . . .
> Indulgences, dispenses, pardons, bulls,—

all the waste paper of the universe in a word.

Milton came home sooner than he meant. He could not "pass his life in foreign amusements while his countrymen were contending for their rights." The Civil War was beginning in earnest. Johnson was amused at this point. "Let not our veneration for Milton," he said, "forbid us to look with some degree of merriment on great promises and small performance, on the man who hastens home, because his countrymen are contending for their liberty, and, when he reaches the scene of action, vapours away his patriotism in a private boarding-school." Johnson's veneration permitted a good deal. Milton's "political notions," he said, "were those of an acrimonious and surly republican." His "republicanism was, I am afraid, founded in an envious hatred of greatness, and a sullen desire of independence; in petulance impatient of controul, and pride disdainful of superiority. He hated monarchs in the state, and prelates in the church; for he hated all whom he was required to obey. It is to be suspected, that his predominant desire was to destroy rather than establish, and that he felt not so much the love of liberty as repugnance to authority."[1] Let not our veneration for Johnson forbid us to remember who laid down the canon of criticism that "the dog is a Whig"[2] and who owned that "he would rather praise a man of Oxford than of Cambridge."[3] But he could praise Milton to a foreigner.[4]

If vapouring in a private boarding-school had been the sum of Milton's energies on behalf of the liberties of his country, he would have been less unpopular, but by now he was thoroughly severed from the Church of England. In 1641 and 1642 he brought out five tracts on the religious situation. Much has been said of Milton's methods and tone in controversy—sometimes unjustly, for we forget the age and the tension of the times. I shall not characterize either style or tone, but will try to let the reader hear Milton himself and decide on his own account, if he wishes, what he will think.

The first was *Of Reformation in England and the Causes that have hitherto hindered it*, published in May, and followed in June by *Of Prelatical Episcopacy*. The latter dealt with Ussher. It has always been supposed to stand in Milton's way that he is a learned poet, but as learning went in those days he did not pass for a very learned man. He preferred principles to authority, and was unwilling "to club quotations with Men whose learning and belief lies in marginal stuffings: who when they have, like good sumpters, laid ye down their horse-load of Citations and Fathers at your door, with a Rapsody of who and who were Bishops here or there, ye may take off their Pack-saddles; their day's work is

---

[1] It is always curious to realize how unintelligible to some minds thought-out political principles remain. All this of Johnson's is still considered worth saying.

[2] *Journey in the Hebrides*, 24 Sept.

[3] Murphy quotes this; see *Johnsonian Miscellanies*, by Birkbeck Hill, vol. i. p. 456, and *cf.* Mrs Piozzi in the same volume, p. 168.

[4] Mrs Piozzi, *ib.* i. 216.

done, and Episcopacy, as they think, stoutly vindicated."[1] So now he turns on Ussher—" suppose we should now, neglecting that which is clear in Scripture that a Bishop and *Presbyter* is all one both in Name and Office . . . suppose . . . we should by the uncertain, and corrupted Writings of succeeding times, determine that Bishop and *Presbyter* are different, because we dare not deny what *Ignatius*, or rather the *Perkin Warbeck* of *Ignatius* says; then must we be constrain'd to take upon our selves a thousand Superstitions and Falsities which the Papists will prove us down in from as good Authorities, and as ancient."[2] Now here he is abreast of modern scholarship as to Bishop and Presbyter, but it was the taunt about Ignatius that hit Ussher and set him to re-examine the Ignatian epistles. Milton was ahead of him, but he caught up and acknowledged six of the epistles to be interpolated and the remaining nine Perkin Warbecks as Milton said.

Similarly, to anticipate a little, when Milton wrote his *Eikonoclastes* (1649) to counteract the effect of *Eikon Basilike*, quite apart from one or two hints which he gives that the whole thing was a forgery, he pointed out another defect. "Who would have imagin'd so little fear in him of the true all-seeing Deity, so little reverence of the Holy Ghost, whose office is to dictate and present our Christian Prayers, so little care of truth in his last words, or honour to himself, or to his Friends or sense of his afflictions, or of that sad hour that was upon him, as immediately before his Death to pop into the hand of that grave Bishop who attended him, as a special Relique of his Saintly Exercises, a Prayer stolen word for word from the mouth of a Heathen Woman praying to a Heathen God; and that in no serious Book, but in the vain amatorious Poem of Sir *Philip Sidney's Arcadia* "?[3]

---

[1] *Reason of Church Government*, bk. ii. Prose i. 61.
"Deep-versed in books and shallow in himself."—*P. R.* iv. 327.
[2] *Of Prelatical Episcopacy*, Prose i. 37.
[3] *Eikonoklastes*, ch. i., Prose i. 368.

This was a bad slip. Gauden should have gone farther afield for plagiarism, if he could not make up a prayer himself. All the replies, as to the value of the *Arcadia* and the suitability of borrowing prayers intended for other gods, evade the point of the royal liar crowning a career of lies by a lie on the scaffold. This was met however by a lie—a Papist renegade was got to swear that Milton himself interpolated the prayer of Pamela in the *Eikon* when it was printing. Even Johnson palmed this off again on his public in 1780.

Milton, like Cromwell, had the type of mind that moves onward, as events teach or principles grow clear. If in 1641 he looked favourably on Presbyterianism, the conduct of the English Presbyterians cured that—" New Presbyter is but old Priest writ large" was a verdict borne out by history. He moved on toward the Independents and perhaps past them. It is a curious thing that in the posthumous *Treatise of Christian Doctrine*, published in 1823, an assertion of the inferiority of the Son to the Father was found, which was counted semi-Arian, while he suggested that polygamy is not contrary to morality, though inexpedient. Such views may shock, but why should they not be considered? What *is* marriage? Was he not living, as many Englishmen have lived, under a polygamous monarchy?

But we have reached the point of Milton's marriage. In May 1643 he very unexpectedly married a girl of seventeen. It was a blunder of the most dreadful kind. What it meant is best seen in the parable which he attributes to "the ancient Sages"[1]—a passage that moves one more and more as one realizes the passion within it.

"Love, if he be not twin-born, yet hath a brother wondrous like him, call'd *Anteros;* whom while he seeks all about, his chance is to meet with many false and feigning desires that wander singly up and down in his

[1] In *The Doctrine and Discipline of Divorce*, Prose i. 174. The passage was added in the second edition.

likeness: By them in their borrow'd garb, Love though not wholly blind, as Poets wrong him, yet having but one eye, as being born an Archer aiming, and that eye not the quickest in this dark Region here below, which is not Love's proper sphere, partly out of the simplicity and credulity which is native to him, often deceiv'd, imbraces and consorts him with these obvious and suborned Striplings, as if they were his Mother's own sons; for so he thinks them, while they subtilly keep themselves most on his blind side. But after a while, as his manner is, when soaring up into the high Tower of his *Apogæum*, above the shadow of the Earth, he darts out the direct rays of his then most piercing eyesight upon the impostures, and trim disguizes that were us'd with him, and discerns that this is not his genuine brother, as he imagin'd. He has no longer the power to hold fellowship with such a personated Mate; for strait his arrows lose their golden heads, and shed their purple feathers, his silken Braids untwine, and slip their knots, and that original and fiery virtue given him by Fate all on a sudden goes out, and leaves him undeified and despoil'd of all his force, till finding *Anteros* at last, he kindles and repairs the almost faded ammunition of his Deity by the reflection of a co-equal and *homogeneal* fire."

Few fables can be so literally true. What had happened was this: Mary Powell (born Jan. 24, 1625-6) came of a Royalist stock, bred in Royalist ways. She was young and pretty—and there was an end of her qualifications. From the hour of marriage, it seems, she refused to be Milton's wife in any sense of the term, and left him altogether after a few weeks. For two years or more she refused to come near him or to see him. The shock to Milton was intense. He was no anchorite or celibate,

> Whatever hypocrites austerely talk
> Of purity, and place, and innocence,

Defaming as impure what God declares
Pure, and commands to some, leaves free to all.
(*P. L.*, iv. 744.)

The great hymn to wedded Love that follows is famous, and it is the intense expression of the poet's real feeling. The "gentlest end of marriage" was companionship of soul, and though Milton's soul may be likened to a star that dwelt apart, it remains that he was keenly sensitive to solitude—"it is not good for man to be alone" is a text on which *Paradise Lost* is a commentary. The fall itself began in solitude. Now this girl bound Milton to herself by marriage, and then refused him everything that marriage implies. Was that marriage? Then what is marriage? Is it marriage simply in virtue of being irrevocable? Why should it be irrevocable?

Milton, here as everywhere, when a question was raised, struck right to the heart of it, regardless of the circumference and its traditions and decencies. He produced his tract on *The Doctrine and Discipline of Divorce*, and followed it up with others, raising problems that unreflective traditionalists would count it sin even to mention. But after all if marriage is sacred, it can be discussed, and it is well to know on what rests its sacredness. Milton's weakness here was just that his soul was like a star and dwelt apart—what could a star-soul know of the sordid vulgarity and selfishness of common men and ordinary women? Such people realize why marriage must be sacred even when it is no marriage.

"A barbarous noise of owls, and cuckoos, asses, apes, and dogs" at once environed Milton. In plainer terms, the Presbyterians, enemies for the time of freedom in thinking and printing alike, set about denouncing toleration and demanding the prohibition of "unlicensed printing." It took two Stuart kings to bring them to a sounder mood. Cromwell was before them—" in things of the mind," he said, "we look for no compulsion but that of light and reason."

Milton's reply was his *Areopagitica,* " a speech for the Liberty of Unlicensed Printing." "Books," he says, "are as lively, and as vigorously productive, as those fabulous Dragons teeth; and being sown up and down may chance to spring up armed Men." "As good almost kill a Man as kill a good Book." "Revolutions of ages do not oft recover the loss of a rejected Truth." "Authorised books," he quotes this from Bacon, "are but the language of the times," and he points his moral with the picture of Galileo in prison, the victim of a system of licensed thinking. No, Truth must be left unrestrained. "Truth is compar'd in Scripture to a *streaming fountain*; if her waters flow not in a perpetual progression, they sicken into a muddy pool of Conformity and Tradition." "Give me the liberty to know, to utter and to argue freely according to conscience, above all liberties."

On 24th June 1646 Oxford surrendered, and the King's cause was lost. The Powells, like other royalists, began to be in distress and to look about them. One day, when Milton was visiting a friend's house, a door opened, and Mary Powell was on her knees before him, praying forgiveness. Milton was a poet, and his imagination reacted to the stimulus. Here was repentance, love, and a true wife at last. He relented, forgave her, and took her back. Then the meaning came out. It was a well-played scene, and it was successful. The Powells encamped themselves in Mary's house, and with them Milton had to live, to eat his meals, and to hear their Cavalier talk. No one can imagine that they would help much to draw husband and wife together—

> His zeal
> None seconded, as out of season judged,
> Or singular and rash.   (*P. L.*, v. 849.)

Milton must have remained quite unintelligible to her; and he must have realized that a man can be as solitary with a wife as without. If there is asperity in his pamphlets against church and king, if in Eve and Dalilah he draws the folly and falsity of women, who shall say it is strange? Dalilah and her Philistines, bed and board—"bound fast to an uncomplying discord of nature ... to an Image of Earth and Fleam"[1]—and his children her true breed! It was seven years before the hand of God took Mary Powell away, and Milton was free. He was free, but he was blind.

> O dark, dark, dark, amid the blaze of noon,
> Irrecoverably dark, total eclipse,
> Without all hope of day! (*S. A.*, 80.)

He had been Latin Secretary to the Protector, and pamphleteer-in-general to the cause of Liberty. Now it was the Massacre in Piedmont that called forth his energy, now the defence of England against sentimentalists, *Eikon*-worshippers, and foreign revilers hired by Charles II. Now it was taunt for taunt in Latin with Salmasius, now in English the discussion of the *Tenure of Kings* (1648-9). A few critical sentences may be gathered from the last, for they show how the poet's mind worked.

"No man who knows aught, can be so stupid to deny that all Men naturally were born free, being the image and resemblance of God himself."[2]

"It being thus manifest that the power of Kings and Magistrates is nothing else, but what is only derivative, transferr'd and committed to them in trust from the People to the common good of them all, in whom the

---

[1] *Doctrine and Discipline of Divorce*, bk. i. ch. iv., Prose i. 173.

[2] Prose i. 311. John Morley (*Cromwell*, 229) not unnaturally sees here an anticipation of Rousseau. Compare also the passage about "a mutual bond of amity and brotherhood between man and man over all the world." Prose i. 316.

power yet remains fundamentally and cannot be taken from them, without a violation of their natural Birthright. . . .

"Unless the People must be thought created all for him, he not for them, and they all in one body inferior to him single. . . .

"It follows lastly, that since the King or Magistrate holds his authority of the people, both originally and naturally for their good in the first place, and not his own, then may the people as oft as they shall judge it for the best, either chuse him or reject him, retain him or depose him, though no Tyrant, meerly by the liberty and right of free-born men to be govern'd as seems them best."

It is sometimes said that Milton's prose works are obsolete. Is an ideal obsolete before it is realized? Are we yet as clear in insight and as free from cant as "the blind man who wrote Latin," or is it still to be said that "the ghost of a linen decency yet haunts us?"[1]

Two great sonnets commemorate how Milton considered how his light was spent. That written to Cyriack Skinner illustrates his mind in one or two ways. He emphasizes that his eyes are "clear to outward view of blemish and of spot." In his *Defensio Secunda* he repeats this—he had been taunted with being

monstrum, horrendum, informe, ingens, cui lumen ademptum

—he had never expected to be matched with the Cyclops, he says, and no one who had ever seen him had called him *deformis*; his eyes indeed were blind, but *ita sine nube clari ac lucidi, ut eorum qui acutissimum cernunt.*[2]

It is always a moving thing to take up a book which a friend has used and marked, and to "read where the quiet hand points." Charles Lamb, returning some volumes of Milton to Coleridge, says in his letter that if

---

[1] *Areopagitica*, Prose i. 159.   [2] Prose ii. 323.

MILTON

Coleridge finds them " in certain parts dirtied and soiled with a crumb of right Gloucester blacked in the candle (my usual supper), or peradventure a stray ash of tobacco wafted, look to that passage more especially: depend upon it, it contains good matter." Lamb retains for the present the Latin works, but calls attention to a passage in the second *Defensio*.[1] " It begins whimsically, with poetical flourishes about Tiresias and other blind worthies (which still are mainly interesting as displaying his singular mind, and in what degree poetry entered into his daily soul, not by fits and impulses, but engrained and innate); but the concluding page . . . divested of all brags and flourishes, gives so rational, so true an enumeration of his comforts, so human, that it cannot be read without the deepest interest. Take one touch of the religious part: 'Et sane haud ultima Dei cura cæci— (*we blind folks*, I understand it not *nos* for *ego*)—sumus; qui nos, quominus quicquam aliud præter ipsum cernere valemus, eo clementius atque benignius respicere dignatur . . . nec tam *oculorum hebetudine* quam *cœlestium alarum umbra* has nobis fecisse tenebras videtur, factas illustrare rursus interiore ac longe præstabiliore lumine haud raro solet. Huc refero, quod et amici officiosius nunc etiam quam solebant, colunt, observant, adsunt." The last word is surely pathetic—the mere presence of his friends was a comfort to him.

Twenty years had passed since Milton came home to serve his country—eighteen or so since he " covenanted with any knowing reader that for some few years he might go on trust with him " for the great life-work in poetry, and the poem was not written. A handful of sonnets is all the twenty years can show, but we must remember what sonnets they are.

But God's strange judgments were not yet done. Milton's light was spent, his talent lodged with him useless, and Patience bids him serve as those who stand and

---

[1] Prose ii. 325.

wait. And then, worst of all, the English nation decided not to have "a free Commonwealth; the manliest, the equallest, the justest Government, the most agreeable to all due Liberty and proportion'd Equality, both Human, Civil, and Christian,"[1] and recalled Charles II. We all know what followed—Clarendon Codes and "Nell-Gwyn-defenders of the faith"—"spiritual laws by carnal power" enforced, and "fair atheists." Milton had described it on the very page on which he eulogizes the Commonwealth.

The poet found himself blind, alone, and in danger, and he tells us how he sang

> With mortal voice, unchanged
> To hoarse or mute, though fallen on evil days,
> On evil days though fallen, and evil tongues,
> In darkness, and with dangers compassed round,
> And solitude.   (*P. L.*, vii. 24.)

Johnson would have us believe this "ungrateful and unjust." "This darkness had his eyes been better employed had undoubtedly deserved compassion"; but "who would pursue with violence an illustrious enemy, depressed by fortune and disarmed by nature?" Who would have Cromwell dug up—dead and so far disarmed by nature—and hang a dead body on a gallows at Tyburn?

> What will not ambition and revenge
> Descend to? (*P. L.*, ix. 168).

Milton probably understood the situation in 1660 as well as Johnson in retrospect. If he did not, there were plenty of people to explain it. "Liberty of Conscience," wrote Roger l'Estrange in 1663, "turns naturally to liberty of government and therefore is not to be endured, especially in a monarchy."[2] In 1683 the University of Oxford

---

[1] *The ready and easy way*, Prose i. 590.
[2] *Toleration Discussed*, p. 102.

publicly burnt Milton's works along with others that maintained that authority is derived from the people.[1]

To be hanged, drawn, and quartered with his friends was one thing, but it was worse to see "God's Englishmen," "a Nation of Prophets, of Sages, and of Worthies," commit themselves body and soul to Belial. Belial was not an austere Puritan god, but "in act more graceful and humane."

> Who more oft than he
> In temples and at altars? . . .
> In courts and palaces he also reigns,
> And in luxurious cities, where the noise
> Of riot ascends above their loftiest towers,
> And injury and outrage; and, when night
> Darkens the streets, then wander forth the sons
> Of Belial, flown with insolence and wine.
>
> (*P. L.*, i. 493.)

If this seem the warped judgment of a disappointed Puritan, John Evelyn was no Puritan, and what the new reign was like may be read in his diary, and what he thought of it.

Thanks perhaps to Andrew Marvell, the acuter phase of danger for Milton passed over, and he was able to settle down to obscurity, poverty and his great poem at last. Slow choosing and beginning late, he had found his inevitable theme. The paper is extant still on which he sketched out long before his alternative plans, and now he could set to work. Years of reading and years of political activity alike had prepared him to think on a great scale. Study has made him master of "those organic Arts which enable men to discourse and write perspicuously, elegantly, and according to the fitted style of lofty, mean and lowly."[2] Life has made him "himself a true poem," and his poetry comes from the whole

---
[1] *Cambridge Modern History*, vi. p. 807.
[2] *Of Education to Master Samuel Hartlib*, Prose i. 138.

man with the untold wealth of suggestion that belongs to a great and manifold nature.

> Es bildet ein Talent sich in der Stille,
> Sich ein Character in dem Strom der Welt,

said Goethe,[1] and Milton's case illustrates this. Great gifts of nature, inexplicable to us here as always, but a great character is here too, buffeted in happiness and misery, trained in high affairs of state to see things

> in clearest ken
> Stretched out to the amplest reach of prospect,
> (*P. L.*, xi. 379),

to think universally, and so to think that he shall become "an Interpreter and Relater of the best and sagest things."

Critics are all at one on Milton's style—there at least, however cramped and narrow the Puritan mind may be, however impossible or grotesque his Heaven and hell and his story from *Genesis* and Lactantius, it is agreed that Milton is great. He sets out to

> assert Eternal Providence
> And justify the ways of God to men,

and we chiefly admire his style,—as if it were a thing detachable.

Dr Johnson indeed tried to shew that Milton's style was not so very wonderful. This drew on him the wrath of the gentle Cowper. "The liveliness of the description, the sweetness of the numbers, the classical spirit of antiquity that prevails in it, go for nothing," writes Cowper of the attack on *Lycidas*, and he concludes a vigorous impeachment of the critic with a cry from the heart—"Oh! I could thresh his old jacket, till I made his pension jingle in his pocket."

There are poets who live by great lines. There is that

---

[1] *Torquato Tasso*, Act I. sc. 2.

MILTON

line of Lucan's which Prescott used nobly of the Spanish conqueror in the New World—

Victrices aquilas alium laturus in orbem,

but Lucan is not a great poet. His best line loses from its context. The clause is worse than the line, the page worse still, the book and the poem worst of all. Now if Milton live in common speech in virtue of the great number of single lines or couplets that every one knows irrespective of context—

> Fallen Cherub, to be weak is miserable. (*P. L.*, i. 157.)
> Better to reign in Hell than serve in Heaven.
> (*P. L.*, i. 272.)
> Not to know me argues yourselves unknown.
> (*P. L.*, iv. 830.)
> And feel that I am happier than I know.
> (*P. L.*, viii. 282.)
> So spake the Fiend and with necessity,
> The tyrant's plea, excused his devilish deeds.
> (*P. L.*, iv. 893.)
> Of whom to be dispraised were no small praise,
> (*P. R.*, iii. 56.)

—or if individual lines haunt the quiet mind for their gentle beauty or appalling grandeur—

> Dreaming by night under the open sky. (*P. L.*, iii. 514.)
> Celestial voices to the midnight air. (*P. L.*, iv. 682.)
> The flaming Seraph fearless though alone.
> (*P. L.*, v. 875.)
> Hurled headlong flaming from the ethereal sky.
> (*P. L.*, i. 45.)

—Milton gains in effect the more, as we read him consecutively.

If we turn to passages, there are those descriptions of Eden, which Tennyson prefers—

> Me rather all that bowery loneliness,
> The brooks of Eden mazily murmuring
> And bloom profuse and cedar arches
> Charm—

though some readers are not at home among so many flowers and so much innocence. Or we can take the hymn of the angels—

> Thee, Father, first they sung, Omnipotent,
> Immutable, Immortal, Infinite,
> Eternal King ; thee, Author of all being,
> Fountain of light, thyself invisible
> Amidst the glorious brightness where thou sitt'st
> Throned inaccessible, but when thou shad'st
> The full blaze of thy beams, and through a cloud
> Drawn round about thee like a radiant shrine
> Dark with excessive bright thy skirts appear,
> Yet dazzle Heaven, that brightest Seraphim
> Approach not, but with both wings veil their eyes.
> (*P. L.* iii. 372.)

Angels begin to be conceivable if we imagine them to sing like this. Or we can stand with the poet while his eye sweeps over vast regions of mankind

> from the destined walls
> Of Cambalu, seat of Cathaian Can,
> And Samarchand by Oxus, Temir's throne,
> To Paquin, of Sinaean Kings, and thence
> To Agra and Lahor of Great Mogul,
> Down to the golden Chersonese, or where
> The Persian in Ecbatan sat, or since
> In Hispahan, or where the Russian Ksar
> In Mosco, or the Sultan in Bizance
> Turchestan-born. (*P. L.*, xi. 387.)

MILTON

The lines are still lines, but they are so interwoven with their variety of pause in sense and syllable and accent, that we do not think of them as lines; the whole piece is one, a cloud that "moveth altogether," but a cloud of strange lights and colours, found in no sky of man's conceiving but Milton's only. And the whole epic is one.

Poetry, Milton wrote to Hartlib, is "less suttle and fine" than Prose or Rhetoric, but "more simple, sensuous, and passionate."[1] "Simple" is the last word that we should apply at first sight to *Paradise Lost*, yet the term is a just one. Milton had long ago disavowed the intention "to make verbal Curiosities the end";[2] he does not use ingenuities, he does not play tricks with his words or his thoughts; he "sets down the thing as it is" —as it is for Milton, we must remember, each thing charged with its own natural endowment of wonder or terror or beauty, and so set down that the reader feels it rather than strays away to admire the poet's skill.

By a poem being sensuous Milton means that it must appeal to our sense of beauty along the lines of our experience. Here, it may be said, much of *Paradise Lost* ought to fail, for much of it must necessarily be foreign to the experience of men. If Heaven is to move us, it must be by its correspondence with what we know. This Raphael suggests himself:

> What surmounts the reach
> Of human sense I shall delineate so,
> By likening spiritual to corporal forms,
> As may express them best—though what if Earth
> Be but the shadow of Heaven, and things therein
> Each to other like more than on Earth is thought?
> (*P. L.*, v. 571.)

In this way we are helped over some of the difficulties

---

[1] *Of Education*, Prose i. 139.
[2] *Reason of Church Government*, II., Prose i. 60.

inherent in the treatment of what lies outside our experience, though the modern reader sometimes moves as uncomfortably in this region as Satan walking with "uneasy steps over the burning marle" (*P. L.*, i. 296).

Yet in Eden, in flower and tree, in bird and animal, in the loveliness of Eve, we find a fuller satisfaction of our need—

> From branch to branch the smaller birds with song
> Solaced the woods, and spread their painted wings
> Till even ; nor then the solemn nightingale
> Ceased warbling, but all night tuned her soft lays.
> Others, on silver lakes and rivers, bathed
> Their downy breast ; the swan, with archèd neck
> Between her white wings mantling proudly, rows
> Her state with oary feet.   (*P. L.*, vii. 433.)

One thing that is always impressive in *Paradise Lost* is the immense range which the poet has over space. The solar system, Ptolemaic or Copernican, is a corner of the vast field over which Satan wages his war on God. When he and his armies were driven from heaven

> Nine days they fell,   (*P. L.*, vi. 871.)

before they reached their goal in

> The dark, unbottomed, infinite abyss.
>   (*P. L.*, i. 405.)

Over all this immeasurable expanse the poet's flight is as sure as Raphael's; he is nowhere lost in the vast inane ; and nowhere does the infinite seem to contract at his coming. All is immense but all is cosmos. Even hell assumes a certain order under his gaze, though it remains vast and uncharted, awful in its unknown spaces. Such is the power of his imagination. It is only in Heaven and in Eden before the Fall that we find it hard to imagine with him. The secret he tells us himself, in *Areopagitica,*

"Good and evil we know in the field of this World grow up together almost inseparably: and the knowledge of good is so involv'd and interwoven with the knowledge of evil, and in so many cunning resemblances hardly to be discern'd, that those confused seeds which were impos'd on *Psyche* as an incessant labour to cull out, and sort asunder, were not more intermix'd. It was from out the rind of one apple tasted, that the knowledge of good and evil, as two twins cleaving together, leap'd forth into the World. And perhaps this is that doom which *Adam* fell into of knowing good and evil, that is to say, of knowing good by evil."[1]

This is exactly the reason of our difficulty. We cannot grasp good without evil, and man's state of innocence perplexes and fatigues. We are uneasy and, as a critic says, are glad to escape in the simile to

> The smell of grain, or tedded grass, or kine,
> Or dairy—

to something familiar, showing the touch of human hands like our own, soiled, helpful, intelligible. It has been said epigrammatically that there is no love in *Paradise Lost*. This is not strictly true, of course, but before the Fall the love of Adam and Eve, however real to themselves, is not to be put in our terms. It is when their sin brings them into our range—when we find our experience in them, the sense "jocund and boon" of wider knowledge and enhanced power that comes with the excitement of disobedience, the exhilaration of limits transcended as it seems, and then the staleness, the paralysis and remorse when "the exhilarating vapour bland" has "exhaled"—the consciousness of the lost ideal and the lower plane—it is then we enter into their life and can identify ourselves with them. It is the first quarrel and the reconciliation in penitence and prayer that make their love real to us. The element of passion

[1] Prose i. 147.

is disentangled—or perhaps we should say, embodied in the only medium we understand.

In Hell things are otherwise. There good is mingled with evil. There is loyalty to Satan among his followers; in Satan there is energy, admiration of beauty, intolerance of tyranny—Milton's own characteristics. Satan feels shame for "his lustre visibly impaired." He "melts," he says, at the harmless innocence of Adam and Eve, and has to excuse his devilish deeds with necessity. Is it possible that a creature with such seeds of good within can be lost? "There shall never be one lost good," said Browning, but we may find ourselves in a tangle of speculation if we listen to him too readily. Milton is nearer the fact; it is the element of good in the evil that gives it its horrible power, and its fascination. It is this that makes it pre-eminently evil—this "use of God against God."

We now come to the general purpose of the poem, for Milton avowed a purpose boldly enough. He would, we remember,

>assert Eternal Providence
>And justify the ways of God to men.

It has been held that he took his story for history, that he believed it all, or most of it, to be literally true. He has taken pains more than once to explain that he is using symbol—

> Who, though with the tongue
> Of Angels, can relate, or to what things
> Liken on Earth conspicuous, that may lift
> Human imagination to such highth?
> (*P. L.*, vi. 297.)

Under the symbol he is giving us a philosophy—a philosophy of human life, of law, disobedience, and doom, these familiar enough, and of "grace prevenient," which is not now so familiar a sound, though, if the fact has ceased to be, Christianity is a thing of the past. But unlike other poets he draws his picture on the background of the universal and eternal, not darkly hinted in inevitable law, but boldly shown, with the clearness of a Canadian landscape where there is no middle distance,—in God the Father, God the Son, Heaven and Hell. It is this explicitness that makes the poem hard reading for the modern temperament. In law we believe, perhaps only too much. It is the basis of our cheap popular sciences and philosophies of Evolution and Environment. But we are not so clear about Moral Law as about physical, and we have little to say of Grace. Milton offends us partly because, like every other generation, we have a strong sense of the value and finality of our own terminology; partly because he is a great deal surer about the spiritual than we are. The physics and astronomy, the non-geological and creationist cosmogony, and so forth, of his poem give us our chance, and we boldly say *Paradise Lost* is impossible. We forget that Milton too had a progressive mind that ranged, at any rate in human experience, a good deal further and more freely than many of us can manage even yet. We forget how he moved over to the Copernican astronomy, and how likely it is that, if we could have made them good to him, he might have adopted our geology and evolution. We forget that we too might be uncomfortable—more so than he—if he boldly threw over the physics and creationism, as he very well might, and challenged us on the spiritual experience. He had had to justify the ways of God to John Milton, and they took a good deal of justification. Samson Agonistes is as likely to reach truth as any pleasant person in an easy chair with a smattering of science.

Our critics tell us to-day that we must dismiss Milton's "fable," that his symbols represent nothing—nothing at all. But if we are to get anything from a poet, we have not only to criticize him by ourselves—an easy and not always very profitable task—but to criticize ourselves by him. Here is a man who thinks in the terms of the eternal, the universal, the infinite, and we say his physics are wrong. How do we think? The influence of Natural Science is strong upon us, with its tendencies to detailed inquiry and to partial and provisional affirmation and its hesitation in general statement. Milton might say that we have no philosophy and no theology, and if he asked us what lay behind all the phænomena we so laboriously study in detail, we should have to tell him that we do not think about it. Which is the greater error, his or ours? Which is the larger, the sounder, the wiser mind? In *Paradise Lost* an attempt is made to get behind the world of phænomena and to think of all existence as a unity, and as a unity in the mind and love of God. The symbol is only symbol, Milton might say, but to suggest that there is nothing behind it is surely to confess that for us the universe has very little meaning. If Milton can induce us to add to our scientific outlook some deep-going spiritual insight, he will not be found quite so obsolete as we are sometimes told.

But after all it is not as a philosopher or a theologian that Milton has to be judged. He is a poet; and whatever in our merely philosophic or theological moods we may make of his work, it is something more. No statement in prose of the philosophy of a poet—even when he makes it himself—is quite the same thing as his poetry. It is like a legal document describing an inheritance. What is there in common between the unpunctuated wilderness of technical terms and the heritage itself with the song of birds about its woods and waters? There is something in common, but who could guess the one from the other—who could enjoy the green and glory of the wood and its voices in "all the whatever-it-is hereinbefore described?" If Milton gave us only a scheme of the universe, we might discuss it and dismiss it. But it is no such document—it is a heritage enjoyed and interpreted by a poet, who has travelled over all its vast regions, with ever-widening intelligence making all his own. This he gives us, but only on the terms of our enjoying it—for in no other way can we enter upon it. The Kingdom of Heaven is only to be had by acceptance, and Nature and Poetry have no other law. When we accept them in earnest, we cease to theorize very much, for we can never be quite certain that we know all that we should know and shall know—the unsuspected depths of wonder and glory and happiness that any chance look may reveal in the most familiar spot. The measure of our enjoyment and expectation of enjoyment gives our right to criticize *Paradise Lost*. The philosophy is there —the cumulative wisdom gathered from life by a great soul—and we can indeed think of it in some degree apart from its expression, but not perfectly; for style is thought, and we have no right to neglect it in judging of a poet's mind. Indeed, what makes a poet so unlike ordinary men is this quality of wholeness, integrity, in his utterance. All counts, and often that most which we at first, and perhaps he to the last, might reckon least.

In the *Areopagitica*[1] Milton had complained that under a system of licensing an author might have to submit his book " to the hasty view of an unleisur'd Licenser, perhaps much his younger, perhaps far his inferior in judgment, perhaps one who never knew the labour of Book-writing." There was no help for it now, and to the licenser *Paradise Lost* was sent. It was to a Rev. Mr Thomas Tompkyns, chaplain to the Archbishop of Canterbury, and author, as it happened, of a pamphlet on " The Inconveniencies of Toleration," that the duty fell of certifying England that Milton was "no Idiot or Seducer." What leisure he had we cannot guess, nor how far he read, but in the first book his eye caught doubtful words and he hesitated. The comet, he there read,

With fear of change
Perplexes monarchs.

[1] Prose i. 151.

However this was explained, and the MS. of the first book is still extant with the *Imprimatur* of Mr Tompkyns.

The publication of his poem at once drew attention to Milton, and thoughtful persons, many of them foreigners, came to see him—Dryden among them. They found him sitting "in a grey coarse Cloth Coat at the Door of his House, in warm sunny Weather, to enjoy the fresh Air," or it might be, "up one pair of Stairs, . . . sitting in an Elbow Chair; black Clothes, and neat enough; pale but not cadaverous; his Hands and Fingers gouty, and with Chalk-stones. Among other Discourse he express'd himself to this purpose, that was he free from the Pain this gave him, his Blindness would be tolerable." When he dictated his verse, we are told, it was often with his leg thrown over the arm of the chair.

Milton had shewn his poem in MS. to Thomas Ellwood, the young Quaker with a conscience about hat-worship. In returning it Ellwood "pleasantly said to him, *Thou hast said much of* Paradise Lost; *but what hast thou to say of* Paradise Found?" From this, Ellwood believed, came *Paradise Regained*. It shows a flagging of powers —but it is a flagging of no ordinary powers. This Milton did not like to hear suggested, and he had an ally in Wordsworth, who "spoke of the *Paradise Regained* as surpassing even the *Paradise Lost* in perfection of execution," pointing out the storm in it, "as the finest of all poetry."[1]

Last came the *Samson Agonistes*, but drama is neither here nor in *Comus* Milton's proper sphere. His Epic has unity and is an integer. His dramas are episodic. Aristotle had said that a poem must have a beginning, a middle, and an end. Wordsworth, following Johnson, held that *Samson Agonistes* has *no middle*, though "the beginning and the end are equally sublime."

[1] *P. R.*, iv. 409. And either tropic now. . . . Ill wast thou shrouded then, O patient Son of God. Knight, *Life of Wordsworth*, vol. iii. p. 258.

Thus the great task was done and the bold promise fulfilled, and after disappointment, blindness, danger, and solitude, the old man could wait in the enjoyment of "the smell of peace toward Mankind" for the end, which came on 8 November 1674, so peacefully that its moment was not recognized. The event made no stir. His work had not been done to win the approval of the men of the Restoration, and he ·had to wait for his fame. But he could afford to wait.

EVELYN

IN 1618 a comet hung over Europe, and years later people traced its effects in the prodigious revolutions, especially in Germany, where "the Swedes broke in, giving umbrage to the rest of the princes, and the whole Christian world cause to deplore it, as never since enjoying perfect tranquillity."[1] Meteors of strange shape and colour perplexed men with fear of change—and comets came and went. "We have had of late several comets," writes Evelyn, "which though I believe appear from natural causes, and of themselves operate not, yet I cannot despise them. They may be warnings from God, as they commonly are forerunners of his animadversions."[2] It was the age of Newton and Halley, but opinion varied "whether comets or blazing stars be generally of such terrible effects, as elder times have conceived them; for since it is found that many, from whence these predictions are drawn, have been above the Moon; ... why since they may be conceived to arise from the effluviums of other Stars, they may not retain the benignity of their Originals;" etc., etc.; "is not absurd to doubt," wrote Sir Thomas Browne.[3] Whatever the truth about comets, other men saw signs of trouble. Milton and Penn saw danger in the fact that men, "to avoid insufferable Grievances at home, are inforc'd by heaps to forsake their Native Country." Altogether it was an age of unrest, trying and perplexing to serious men of every

---

[1] Evelyn's *Diary*, 1624. Quotations from the *Diary* are made from Mr Austin Dobson's edition.
[2] Evelyn's *Diary*, 12 Dec. 1680.
[3] *Pseudodoxia*, bk. vi. ch. 14.

school.[1] Each in turn saw right and wrong in ascendancy and decline; nothing was secure; in politics and religion change followed change. Even among the eternal stars themselves there was the strangest change of all, for the earth was turned out of the centre of her spheres and set revolving through space, and her quiet place was taken by the sun, his chariot unyoked for the last time.

English literature and history are full of the thoughts of the men of this strange epoch. They wrote with unexampled length and learning, ignorance and freedom, upon every subject. Thirty thousand pamphlets are said to have been printed during the Commonwealth alone; and perhaps more lives, diaries and memoirs were written than in any century before. What is stranger is that these lives are of interest still—some indeed were not published till their writers had lain a hundred years in their graves, and their names were nearly if not quite forgotten. Of these one of the most interesting is John Evelyn. He was well known in his day—a grave, upright and godly man, with a good Englishman's concern for public morals, for his fellow-citizens' health and commercial prosperity, for the vindication of his country from the falsehoods of the foreigner, and a certain capacity for business when put to it [2]—and at the same time a *virtuoso*, an inveterate and delightful dabbler in art and science and everything rare and curious—a friend of poets and politicians, of bishops and kings, and secretary for a while of the Royal Society. If his judgments on men and things are not very profound, they may not be the less English for that, and they reveal what is always of moment—the average mind of a generation. He was an English gentleman in everything—in his descent from a family that made their

---

[1] See particularly Evelyn's preface to his *History of Religion*, concluding: "When, I say, I beheld all this, 'my feet were almost gone,'" etc.

[2] As on occasions of the Dutch prisoners and the Fire of London.

wealth by a trade, gunpowder in this case — in his attachment to his country seat and county and his love of London — in his concern for the Church of England, his loyalty to his king and his sincere pleasure in being noticed by that king, and perhaps in his refusal to accept a title. He has the dignity, the sense of responsibility, the grave courtesy and the limited outlook of his order; and he is interesting chiefly because he is representative.

He is often compared with his "particular friend" Mr Pepys; but the comparison rests on their diaries after all—diaries as diverse as they could well be. Mr Pepys, in all else a more effective citizen than his friend, is in his Diary frankly the most original of men; Evelyn is not original at all, and that is one of his great merits. In studying the past we turn naturally to the great and outstanding figures, but after all they are apt to belong to all time. To understand them, we need to set them among their contemporaries; and we are happy indeed when among their contemporaries we can find a man so entirely average as Evelyn, whose diary has yet scarcely a page without something to engage the reader's attention and his friendship. It is curious to read Evelyn and Milton side by side—each English, cultured and learned, each acutely interested in politics and each a pamphleteer. Each gives the reader something by which to judge the other. "Mr Edward Phillips," wrote Evelyn (24 Oct. 1664) "came to be my son's preceptor: this gentleman was nephew to Milton who wrote against Salmasius' *Defensio*; but was not at all infected with his principles, though brought up by him." This was before *Paradise Lost* appeared. *Lycidas, Comus, L'Allegro*, the *Ode on the Nativity*, had long been in print, but the friend of "the great poet Mr Waller,"[1] of "that incomparable poet and virtuous man my very dear friend Abraham Cowley,"[2] and the acquaintance (at least) of "Mr Dryden the poet,"

---

[1] 7 July, 1646.   [2] 1 Aug. 1667.

EVELYN

always saw the pamphleteer in Milton. Thus when Christopher Milton, the renegade and knight, was made a judge by James II., Evelyn notes he is "brother to that Milton who wrote for the Regicides."[1]

"I was born (at Wotton, in the County of Surrey) about twenty minutes past two in the morning, being on Tuesday the 31st and last of October 1620," writes Evelyn, and goes on to particularize as to his parents and his father's "sanguine complexion mixed with a dash of choler," his beard, "his eyes extraordinarily quick and piercing," and so forth; and his mother with "eyes and hair of a lovely black, of constitution more inclined to a religious melancholy or pious sadness"—and of Wotton he adds that the house is "large and ancient, suitable to those hospitable times," and "sweetly environed with delicious streams and venerable woods." He was baptized "in the drawing-room, by Parson Higham, the present incumbent of the parish, according to the forms of the then glorious Church of England." The adverb prepares us for what is to come.

To understand a man, the first thing is to realize what he carries in memory and that is very often a matter of three generations. Memory and association—what has been told us by our fathers and what by the old men, their fathers—these things make our minds. We are sons and grandsons if we are anything, whether we outgrow or betray or cleave to what our fathers and grandfathers have taught us. But it will have to suffice here to hint merely at the seventy years that preceded 1620, and the national memories of Armada and Reformation, of Smithfield fires and Puritan controversies, of English drama and the *Faerie Queene*. Shakespeare was but four years dead, Ben Jonson had seventeen years more to live. Raleigh had fallen in the year of the comet; Bacon lived to see Charles I. on the throne. In 1620 the *Mayflower* took the Pilgrim Fathers to New England. None of

[1] 2 June 1686.

these people are mentioned by Evelyn himself, but they and theirs made his environment. In 1621 Burton's *Anatomy* was first printed. Here is his picture of the England he knew; it is a moralist's picture, and will therefore not be too bright.

"A blessed, a rich country, and one of the fortunate isles; and, for some things, preferred before other countries, for expert seamen, our laborious discoveries, art of navigation, true merchants. . . . We have besides many particular blessings, which our neighbours want—the gospel truly preached, church discipline established, long peace and quietness—free from exactions, foreign fears, invasions, domesticall seditions—well manured, fortified by art, and nature, and now most happy in that fortunate union of England and Scotland," and above all, that other Numa, second Augustus and true Josiah, James I. "Yet, amongst many roses, some thistles grow, some bad weeds and enormities." A Hercules is wanted to put things right, and he sketches at length what he would do if he were that Hercules.

Later on he deepens the gloom of the picture—except that he is such invincibly cheerful company himself. "See the divel," he says, "that will never suffer the church to be quiet or at rest . . . we have a mad giddy company of precisians, schismaticks, and some heretiques even in our bosoms in another extream.

> Dum vitant stulti vitia, in contraria currunt;

That out of too much zeale in opposition to Antichrist . . . will admit of no ceremonies at all, no fasting dayes, no cross in baptism, kneeling at communion, no church musick, etc., no bishops' courts, no church government, raile at all our church discipline, will not hold their tongues, and all for the peace of thee, O Sion. No, not so much as degrees some of them will tolerate, or universities; all humane learning ('tis *cloaca diaboli*) hoods, habits, cap and surpless . . . they abhor, hate and snuff at . . . they make matters of conscience of them, and will rather forsake their livings then subscribe to them."[1] But we had better leave this "company of giddy heads" at once—"Brownists, Barrowists, Familists, and those Amsterdamian sectes and sectaries."[2]

In such an England John Evelyn grew up. In 1631 "there happened now an extraordinary dearth in England, corn bearing an excessive price; and, in imitation of what I had seen my father do, I began to observe matters more punctually, which I did use to set down in a blank almanack." His father wished to send him to Eton,[3] "but, not being so provident for my own benefit, and unreasonably terrified with the report of the severe discipline there, I was sent back to Lewes; which perverseness of mine I have since a thousand times deplored." His mother died in 1635. Two years later he went to Oxford —to Balliol College—and "subscribed the articles and took the oaths." Laud was Chancellor, he says, and the University was under his "exact discipline," and "at this time was the Church of England in her greatest splendour, all things decent, and becoming the Peace, and the persons that governed." He was somewhat backward with his studies, but he found time for "the dancing and vaulting schools."

Eventually Evelyn amassed an immense amount of miscellaneous learning. In a letter to Dr Beale in 1668, he speaks of his eye-sight as impaired "since my too

[1] It is interesting to compare what George Fox has to say here:—"And I was to bring People off from *Jewish Ceremonies*, and from *Heathenish Fables*, and from Mens *Inventions* and *windy Doctrines*, by which they blowed the People about, this way and the other way, from *Sect* to *Sect*, and all their beggarly Rudiments with their *Schools* and *Colledges*, for making *Ministers* of Christ, who are indeed Ministers of their own making, but not of Christ's, And all their *Images* and *Crosses* and *Sprinkling of Infants*, with all their *Holy-Days* (so called) and all their vain *Traditions*. . . ."—George Fox's Journal, folio p. 25.
[2] *Anatomy of Melancholy*, Part 3, Sect. 4, Mem. 1, Subs. 3.
[3] Evelyn, 21 Oct. 1632.

intent poring upon a famous Eclipse of the Sun, about 12 yeares since "—" but besides that, I have treated my eyes very ill neere these 20 yeares, during all which tyme I have rarely put them together, or compos'd them to sleepe before One at night and sometimes much later." When needful, he uses a κολλουριον [1] (which he sets forth) to ease his eyes, and continues—" Indeede, in ye sum'ertime, I have found wonderfull benefit in bathing my head with a decoction of some hot and aromaticall herbs, in a lixivium made of the ashes of vine-branches, and when my head is well washed wth this, I im'ediately cause aboundance of cold fountain-water to be poured upon me *stillatim*, for a good halfe-hour together." He enlarges on the advantage of this practice from personal and other experience. Thus it was he did his reading, which would seem from his writings to have been very wide. He has the habit of the learned of his day of filling his pages with lists of recondite and other authorities. " Onely I will mind you of one passage of Jamblicus . . . and to that purpose Cicero de Nat. Deor: Seneca de Providentiâ, the Golden Verses of Pythagoras, and more expressly Lactantius L. 3 C. 9, where he proves *cultum Dei* to be naturally in Man, making it a formal part of its definition *Animal Rationale Religiosum*. To conclude, Augustine, Clemens, Lactantius, Cyrill, Arnobius, Justin Martyr, of old,—of the neoteriq, Aquinas, Plaessis Morney, Dr Andrews, Grotius, Dr Hammond in a particular opusculum, I. L. Vives, Bradwardine de Causa Dei, Valesius de Sacra Philosophia, Campanella, and our most ingenious Dr Moore, in his Antidote against Atheisme, have all treated on this subject "[2]—a fine list of authorities, with many more in the earlier part of the letter, to be quoted by a man of thirty-seven not a professed theologian. After all this it is a relief—at least to a Cambridge mind—to find him misquoting Lucretius to the havoc of grammar and

---

[1] I keep the Greek type and refrain from adding an accent.
[2] Letter to Mr E. Thurland, 20 Jan. 1656-7.

scansion together in the letter about his eye-sight—
Odorumque Canum Vis.[1]

As his home was so near Oxford, he was not held there so closely as men from the North and from Scotland long were. Thus on the 3rd of November 1640, "a day never to be mentioned without a curse," he saw King Charles ride to open "that long, ungratefull, foolish, and fatal Parliament, the beginning of all our sorrows for twenty yeeres after, and the period of the most happy Monarch in the world; *Quis talia fando!*" In May next year (1641) he "beheld on Tower-hill the fatal stroke which sever'd the wisest head in England from the shoulders of the Earle of Strafford."

In 1641 his father died and Evelyn went to the Low Countries for two or three months. On his way he saw at Chatham "the *Royal Sovereign,* a glorious vessel of burden lately built there, being for defence and ornament, the richest that ever spread cloth before the wind. She carried an hundred brass cannon and was 1200 tons; a rare sailer, the work of the famous Phineas Pett, inventor of the frigate-fashion of building, to this day practised. But what is to be deplored as to this vessel is, that it cost his Majesty the affections of his subjects, perverted by the malcontent great ones, who took occasion to quarrel for his having raised a very slight tax for the building of this, and equipping the rest of the navy, without an Act of Parliament." He was never very much interested in Constitutional questions, nor in political liberty, till James II. threatened danger to the English church.

In Holland he saw something of war, but it was not to his mind, so he "took his leave of the leaguer and *camarades*" and travelled with curious eyes, as ever, for any strange sight. Thus at the fair at Rotterdam he first saw an elephant, and remarked that it was "flexible and nimble in the joints, contrary to vulgar tradition."[2] This was a point much discussed, as the friends of Sir Thomas

---

[1] Letter to Dr Beale, 27 Aug. 1668.   [2] Evelyn, 13 August 1641.

Browne will remember.[1] Evelyn however made sure of the beast's knees on his own account, while he "most of all admired the dexterity and strength of its proboscis."

At Amsterdam he went to see a synagogue.[2] He seems to have been interested in Jews at various places on his travels—in the red hats they were compelled to wear at Avignon[3] and their yellow garb in Rome.[4] He went once to witness the rite of circumcision;[5] and on the other hand he heard a sermon preached to the Jews in San Sisto[6]—at least he was there, for "it is with so much malice in their countenances, spitting, humming, coughing and motion, that it is almost impossible they should hear a word from the preacher. A conversion," he adds, "is very rare." He stood godfather to a convert, "who was believed to be a counterfeit."[7] The Jew was an exotic not yet cultivated in England, and our destinies lay in the hands of other arbiters.

For it was now to be decided who did control England's destinies, the King or the Parliament. Evelyn landed at Dover on 12 October 1641, and found matters advanced. He was in London awhile in 1642, January to March, "studying a little but dancing and fooling more." On 23 October 1642 the battle of Edgehill was fought. Evelyn was not a combatant. He went, he says, in the same month to see the siege of Portsmouth and "the so much celebrated line of communication" London way; he went with horse and arms to the King's army arriving just after the battle of Brentford 12 Nov. 1642, and on the 15th concluding that to go with it to Gloucester "would have left both me and my brothers exposed to ruin without any advantage to his Majesty," he went home. Finally he sent his "black *manège* horse and furniture" to the King at Oxford; and then last of all to avoid signing the Covenant and some other "very unhandsome

---

[1] Sir Thomas Browne, *Pseudodoxia*, bk. iii. ch. i.
[2] 21 Aug. 1641.   [3] Oct. 1644.   [4] May 1645 and 15 Jan. 1645.
[5] 15 Jan. 1645.   [6] 7 Jan. 1645.   [7] 25 Feb. 1645.

things," he obtained a licence from the King and went abroad.[1]

For some years he travelled—mostly in France and Italy—seeing the cities of many men and learning something of their minds on every conceivable subject. Processions and highly artificial gardens he must always see; strange birds and beasts he could not resist—the Duke of Orleans' tortoises (he kept one himself later on, of whose death and its cause he advised the Royal Society[2]),—bears, tigers, and lions "in a deep-walled court" at Florence,[3]—the *manucodiata* or bird of Paradise, stuffed specimens at Naples.[4] There were discomforts in travel. In the Forest of Orleans he and his party were attacked by brigands and four of them were killed.[5] To pass the oak-woods of the Campagna they "were fain to hire a strong convoy of about thirty firelocks" because of the banditti.[6] When they were at Marseilles, where they visited the galleys and the galley-slaves—"so many hundreds of miserably naked persons . . . doubly chained about their middle and legs"—they had to buy "umbrellas against the heats," and "consult of their journey to Cannes by land, for fear of the Picaroon Turks, who make prize of many small vessels about these parts."[7] At Venice Evelyn was shot at from a gondola.[8] In the fens near Ferrara "we were so pestered with those flying glow-worms, called *lucciole*, that one who had never heard of them, would think the country full of sparks of fire. Beating some of them down, and applying them to a book, I could read in the dark by the light they afforded."[9] Homeward bound they crossed the Alps, "through strange,

---

[1] 11 Nov. 1643 at Calais.

[2] The Duke's tortoises, 1 April 1644. Evelyn's tortoise, *Miscell. Writings*, p. 696. He looked on it as a kind of *plant-animal*; it happened to be "obstructed by a vine-root from mining" deep enough, and so died, after many winters safely past.

[3] 25 Oct. 1644.   [4] 4 Feb. 1645.   [5] April 1644.
[6] 29 Jan. 1645.   [7] Oct. 1644.   [8] Jan. 1646.
[9] May 1645.

horrid and fearful crags and tracts," "cataracts of stupendous depth" and "almost inaccessible heights," ways "covered with snow since the Creation," and here they got into trouble about a dead goat. Finally at Geneva Evelyn had the smallpox.

But there is no doubt he enjoyed his travels. He laid up observations of architecture and painting which stood him in good stead long after, and he kept an open eye for the Roman Catholic religion. He was shown endless relics, "and, to omit no fine thing, the just length of the Virgin Mary's foot as it seems her shoemaker affirmed,"[1] "St Thomas's doubting finger . . . some of Judas's pieces of silver; and many more, if one had faith to believe it."[2] He kissed the Pope's toe, and "being sufficiently blessed with his thumb and two fingers for that day, I returned home to dinner."[3] He saw "the Inquisition-house prison, the inside whereof, I thank God, I am not curious to see."[4] On the other side he remarked upon "the Church government" at Geneva, which "is severely Presbyterian, after the discipline of Calvin and Beza, who set it up, but nothing so rigid as either our Scots or English sectaries of that denomination."[5]

He practised painting and learnt to play on the theorbo. He saw and described Vesuvius, and he visited the Grotto del Cane and saw the regular experiment tried on two dogs there. He studied anatomy at Padua. His design to visit the Holy Land and other parts of Syria, Egypt and Turkey was frustrated to his great mortification,[6] so that Naples was "the non ultra of his travels."

He did not at once return to England, but stayed in Paris with the Royalist refugees, and amongst them he found a wife. The lady was Mary, the daughter of Sir Richard Browne. On the 10th of June 1647 "we concluded about my marriage"—the pronouns imply

[1] 19 Nov. 1644.   [2] 27 Febr. 1645.   [3] 4 May 1645.
[4] 12 Dec. 1644. [5] June 1646.   [6] June 1645.

Sir Richard rather than Miss Mary—and, on Thursday the 27th, Earle of the *Microcosmographie* " married us." Mrs Evelyn was very young, her husband says—she seems in fact to have been twelve years old—so she stayed on at her father's. Sixty years later, in a will dated 9 Febr. 1708, she spoke of her husband. "His care of my education was such as might become a father, a lover, a friend, and husband, for instruction, tenderness, affection and fidelity to the last moment of his life; which obligation I mention with a gratitude to his memory, ever dear to me; and I must not omit to own the sense I have of my Parents care and goodnesse in placing me in such worthy hands." A glowing "Character of Mrs Evelyn" was written by her son's tutor at Oxford, and some of her letters survive. These, like the printed letters of her husband, are mostly of the full-dress order —kept in both cases, one feels, in virtue of this fact— and, though she can write directly enough to her son, for most readers to-day it will be enough to realize that Mrs Evelyn's letters quite deserve the praise of Dr Bohun: " Y^e periods flowing and long, after the Ciceronian way."

Leaving his little wife in France, Evelyn crossed to England, where he stayed for some two years. At Hampton Court, 5 Octr. 1647, he "had the honour to kiss his Majesty's hand, and give him an account of several things I had in charge, he being now in the power of those execrable villains who not long after murdered him." To this event he alludes a few pages further on, for his diary is rather thin at this period. "The villainy of the rebels proceeding now so far as to try, condemn and murder our excellent King on the 30th of this month [January 1649], struck me with such a horror that I kept the day of his martyrdom a fast, and would not be present at that execrable wickedness; receiving the sad account of it from my brother George and Mr Owen, who came to visit me this afternoon, and recounted all the circumstances." The passage is a curious one with its conflict of feelings; for he was a born sight-seer. Pepys saw the spectacle, he half implies, by accident.[1]

A few days earlier Evelyn had published a translation from the French, *Of Liberty and Servitude*, "for the preface of which I was severely threatened."

On the 30th of May he records that "Unkingship was proclaimed." In June he obtained "a pass from the rebel Bradshaw then in great power," and in July set off for France and his wife. He reached Paris on August 1st, and then—"18th August. I went to St Germain to kiss his Majesty's hand; in the coach, which was my Lord Wilmot's, went Mrs Barlow, the King's mistress, and mother to the Duke of Monmouth, a brown, beautiful, bold, but insipid creature." So began a long acquaintance with Charles II., for whom his feeling was always one of respect, tempered by a definite opinion as to Mrs Barlow and her many successors.

In Paris his diary grows more interesting, with several accounts of street brawls, in which the sword was used, and of visits to curious sights—processions, works of art, "the operation of cutting for the stone," a conjuror, "a dromedary, a very monstrous beast much like a camel but larger," and an examination by torture, of which he gives elaborate details. He made a short visit to England in 1650, remarking on his journey upon the misery of the French peasants, plundered freely by tattered and ill-paid soldiers. He had his portrait engraved by Nanteuil (13 June 1650). It is from this that Carlyle drew "a certain slender young man, of pale intelligent look not without an air of dandyism, by name John Evelyn."[2] Another painter, Bourdon, painted Mrs Evelyn—a portrait that had adventures, for it was taken by pirates on its way to England and afterwards recovered by a curious chance.[3]

---
[1] Pepys, 13 Oct. 1660, on hanging of Harrison.
[2] *Historical Sketches*, 340.
[3] 27 Febr. 1649, 3 Febr. 1652, 15 April 1652.

EVELYN

"1st December [1651]. I now resolved to return to England." A brief but significant entry. Cromwell's "crowning mercy,"[1] the decisive battle of Worcester, was won on 3 Septr. 1651. Evelyn was a Royalist, but not an extremist; he had the English gift of commonsense, and the Royalist cause seemed hopeless. He was tired of exile and he compromised. He may have fancied he could be of some use to his King in England, but he made his peace with Cromwell's government as far as was necessary. It was not hard to do. "Cromwell's was the most tolerant government which had existed in England since the Reformation," says Professor Firth,[2] and Evelyn was conspicuously not a dangerous person. Sir Richard Browne's lease from the Crown of Sayes Court at Deptford had been seized by the Parliament. Evelyn compounded for it for £3500 (22 Febr. 1653), having extracted a promise from Charles II. "that if it ever pleased God to restore him, he would secure it to us in fee-farm."[3] But, as Burnet said, Charles "had a softness of temper that charmed all who came near him till they found how little they could depend on good looks, kind words and fair promises; in which he was liberal to excess, because he intended nothing by them but to get rid of importunities and to silence all farther pressing upon him."[4] So Evelyn found more than once.

Now settled at Sayes Court (1652), where he lived continuously for nearly half a century, Evelyn took his wife for a tour through England. York and Bristol were the furthest points reached. Bristol, he found, "emulated London"; being "wholly mercantile, as standing near the famous Severn commodiously for Ireland and the Western world. Here I first saw the manner of refining

---

[1] Cromwell's Letter to Wm. Lenthall, 4 Septr. 1651.

[2] *Cromwell*, p. 367. Compare also Oliver's tolerance of George Fox. Cambridge edition of Fox's Journal, i. p. 159.

[3] Evelyn, 9 March 1652.

[4] *History of His Own Times*, vol. i. p. 93 (ed. 1724).

sugar and casting it into loaves." He visited the rock of St Vincent, "the precipice whereof is equal to anything of that nature I have seen in the most confragose cataracts of the Alps, the river gliding between them at an extraordinary depth. Here we went searching for diamonds, and to the Hot Wells, at its foot. There is also on the side of this horrid Alp a very romantic seat."[1] At Cambridge he "went first to St John's College, well built of brick, and library, which I think is the fairest of that University." (So thought Mary Lamb.) In the St John's library he saw "a vast old song-book, or Service, and some fair manuscripts."[2] The vast old song-book still lies there on its table, a familiar object.

Though now living in comparative peace, Evelyn was not pleased with things in England. There was the state of the Church. He complains again and again that the pulpits are "full of novelties and novices" (4 Aug. 1650), "filled with sectaries of all sorts, blasphemous and ignorant mechanics" (3 Aug. 1656), who preached "feculent stuff" (4 December 1654). "There was now nothing practical preached, or that pressed reformation of life, but high and speculative points and strains that few understood, which left the people very ignorant and of no steady principles, the source of all our sects and divisions, for there was much envy and uncharity in the world."[3] Such was "the madness of the Anabaptists, Quakers, Fifth Monarchy men, and a cento of unheard-of heresies beside"—"these equivocal Christians and enthusiasts."[4]

---

[1] 27 June 1654.   [2] 31 Aug. 1654.   [3] 2 Nov. 1657.
[4] *A Character of England*, Misc. Works, pp. 152-156.

>Next I turn'd Anabaptist
>And pray'd by the spirit;
>>To preach and print,
>>Make mouths and squint
>Was thought a mighty merit.
>We slighted steeple-houses;

There are the Independents, "a refined and apostate sort of Presbyters"—"these are those pretenders to the Spirit,[1] into whose party do's the vilest person living no sooner adscribe himself, but he is, *ipso facto*, dub'd a saint, hallow'd and dear to God."

There are the Quakers, rejecting Scripture, and guided "by the lights and impulses within," who will not use arms or take any oath—"*thou* and *thee* is their language to their greatest King, without baring the head, or using the least respect"—"a frugal, plain, silent, yet crafty sect allowing their women to preach, pretending the most primitive simplicity."[2]

Other men made similar complaints. Witness that delightful page of Walton, where he tells how he met Dr Robert Sanderson "in sad-coloured clothes, and, God knows, far from being costly," and how "it began to rain,—and immediately the wind rose, and the rain increased so much, that both became so inconvenient, as to force us into a cleanly house, where we had bread, cheese, ale, and a fire for our money"—and a good talk over the scandal of Parliament abolishing the Liturgy, and how "no minister was now thought godly that did not decry it and at least pretend to make better prayers *ex tempore*."

> Thou dost a chaos, and confusion now,
> A Babel, and a Bedlam, grow—

said Cowley, addressing his native land.

> Stables we met together in—
> With yea and nay
> We did betray
> Our Presbyterian brethren.
> "The Mad Sectary," a song of 1677
> (London's Triumphs, Jordan).

[1] *Cf.* Selden, *Table Talk*, § 111, 5. "Preaching by the Spirit (as they call it) is most esteemed by the common people, because they cannot abide Art or Learning, which they have not been bred up in."

[2] Evelyn, *History of Religion*, vol. ii. p. 265.

Yet the sacrament was administered in private houses and some churches pretty freely, as Evelyn shows by his frequent references; and Cromwell's people knew it and winked at it. Things were bad under "Julianus Redivivus," as Evelyn calls him; yet life had its alleviations. There was the garden, and even rebels might enjoy the "purest of pleasures." For instance: "15th [May 1657]. Lawrence, President of Oliver's Council, and some other of his Court-Lords came in the afternoon to see my garden and plantations."[1] Three days later Evelyn records seeing "a sort of cat brought from the East Indies shaped and snouted much like the Egyptian racoon, etc." In August it is a "way-wiser," showing the number of miles "by an index as we went on"; and in September the "funamble Turk" and a "hairy woman" from Augsburg.

But at last Oliver died on his day of Crowning Mercies; and the question was what should come next, and what after that? Evelyn wrote an *Apology for the Royal Party* in 1659, on behalf of Charles II. "Did ever any man observe the least inclination of revenge in his breast? ... Do but reason a little with your self, and consider sadly, whether a young Prince, mortified by so many afflictions, disciplin'd by so much experience, and instructed by the miscarriages of others, be not the most excellently qualified to govern. ... For his vertues and morality I provoak the most refined family in this nation to produce me a relation of more piety and moderation; show me a fraternity more spotlesse in their honour, and freer from the exorbitances of youth then these three brothers, so conspicuous to all the world for their temperance, magnanimity, constancy and understanding."[2]

It has been made a reproach against Evelyn that he

---

[1] It may be added that Evelyn had friendly relations also with Wilkins, the moderate brother-in-law of the "tyrant."
[2] *Misc. Works*, 185-187.

flattered the royal family, and the charge would be hard to rebut. Something may be allowed for the phrase of the day, and something too to the writer who would uphold the credit of the leader of his party; and, besides, when have men ever spoken the truth about their kings till death or exile has made it safe? Evelyn's language finds an echo in Cowley's *Ode upon His Majesties Restoration and Return*, so it was probably no private property.

> As a choise *Medal* for *Heaven's Treasury*
> *God* did *stamp* first upon one side of *Thee*
> The *Image* of his *suffering Humanity* :
> On th' other side, turn'd now to sight, does shine
> The *glorious Image* of his *Power Divine*;

while the King and his brothers seem to the poet "like *Heavenly Saints* even in their *Purgatory*" or the three Judæan Youths in the Chaldæan furnace.

Mr Pepys has described the King's voyage to England with a fresh gale and most happy weather, how he was very active and stirring ("quite contrary to what I thought him to have been"), and how "upon the quarter-deck he fell into discourse of his escape from Worcester." Evelyn, on 29 May 1660, records the triumphal entry into London—"I stood in the Strand and beheld it, and blessed God. . . . It was the Lord's doing," and there had been nothing like it since the return of the Jews from Babylon. He was presented to his King on June 4th. Clarendon ends his history with the Restoration, and predicts that no nation can ever be more happy "if God shall be pleased to add establishment and perpetuity to the blessings he then restored."

Before the year was out the Regicides "suffered for reward of their iniquities"—"I saw not their execution, but met their quarters,[1] mangled, and cut, and reeking, as they were brought from the gallows in baskets on the

---

[1] The reader who is interested in this form of punishment can consult Ellwood (ed. Crump), p. 114.

hurdle. Oh the miraculous providence of God!"[1] The spectacle was spread over several days. Then on 30 Jan. 1661 "the carcasses of those arch-rebells, Cromwell, Bradshaw, and Ireton," were "dragg'd out of their superb tombs in Westminster among the Kings, to Tyburne, and hang'd on the gallows there from 9 in ye morning till 6 at night, and then buried under that fatal and ignominious monument." Pepys condemned this step,[2] but Evelyn cries out on "the stupendous and inscrutable judgments of God,"—" look back at October 22, 1658." This is the day on which he says he saw Cromwell buried, though that was done on 23 November,—a blunder in dates among several others, which suggest Evelyn was not always as punctual with his diary as his father might have urged. "Look back at October 22, 1658, and be astonished! and fear God and honour the King; but meddle not with them who are given to change." He hardly needed this admonition to himself, but the note of triumph at the insult offered to the body of a great Englishman is not pleasant. However, if this sort of thing pleased Royalists, it did not hurt Cromwell. It at least showed the difference between him and his critics.

The restoration of the King meant the restoration of the Church of England—a rather more effectual restoration than Charles wished, but he had no choice till he found another source of supply than his Parliament. The passing and enforcement of the Clarendon Code Evelyn

---

[1] 17 Oct. 1660; *cf.* George Fox, 1660 (folio p. 226).
"When we came to Charing-Cross, there were Multitudes of People gathered together to see the *Burning* of the *Bowels* of some of them that had been the *Old King's Judges*, and had been *hanged, drawn* and *quartered.*
"We went next Morning to *Judge Mallet's Chamber*, who was putting on his *Red Gown*, to go sit upon some more of the *King's Judges*. He was then very peevish and froward. . . ."

[2] Pepys, recording the vote of Parliament that this should be done, added "which (methinks) do trouble me that a man of so great courage as he was, should have that dishonour, though otherwise he might deserve it enough," and he did not go to the sight. Mrs Pepys went.

hardly notices. Pepys, when he saw Dissenters dragged through the streets, wrote: "They go like lambs, without any resistance. I would to God they would conform, or be more wise and not be catched."[1] Evelyn's thoughts were elsewhere. "Now the service was performed with music, voices, etc. as formerly"[2]—"after sermon, the Bishop (Dr Wren) gave us the blessing very pontifically."[3] "The Scottish Covenant was burnt by the common hangman in divers places in London. Oh, prodigious change!"[4] He hears a sermon to the effect that "the Church of England was, for purity of doctrine, substance, decency and beauty, the most perfect under Heaven";[5] and another in which the Dean of Windsor showed "how the neglect of executing justice on offenders (by which he insinuated such of the old King's murderers as were yet reprieved and in the Tower) was a main cause of God's punishing a land."[6] On 17 Aug. 1662 he records that "our vicar" read the abjuration of the Covenant, required by Parliament on penalty of his losing his living. Two thousand clergy refused.

Ten years later, when Charles II. issued his Declaration of Indulgence in favour of universal toleration,[7] it was not the constitutional usurpation involved that Evelyn resented. He looked at it merely as it affected the Church. "It has proved, and was then evidently foreseen, to the extreme weakening of the Church of England and its Episcopal Government, as it was projected.... I think there might be some relaxations without the least prejudice to the present Establishment, discreetly limited, but to let go the reins in this manner, and then to imagine they could take them up again as easily, was a false policy, and greatly destructive. The truth is, our Bishops slipped the occasion; for, had they held a steady hand

---

[1] Pepys, 7 August 1664.
[2] Evelyn, 25 Nov. 1660.
[3] 10 Febr. 1661.
[4] 22 May 1661.
[5] 10 Nov. 1661.
[6] 15 Jan. 1662.
[7] Burnet, *Own Times* (1724), vol. i. p. 307.

upon his Majesty's restoration, as they might easily have done, the Church of England had emerged and flourished without interruption." [1]

All through these two uneasy reigns he watched Papist intrigue with concern. In 1665 he published a translation of *The Mystery of Jesuitism* for which Charles volunteered his thanks—" he had carried [it] two days in his pocket, read it, and encouraged me; at which I did not a little wonder." [2] One can imagine how the "peculiarly bright black eyes" [3] of the cleverest of English kings looked through his faithful subject. But Evelyn's suspicions, like many other men's, grew keener as time went on. After the passing of the Test Act, 1673, "against the increase of Popery" he speaks of the "exceeding grief and scandal to the whole nation that the heir of it [James II.], and the son of a martyr for the Protestant religion, should apostatise. What the consequence of this will be God only knows and wise men dread." [4]

There was a great deal to disquiet a sober and respectable Royalist. Charles came to Sayes Court once "to honour my poor villa with his presence, viewing the gardens and even every room of the house, and was pleased to take a small refreshment." [5] Charles was always courteous to the *virtuoso*, many of whose tastes he shared; he consulted him as to rebuilding Whitehall and other matters,—he even, the diarist says, "was pleased to give me a piece [of King-pine from Barbados] off his own plate to taste of" [6]—and he promised to make Mrs Evelyn "Lady of the Jewels (a very honourable charge) to the future Queen (but which he never performed)." [7] But Evelyn was uneasy. As early as January 1662, he deplores the gambling at Court, and it did not grow less,[8] nor other evils.

The fall of Clarendon, "my particular kind friend on all

---

[1] 12 March 1672. [2] 25 Jan. 1665. [3] Osmund Airy, *Charles II.*, p. 386.
[4] Jan. 1673. [5] 30 April 1663. [6] 19 Aug. 1668.
[7] 31 March 1661. [8] *Cf.* 8 Jan. 1668.

occasions," troubled him—"He had enemies at Court especially the buffoons and ladies of pleasure because he thwarted some of them and stood in their way; I could name some of them."[1] In 1670 a new figure appears (4 Nov.)—"I now also saw that famous beauty, but in my opinion of a childish, simple and baby face, Mlle Kéroualle, lately Maid of Honour to Madame and now to be so to the Queen." Ten months later Evelyn was staying at Euston with Lord Arlington, while the King was at Newmarket. There was visiting between the two places, and Mademoiselle Kéroualle was much seen. Indeed, Evelyn has to repudiate with vigour the story that he was present at her mock-marriage with the King, when "the stocking was thrown," and "she was first made *a Miss*," but he remarked freedoms enough in what went on.[2] This was no ordinary addition to the harem; it was an international affair arranged by Louis XIV. "A young Cambridge divine preached an excellent sermon" to the King next Sunday. Some years later the parents of the lady were entertained by Sir Richard Browne, Mrs Evelyn's father; she "was now made Duchess of Portsmouth and in the height of her favour."[3] Twice over Evelyn records his being in the Duchess's apartment at Whitehall, rich and splendid beyond the Queen's.[4] He has one or two references to other ladies. He had met the King one day and walked with him through St James's Park, "where I both saw and heard a very familiar discourse between . . . [Evelyn leaves a gap here] and Mrs Nelly, as they called an impudent comedian, she looking out of her garden on a terrace at the top of the wall, and . . . standing on the green walk under it. I was heartily sorry at the scene."[5]

More and more he suspects mischief. Why was Tilbury Fort built, "a royal work, indeed, and such as

---

[1] 27 Aug. 1667. *Cf.* Burnet, *Own Times* (1724), vol. i. p. 257.
[2] Oct. 1671. [3] 15 June 1675.
[4] 10 Sept. 1675; 4 Oct. 1683. [5] 1 March 1671.

will one day bridle a great city to the purpose, before they are aware?"[1] And the army encamped on Hounslow Heath was "designed against France, in pretence at least."[2] He meets Titus Oates, "a bold man, and, in my thoughts, furiously indiscreet"[3]—and then Sir Edmund Berry Godfrey was "found strangled, as was manifest by the Papists."[4] Then the King took away the "ancient privileges" of London,[5] as Diabolus did those of Mansoul in the *Holy War*. It was an anxious time.

Meanwhile, of course, there were incidents of lighter nature—a new fair at Blackheath,[6] a rhinoceros and a crocodile in London,[7] meetings of the Royal Society, of which Evelyn was a member from the first, active, proud, and useful.

And now Charles died on 6 February 1685—somewhat suddenly—a week after Evelyn had paid his last visit to the court. This is his account of it: "I can never forget the inexpressible luxury and profaneness, gaming and all dissoluteness, and as it were total forgetfulness of God (it being Sunday evening) which this day se'nnight I was witness of, the King sitting and toying with his concubines, Portsmouth, Cleveland, and Mazarin, etc., a French boy singing love-songs, in that glorious gallery, whilst about twenty of the great courtiers and other dissolute persons were at basset round a large table, a bank of at least £2000 in gold before them; upon which two gentlemen who were with me made reflections with astonishment. Six days after, was all in the dust."[8] So he moralizes, but he does not explain why he frequented such scenes—why he of all men should go to such profanities as the marriage by the

---

[1] 21 March 1672.   [2] 29 June 1678.
[3] 1 Oct. 1678.   [4] 21 Oct. 1678.
[5] 18 June 1683. *Cf.* Burnet, *Own Times* (1724), vol. i. p. 527, on the surrender of Charters by Corporations.
[6] 1 May 1683.   [7] 22 Oct. 1684.
[8] On death of Charles, Burnet, *Own Times* (1724), vol. i. p. 606.

Archbishop of Canterbury of a little girl of five to a nine-year-old bastard of the King, and other scenes of wickedness.

It would be too long to set out all the notes with which he follows the progress of history in James's reign —the defeat of Monmouth and his Anabaptists and poor cloth-workers—how Dryden and Mrs Nelly go to mass and are no loss to the Church, and Judge Jeffreys goes "thorough stitch"[1]—how the French persecution is more inhuman than ever, and James silences divers excellent divines in England—while the Popish service is publicly held at Whitehall, and Popish Justices of the Peace established in all counties, "so furiously do the Jesuits drive"—and the army is doubtless kept and increased in order to bring in and countenance Popery—and then how the Seven Bishops are sent to the Tower and Evelyn visits them, not his only public stand at this time. By and by there comes the entry: "10th [June 1688]. A *young Prince* born, which will cause disputes"; and later, in September, a report is current in London that the Prince of Orange has landed. Irish and Scots soldiers are sent for by James. "It brought the people to so desperate a pass, that they seemed passionately to long for and desire the landing of that Prince, whom they looked on to be their deliverer from Popish tyranny, praying incessantly for an East wind, which was said to be the only hindrance of his expedition." The story is familiar, but, interesting as Evelyn's journal is from end to end, it is seldom more so than in these years. Finally "18th [Dec. 1688]. I saw the King take barge to Gravesend at twelve o'clock—a sad sight! The Prince comes to St James's, and fills Whitehall with Dutch guards.... All the world go to see the Prince at St James's, where there is a great court. There I saw him

---

[1] Evelyn dined with him all the same, and "was used with great respect," 31 Oct. 1685—this after the Monmouth trials. Jeffreys "is of nature cruel and a slave of the Court."

and several of my acquaintance who came over with him." So ends a great story.

Mr Pepys from time to time records conversations with Evelyn on public affairs. His first visit to Sayes Court was on 5 May 1665—Mr Evelyn "being abroad, we walked in his garden, and a lovely noble ground he hath indeed. And among other rarities, a hive of bees, so as being hived in glass, you may see the bees making their honey and comb mighty pleasantly." On 5 November (Lord's day) 1665 he found the owner at home, not for the first time, and he was shown all sorts of things—"the whole secret of mezzo-tinto,"—a "Hortus Hyemalis"—and so forth. "In fine, a most excellent person he is, and must be allowed a little for his conceitedness; but he may well be so, being a man so much above others. He read me, though with too much gusto, some little poems of his own that were not transcendant, yet one or two very pretty epigrams. . . . Here comes in, in the middle of our discourse Captain Cocke, as drunk as a dogg, but could stand and talk and laugh." Pepys rides in Evelyn's coach, "all the way having fine discourse of trees and the nature of vegetables."[1] Above all, with the solemn interest of English moralists impressed with a sense of public concern, they talked "of the vanity and vices of the Court"[2]—of the Duke of York and my Lady Denham—"good Mr Evelyn cries out against it and calls it bitchering."[3] Once Pepys records at some length two hours of Mr Evelyn's narrative of Court life—the passage forming a significant commentary on the few lines which Evelyn quoted in his memoir of young Mrs Godolphin. When a girl, this lady was Maid of Honour to the first Duchess of York, and she then wrote "under her own faire hand": "Be sure never to talk to the King; when they speak filthyly, tho' I be laugh'd att, looke grave, remembring that of

[1] Pepys, 5 Oct. 1665. [2] Pepys, 29 Jan. 1666.
[3] Pepys, 26 Sept. 1666.

Micha, there wyll a time come when the Lord will bind vp his jewells."[1] Evelyn's words, recorded by Pepys, not himself, are striking. Little wonder that he, as Pepys says, "did believe we should soon see ourselves fall into a Commonwealth again."[2]

The two men had many tastes in common. Evelyn's book "about directions for gathering a Library" is indeed "above my reach, but his epistle to my Lord Chancellor is a very fine piece."[3] Evelyn could always manage a magnificent preface—like a letter in the grand style to the *Times* written by a gentleman of his type in the days before modernity quite prevailed. But, whatever the reach of the books, or the "conceitedness" of their fanciful author—"the more I know him the more I love him," writes Pepys in 1666 (29 April). Evelyn's most enormous letter is to Pepys—18 quarto pages of print—on Pepys' wish to have his portrait done by Kneller to adorn his Library among "the Boyles, the Gales, and the Newtons of our Nation: what, in God's name should a planter of Colewort do amongst such Worthies?" The picture was painted. The spare elderly man is still to be seen, with his *Sylva* in his hand. Books which Evelyn lent to Pepys are now in the Pepysian Library at Magdalene College. On 26 May 1702, Evelyn, nearly eighty-two years old himself, records the death of his old friend—"a very worthy, industrious and curious person, none in England excelling him in knowledge of the navy . . universally beloved, hospitable, generous, learned in many things, skilled in music, a very great cherisher of learned men."

Pepys was only one of many notable friends. There was Jeremy Taylor, whom Evelyn befriended more than once when that injudicious genius got into trouble in the Commonwealth, and who has left an interesting testimony

---

[1] *The Life of Mrs Godolphin*, by Evelyn, p. 22. She is a little shaky on the Old Testament.

[2] Pepys, 30 Nov. 1667.   [3] Pepys, 5 Oct. 1665.

to his friend's *Tusculanum*, remarking on "the prettinesse of your aboad"—"I am pleased indeed at the order and the cleanenesse of all your outward things."[1] There was Sir Thomas Browne.[2] There was Henry Howard, afterwards Duke of Norfolk, whom he induced to give the Arundel marbles to Oxford. There was Cowley, to whom he appealed for an Ode in honour of the Royal Society—"can he desire a nobler or a fuller Argument either for the softest Aires or the loudest Echoes, for the smoothest or briskest strokes of his Pindaric Lyre?"[3] Cowley wrote the Ode, but it is not a triumph of the Pindaric style. Its briskest stroke is the sex attributed to Philosophy—

> Philosophy, I say, and call it, He,
> For whatso'ere the Painters Fancy be,
> It a Male-virtue seemes to me.

This brings us back to the Royal Society and Evelyn's many works undertaken in its honour and for the public good. In those late hours he kept in his quiet house he must have written as much as he read—and always with an eye to the nation's welfare. Sir Peter Wyche was chairman of a committee appointed by the Royal Society to consider of the improvement of the English tongue, and Evelyn sent him a dozen suggestions—one, alas! advocating what we call the American spelling of Honour.[4] Or he has a touch at Fashion in a tract entitled *Tyrannus or the Mode*—"methinks a French Taylor with his ell in his hand, looks like the Enchantress Circe over the companions of Ulysses and changes them into as many forms"; but "why should I dance after a Monsieurs flajolet?" The tract shows Evelyn in his most entertaining mood, but he has a serious remark on the "two Millions of Treasure" "lost in Gold and Silver lace" or

---

[1] Letter of Jeremy Taylor, 16 April 1656.
[2] 18 Oct. 1671.   [3] Letter of 12 March 1667.
[4] Letter of 20 June 1665.

sent abroad for "foreign silkes."[1] But one of his chief concerns was the smoke of London—"that hellish and dismall cloud of sea-coal" that hangs over a beautiful city, till "almost one-half of them who perish in London, dye of phthisical and pulmonic distempers," and "the inhabitants are never free from coughs and importunate rheumatisms, spitting of impostumated and corrupt matter." He has plans to deal with it which he sets out in his *Fumifugium*.[2] He would remove to a distance "such as in their works and fournaces use great quantities of sea-cole"—viz. "brewers, diers, sope and salt-boylers, lime-burners and the like"—and plant gardens round the city with fragrant shrubs. In his *Sylva*, to protect the Royal forests he urges similarly the removal of the iron-mills; "if that at least be true which some have affirmed that we had better iron and cheaper from foreigners when those works were strangers amongst us." He thinks that the New-English, who have a "surfeit of the woods which we want," might "supply us with iron for the peace of our days; whilst his Majesty becomes the great sovereign of the ocean, free commerce, *nemorum vindex et instaurator magnus*."[3] For he saw danger to England in the loss of her forests and wrote his *Sylva* to promote their preservation and extension; and he reminded King Charles in the preface to the fourth edition "how many Millions of Timber - Trees (beside infinite others)" have been planted as a result of his writing. The *Sylva* was long a popular work. Elsewhere he finds as beneficent results due to his care, in the many artists set to work to perfect "the new way of graving called Mezzo Tinto" by his account of it in his *Sculptura*.[4] This claim is however dismissed to-day with some incisiveness.[5] One of his

[1] Printed after his letters by Bray.
[2] In his *Miscellaneous Works*, pp. 207-242. It is interesting to find the total production of coal in England in 1660 estimated at less than 2¼ million tons.
[3] *Sylva*, book iii. ch. 7.   [4] Diary, 13 March 1661.
[5] See C. F. Bell's edition of *Sculptura* (1906), Introduction.

latest works to reach the Press in full was his *History of Religion*, a long inquiry, provoked by the events of his day, into the reality of God and religion generally, in which he reaches the conclusion that " we have no Master but Christ, no religion but Christian, no rule but Scripture, no law but right reason," and that " the present Church of England " is " the most purged, refined and reformed." [1] But his great works have passed away ; the thought was not so original, nor the style so individual, as to safeguard them. It is by gardens and trees and by his diary that he is best remembered.

Public life and private life—his friends, his books, his children—fill his diary. The wonderful promise and early death of his first little Richard ; the death of a second little Richard some few months old ; the loss by smallpox of two other children ; John the younger's going to Oxford ; the marriage of Susanna ; the verses in Greek that John wrote, and the English rhymes of Mary—these show Evelyn on another side with which every reader must sympathize. " Here ends the joy of my life, and for which I go even mourning to the grave," he wrote, 27 January 1658, when Richard died ; but life had much more of joy and sorrow for him before he died himself, 27 February 1706, eighty-five years old, but still full of interests. The last entry in the diary belongs to 3rd February, and consists of the notes of sermons heard that Sunday morning and afternoon.

But let us go back to an earlier day and take farewell of him in his garden, with Abraham Cowley.[2]

> Happy art Thou, whom God does bless
> Wth ye full choice of thine own happiness!
> And happier yet, because thou 'rt blest
> Wth prudence how to choos the best!

---

[1] *History of Religion*, ii. 312, 313.
[2] *The Garden*, dated 16 Aug. 1666 (printed among Evelyn's *Misc. Works*, p. 436).

EVELYN

In Books and Gardens thou hast plac'd aright
    (Things which thou well dost understand,
And both dost make wth thy industrious hand)
    Thy noble innocent delight :
And in thy virtuous Wife, where thou again dost meet
    Both pleasures more refin'd and sweet :
    The fairest gardens in her looks
    And in her mind the wisest books.

BUNYAN

I

"A N⁰. 1660.—But upon yᵉ 29th day of the 3d month, An°. 1660, when King *Charles* II was brought from his exile againe into yᵉ *Nation* and to yᵉ Crown, *Then* Sathan stirred up adversaryes against us and our *Trouble* or *Persecution* began."

So writes Edward Terrill in the records of the Baptist church in Broadmead in the city of Bristol. By 1670 Terrill records seven persecutions, and by 1681 he has to add two more. Yet, in a Declaration given at Breda on the 4/14th day of April 1660, the words of King Charles are still to be read: "We do declare a liberty to tender consciences; and that no man shall be disquieted, or called in question, for differences of opinion in matters of religion which do not disturb the peace of the kingdom; and that we shall be ready to consent to such an act of Parliament, as, upon mature deliberation, shall be offered to us, for the full granting that indulgence."[1]

Freedom in religious life was not a matter of much moment to King Charles—as yet, and his first Parliament, which sat for eighteen years, sent him no such Act. On the contrary, it passed in its first five years the series of Acts known as the Clarendon Code.[2] The Corporation Act (1661) closed the municipal bodies, which ruled the towns and usually controlled the choice of members of Parliament, against all who would not receive the Communion by the rites of the Church of England. Some time

---

[1] See Clarendon, *History*, bk. xvi.
[2] See G. M. Trevelyan, *England under the Stuarts*, p. 341.

later, the King began to remodel the charters of the towns —a thing never before attempted in this country. The Uniformity Act (1662) turned two thousand Puritan clergy out of their livings.[1] The Conventicle Act (1664) punished attendance at religious rites other than those of the Church, by imprisonment, by transportation on the third offence, and death if the criminal returned. The Five Mile Act (1665) forbade any clergyman or schoolmaster to come within five miles of a city or corporate town, unless he declared that he would not "at any time endeavour any alteration of Government either in Church or State." The Code was not only passed into law; it was administered, and it was followed up by further legislation. In March 1670 the Conventicle Act was renewed with added severities by Parliament.[2] In 1673 the Test Act was passed, which forbade civil or military office under the crown to any who would not take the Anglican sacraments. So the laws were made which cut the nation in two, and Dissenters were kept out of office by Test Acts till 1828, and out of the Universities still longer. "There was no excuse of self-defence," says Professor Gwatkin, "persecution was pure and simple revenge on the defeated party; and of mere revenge the better sort of churchmen would sooner or later be ashamed."[3]

Laud, between 1628 and 1640, had driven twenty thousand Puritans to America,[4] and now others followed them. The argument from the danger of emigration recurs in the pamphlets for toleration.[5] But the most remained in England, cut off from the national life, but not from hope. It is in such simple narratives as the *Broadmead Records* that we read at what cost they maintained the principle of religious liberty. Bishops, judges, justices,

---

[1] "The Act for Uniformity is lately printed, which, it is thought, will make mad work among the Presbyterian ministers," Pepys, 31 May 1662.
[2] See Ellwood's History on this, under the year 1670.
[3] *Cambridge Modern History*, vol. v. p. 330.
[4] This would be about the population of Bristol in 1640.
[5] E.g. it is used by Penn in his *England's Present Interests Discovered*.

train-bands and informers[1] harried the Bristol Baptists out of their meeting-house, from the Somerset bank of the Avon to the Gloucestershire side and back again. One day's record will suffice. "We resolved to keep a Day at Mr Jackson's, over y⁵ Down. But Sandford, an Inn-keeper at Westbury, hearing of our Meeting, sent y⁵ Bailiff of y⁵ hundred and ½ a dozen more to disturb us after we had spent about 3 hours. When they came into y⁵ Court, Aldm. Yate's Wife advised us to retire into y⁵ Garden and disperse. So we did, and met again in a Valley on Durdham Down, and continued in Peace till about 5." This is a picture of what went on all over England. Dissenters, men and women, were put into prisons by thousands, and hundreds of them died there.[2] For the moment it was the extremists who ruled, and vengeance and extermination were their objects.

In some parts of the country there was little disposition to wait the lead of Parliament. In Bedford there was a notable minister—a converted tinker, John Bunyan, and he, on the Restoration of Charles II and the Church, became a marked man at once. What befell him is recorded by himself in a short document first printed in 1765.[3]

"Upon the 12th of this instant November, 1660, I was desired by some of the friends in the country to come to teach at *Samsell*, by *Harlington*, in *Bedfordshire*. To whom I made a promise, if the Lord permitted, to be with them on the time aforesaid. The justice hearing

---

[1] Compare Ellwood's account of the informers in Buckinghamshire in 1670.

[2] Letter of George Fox to the King, 1662 (1st edn. in folio, p. 250). "There have *suffered* for good Conscience-sake, and for bearing *Testimony* to the *Truth* as it is in Jesus, *Three Thousand, One Hundred, Seventy Three Persons*"; these "under the Changeable *Powers* before thee," and "in thy Name since thy Arrival, by such as thought to ingratiate themselves thereby to thee, *Three Thousand, Sixty and Eight Persons*. Besides this, our *Meetings* are daily *broken up* by Men with *Clubs* and *Arms*," etc.

[3] In all the quotations from *Grace Abounding*, the *Pilgrim's Progress* and the *Holy War*, italics, capitals and spelling are given as Bunyan left them— here taken from Dr Brown's editions (Cambridge English Classics).

thereof, (whose name is Mr *Francis Wingate*) forthwith issued out his warrant to take me, and bring me before him, and in the mean time to keep a very strong watch about the house where the meeting should be." Bunyan had warning of what was on foot, and he recalls how he thought over what should be his course. " I walked into the close, where I somewhat seriously considering the matter, this came into my mind : That I had shewed myself hearty and courageous in my preaching, and had, blessed be Grace, made it my business, to encourage others ; therefore thought I, if I should now run and make an escape, it will be of a very ill savour in the country. . . . Besides I thought, that seeing God of his mercy should chuse me to go upon the forlorn hope in this country ; that is, to be the first, that should be opposed, for the Gospel ; if I should fly, it might be a discouragement to the whole body that might follow after." [1]

So he went to his meeting and was at once arrested and brought to Mr Wingate, the justice, who " said that he would break the neck of our meetings." As Bunyan would not consent to leave off preaching, he could not well be released on sureties, as the bonds would inevitably be forfeited. " Now while my mittimus [2] was a making . . . in comes an old enemy to the truth Dr *Lindale*," the vicar of Harlington, and he " fell to taunting at me with many reviling terms." Amongst other things the vicar reminded him of " one Alexander a Coppersmith "— " aiming 'tis like at me, because I was a Tinker." On the way to the jail, two friends met him, and had him taken back to the justice, to make another attempt for his liberty. " As I went, I lift up my heart to God for light and strength, to be kept, that I might not do any thing that might either dishonour him, or wrong my own soul, or be

---

[1] Compare the feeling of Hardcastle in Bristol Gaol : appendix to *Broadmead Records*, p. 324.

[2] As the question has been raised, how much Latin did Bunyan know, it is interesting to note what Latin he had, and where he learnt it. *Cf.* p. 140.

a grief or discouragement to any that was inclining after the Lord Jesus Christ."

This time he had an encounter with Mr Foster of Bedford, who pretended some friendliness. The description of their meeting, and the conversation that followed, are full of life and character, but space forbids quotation. Foster told him that he did not understand the Scriptures —" for how (said he) can you understand them when you know not the original Greek? etc." The question suggests a curious note in George Fox's *Journal* (1646)—" As I was walking in a Field on a *First-day* Morning, the Lord opened unto me, ' *That being bred at* Oxford *or* Cambridge, *was not enough to fit and qualifie Men to be Ministers of Christ*,' and I stranged at it, because it was the Common Belief of the People . . . That which was opened in me, I saw, struck at the *Priest's Ministry*." [1]

Bunyan was not to be cajoled or frightened, and he was led away to prison " with God's comfort in my poor soul"; for, "before I went down to the justice, I begged of God, that if I might do more good by being at liberty than in prison, that then I might be set at liberty: But, if not, his will be done; for I was not without hopes but that my imprisonment might be an awakening to the Saints in the country, therefore I could not tell what to chuse. Only I in that matter did commit the thing to God. And verily at my return, I did meet my God sweetly in the prison again."

Seven weeks later he was brought before the Justices. He was prosecuted under an Act of the 35th year of Elizabeth. His indictment ran : " That John Bunyan, of the town of Bedford, labourer, . . . he hath (since such a

---

[1] George Fox, folio, p. 5. As Bunyan says elsewhere: "Some men despise the Lazaruses of our Lord Jesus Christ because they are not gentlemen, because they cannot with Pontius Pilate speak Hebrew, Greek and Latin." It is interesting to find the same sort of criticism a century earlier in a sermon of Latimer's. "But some will say, 'Our curate is naught; an ass-head; a dodipole; a lack-latin, and can do nothing.'"—*Sermon* xvi. (vol. i. p. 304).

time) devilishly and perniciously abstained from coming to church to hear divine service, and is a common upholder of several unlawful meetings and conventicles, to the great disturbance and distraction of the good subjects of this kingdom, contrary to the laws of our sovereign lord, the king, etc."[1] So Bunyan reports it in his *Relation of Imprisonment*. Dissenters had during this period ample opportunity to acquaint themselves with the laws that bore upon them; and they were sometimes able by legal knowledge to escape injustice, though, as Terrill says, "Wee saw by experience, ye Judges as well as ye Justices were resolved to tread us downe, because we would not conforme to their worship; that as Christians wee should have no peaceable enjoyment, and as men wee should have no justice" (1 Aug. 1675). In the *Pilgrim's Progress* and the *Holy War* the trial-scenes are very precisely done. Bunyan's justices sent him back to prison, warning him of the risk of banishment, and the further risk attending return,—in which case "you must stretch by the neck for it, I tell you plainly."[2]

After twelve more weeks, Cobb, the Clerk of the Peace, came to talk him into reason. "What benefit will it be to your friends, or what good can you do to them, if you should be sent away beyond the seas into *Spain* or *Constantinople*, or some other remote part of the world? Pray be ruled." The banishment would probably have been westward in reality.[3] Bunyan had heard of Giant

[1] *Cf.* the story of the Mittimus made at Lancaster for George Fox, 1660 (Fox, folio, pp. 218-229)," *suspected to be a common Disturber of the Peace of this Nation, an Enemy to our Sovereign Lord the* King, *and a chief Upholder of the* Quakers Sect ; *and that he, together with others of his Fanatick Opinion, have of late endeavoured to make Insurrections in those parts of the Country, and to Imbroil the whole Kingdom in Blood.*"

[2] This kind of threat addressed to George Fox, e.g. in Scarborough Castle, 1666 (folio, p. 303): "And the *Officers* would often be *threatening* me, that *I should be* hanged *over the Wall* . . . they talked much then of *hanging* me. But I told them, 'If that was it they desired, and it was permitted them, I was *ready*.'"

[3] Transportations of Friends "to *Barbados*, and to *Jamaica*, and to *Mevis*, and the *Lord blessed* them there" (G. Fox, folio, p. 304).

Pope, as we know, and of the Turks and " Mahomet their Saviour" (*G. A.* § 98), but he was obdurate. " Sir," said I, " the law hath provided two ways of obeying: The one to do that which I in my conscience do believe that I am bound to do, actively; and where I cannot obey it actively, there I am willing to lie down and to suffer what they shall do unto me."[1]

What his imprisonment cost Bunyan we can read in an appendix to *Grace Abounding*. " The parting with my Wife and poor Children hath often been to me in this place, as the pulling the Flesh from my Bones; and that not only because I am somewhat too too fond of these great Mercies,[2] but also because I should have often brought to my mind the many hardships, miseries and wants that my poor Family was like to meet with, should I be taken from them, *especially my poor blind Child*, who lay nearer my heart than all I had besides; O the thoughts of the hardship I thought my blind one might go under, would break up my heart to pieces. . . . But yet recalling my self, thought I, I must venture you all with God, though it goeth to the quick to leave you; O I saw in this condition, I was as a man who was pulling down his House upon the head of his Wife and Children; yet thought I, I must do it, I must do it " (*G. A.* §§ 328, 329).[3]

What a prison was in those days may be read here and there in the Journal of George Fox. A humorous

---

[1] Twelve years later he was of the same mind. "But if nothing will do, unless I make of my conscience a continual butchery and slaughter-shop, unless putting out my own eyes I commit me to the blind to lead me, as I doubt not is desired by some [Offor omits 'not'] I have determined, the Almighty God being my help and shield, yet to suffer, if frail life might continue so long, even till the moss shall grow on mine eyebrows, rather than thus to violate my faith and principles." In preface to *A Confession of my faith and a reason of my practice*, 1672 (in Offor, vol. ii. p. 594). See Brown, *John Bunyan*, p. 240.

[2] Compare letter of Cromwell to Lord Wharton, 1 Jan. 1649 (end):
"My service to the dear little Lady: I wish you make her not a greater temptation than she is. Take heed of all relations. Mercies should not be temptations: yet we too oft make them so."—Lomas, i. 522.

[3] *Cf.* Letter of G. Fox to his wife from Worcester Gaol, 1673 (folio, p. 389).

but vivid description of it will be found in Earle's *Microcosmographie*, and Thomas Ellwood's account of it is better still.[1] When Giant Despair put Christian and Hopeful "into a very dark Dungeon, nasty and stinking to the Spirits of these two men," Bunyan may have described their position from recent memories.[2]

The present situation was not all. Looking back, Bunyan tells us that "I being but a young Prisoner, and not acquainted with the Laws, had this lay much upon my Spirit, That my Imprisonment might end at the Gallows for ought that I could tell." He was afraid of himself—"*if I should make a scrambling shift to clamber up the Ladder, yet I should either with quaking or other symptoms of fainting, give occasion to the Enemy to reproach the Way of God and his People for their Timorousness. This therefore lay with great trouble upon me, for methought I was ashamed to die with a pale Face, and tottering knees, for such a Cause as this*" (*G.A* § 335[3]). The Tempter followed this up with the question, But whither must you go, when you die? and he was "tossed for many weeks." At last he found comfort in the thought that this was God's affair—"I was bound, but he was free, yea, 't was my Duty to stand to his Word, whether he would ever look upon me or save me at the last: Wherefore, thought I, save the point of being thus, I am for going on, and venturing my eternal State with Christ, whether I have comfort here or no; if God doth not come in, thought I, *I will leap off the Ladder even blindfold into Eternity, sink or swim, come Heaven, come Hell; Lord Jesus, if thou wilt catch me, do; if not, I will venture for thy Name*" (*G.A.* § 338).

[1] *Cf.* also Ellwood's account of Newgate in 1662 (Crump's edition, pp. 106-14).

[2] The same adjectives of Nottingham Gaol in George Fox, 1649: "The Officers came, and took me away, and put me into a *nasty, stinking Prison*; the smell whereof got so into my Nose and Throat, that it very much annoyed me." Folio edn. p. 26. Earle also emphasizes the "ill smells."

[3] The italics here and elsewhere in this essay are Bunyan's own.

"I am for going on." 'Αλλὰ καὶ ἔμπης οὐ λήξω, says Achilles in a great passage of the *Iliad*. Death is imminent, he is told, if he does not forbear to fight against Troy; and he knows it, he rejoins, "and for all that, I will not forbear." And Achilles had not the public shame of rope and ladder before him, nor the chance of eternal hell.

It did not, of course, come to the gallows, but twelve years of imprisonment lay before Bunyan, with the break of a few weeks in 1666.

Prison, if in many ways fouler and harder then than now, had less system about it. The feeding of the prisoners was contracted for by the jailer, and they were starved and badly kept. But it was possible sometimes for a prisoner to have a day outside. Bunyan was now and then let out of the Bedford County Jail (it was not the town jail on the bridge yet), as Francis Holcroft was allowed out of the neighbouring jail at Cambridge, to preach quietly in some village and return.

Comfort came to Bunyan long before release. While still in prison (1665), he wrote a set of verses to a friend outside, who had encouraged him "to hold his head above the flood." Bunyan's verse is not like his prose. It is of the conscientious order; it rhymes with desperate purpose, and the length of the lines is carefully measured; a syllable is a syllable with him and has to do a syllable's duties. Like the prisoners in a modern British jail, his syllables are treated with paralysing regularity. But now and then he rises—as in some of the lines prefixed to the *Holy War* and the piece called *The Child with the Bird at the Bush* in his *Rhymes for Boys and Girls*. A few stanzas from the prison set may illustrate at once his methods in verse, and, what is more, his contentment and freedom of mind

> The prison very sweet to me
>   Hath been since I came here,
> And so would also hanging be,
>   If God would there appear.   (Stanza 18)

BUNYAN

When they do talk of banishment,
  Of death, and such-like things;
Then to me God sends heart's content
  That like a fountain springs.   (20)

God sometimes visits prisons more
  Than lordly palaces,
He often knocketh at our door
  When he their houses miss.[1]   (27)

The truth and life of heavenly things
  Lift up our hearts on high,
And carry us on eagles' wings,
  Beyond carnality.   (28)

By which means God doth frusturate
  That which our foes expect;
Namely, our turning th' Apostate,
  Like those of Judas' sect.   (30)

The *truth* and I were both here cast
  Together, and we do
Lie arm in arm, and so hold fast
  Each other; this is true.   (33)

This gaol to us is as a hill,
  From whence we plainly see
Beyond this world, and take our fill
  Of things that lasting be.   (34)
      (*Prison Meditations.*)

Thus Bunyan found, with many before and since, that shame can take men deeper than the shows of things, and that when, robbed of the ordinary satisfactions, a chance comes to us of seeing things in earnest, as they are, *sub specie aeternitatis.* The years in prison were not

[1] There seems to be historical evidence for this in the reign of Charles II.

lost time—"I never had in all my life so great an in-let into the Word of God as now: them Scriptures that I saw nothing in before, are made in this place and state to shine upon me; Jesus Christ also was never more real and apparent than now; here I have seen him and felt him indeed: O that word, *We have not preached unto you cunningly devised Fables*, 2 Pet. i. 16."[1]

This brings us, of course, to *Grace Abounding*, the first of Bunyan's great works. The many volumes of his homiletic writings fall very far short of his masterpieces, and it is on these that our attention must be concentrated. Their dates should first be noted. *Grace Abounding* was first printed in 1666. Ten years later, after three years of liberty with a licence to preach, Bunyan, as Dr John Brown surmised, had a third term of imprisonment, this time in the famous jail on Bedford bridge. The evidence for this had to be carefully gathered from hints and traditions, and then the theory of a third imprisonment received startling confirmation, for the actual warrant was discovered, couched in the same old jargoning style as the first. Bunyan, then, having "lighted on a certain Place, where was a Den," dreamed his dream. The *Pilgrim's Progress*—the first part—was published in 1678. Two years later, a free man now for the rest of his days as it proved, he issued *The Life and Death of Mr Badman*, as a pendant to his Pilgrim. In 1682, *The Holy War* came out, and in 1685 the second part of *The Pilgrim's Progress*.

These books are historical documents of great value, as significant and as valid as the journal of Samuel Pepys, though they represent another region of English society than that in which Mr Pepys moved—not always in the straightest line toward the Celestial City. They are

[1] A fellow-prisoner wrote (cp. J. Brown, *Bunyan*, p. 170) on the occasion of 60 new prisoners being added in a batch—"in the midst of the hurry which so many newcomers occasioned, I have heard Mr Bunyan both preach and pray with that mighty Spirit of Faith and Plerophory of Divine Assistance that has made me stand and wonder."

pictures of life as seen in street and house, inn and field. An immense tide of religious experience had flowed over England a century before and was still flowing. Indeed it is not till we reach Bunyan and George Fox, and catch at last the authentic voices of men of the people, unlettered and un-Latined, that we learn what the Reformation had meant. The two men were contemporaries (Fox, 1624-1689, and Bunyan 1628-1688), both children of devout parents. Of his father George Fox says, "there was a *Seed* of *God* in him. The Neighbours called him *Righteous Christer* [Christopher was his name]. My Mother was an upright Woman; her Maiden-name was *Mary Lago*, of the Family of the *Lago's*, and of the Stock of the *Martyrs*."[1] Bunyan's father was a good quiet man, perhaps of less moment, but he records that his first wife's father "was counted godly" and left his daughter two books, *The Plain Man's Pathway to Heaven* and *The Practice of Piety* (*G. A.* § 15)—the former a dialogue not without influence on Bunyan's literary work. Foxe's *Book of Martyrs* and Luther's *Commentaries* were read. Bunyan's words on Luther's book on *Galatians* are significant—"I found my condition, in his experience, so largely and profoundly handled, as if his Book had been written out of my heart. This made me marvel; for thus thought I, *This Man could not know anything of the state of Christians now, but must needs write and speak the experience of former days*" (*G. A.* § 131). In the heart of the common people was an intense spiritual life, and they were conscious of a past behind them—they were the children and successors of men of like experience, of men who had paid dearly for their religion and suffered the loss of all things for it. "I knew your Husband's Father," says Gaius to Christiana, "yea, also his Father's Father. Many have been good of this stock, their Ancestors dwelt first at *Antioch*." "I would have

---

[1] Apparently he means the connexion of Robert Glover who was burned at Mancetter in Queen Mary's reign.

him . . . read a little history," was Oliver Cromwell's idea for his son's education.[1]

But, if Fox and Bunyan and Terrill shed light on the history that preceded them, so they do on the subsequent history of English religion. Men may judge, as they will or must, of English Dissent, but till they are at the heart of that experience which is recorded in *Grace Abounding*, the *Pilgrim's Progress* and Fox's *Journal*, their judgements will be external and of little value. In few other books is the religious life, that is the historic source and the continuing reason and inspiration of the Dissenting communities, to be read so clearly and so truly. It is only as they breed true to this type that these communities can live at all, or that it is desirable they should live.

Bunyan, like many other men, wrote all his books out of the experience of an individual soul. In the preface to *Badman* he says that he has "as little as may be gone out of the road of mine own observation of things." The four great books owe their brilliance and originality to the one indelible experience out of which they are written. Christian and Mansoul go through the same depths of affliction and conflict as Bunyan himself, and reach the same peace and reconciliation. But, volume by volume, there is a difference. The writer looks back from time to time upon the scene of the conflict, but each time from a higher and a happier level.[2] The memory of what he went through is ineffaceable, but it is no longer his only memory; it is enriched with others; he has a larger, a more varied and a more restful mind. For the years

[1] Carlyle's *Letters and Speeches of Cromwell* (ed. Lomas), i. 451.
[2] *Cf.* P. T. Forsyth, *Christ on Parnassus*, p. 93, on "the great outburst of humour in Art in the Middle Age," due to the new feeling of the Infinite. "It could not happen in the first years of Christianity, for then the Infinite was too near and solemnizing a presence. The soul was absorbed and engaged with God. But when the newness of the divine Presence was removed without taking away the security, and the dazzled eyes returned to the light and objects of common earth, then the disparity, the contrast began to be felt; and it was joined with a great pity; and then stole over the face of Europe the dawn of that tender and sympathetic smile. . . ."

interpreted his experience, and he came to see it more and more in the sunshine. The peace, for which he had struggled so hard, did not pass away. It became more sure with years, and as he grew more conscious of its sureness and of his own salvation, he remembered the past with deepening happiness. And, in this increasing sunshine, every faculty within him flowered—his humour, his geniality and his humanity have more and more freedom and fulness. There is a gaiety even in Christian's adventures which Bunyan had hardly known twenty years before. The *Holy War* has more of it still—it breaks out in the despatches and dialogues and descriptions. As for Christiana and her boys, they have far too happy a life of it to please some critics. "One smiled and another smiled and they all smiled for joy"; and they "had the weather very comfortable to them."

II

Grace Abounding must be one of the truest and strongest of all spiritual autobiographies. Other men have had conflicts and reached the Celestial City, but few have had such a mastery of language, such a gift of seeing and hearing everything again as they write, such a force of sheer simplicity and truth. "I could," he says, "have stepped into a Stile much higher than this, in which I have here discoursed, and could have adorned all things more than here I have seemed to do; but I dare not: God did not play in tempting of me; neither did I play when I sunk as into a bottomless Pit, when *the Pangs of Hell caught hold upon me*; wherefore I may not play in relating of them, but be plain and simple, and lay down the thing as it was[1]: He that liketh it, let him receive it; and he that does not, let him produce a better. Farewel." "If the fact be so," Cromwell once said, "why

[1] *Cf.* beg. of Bunyan's *Holy City*: "In my dealing with this mystery, I shall not meddle where I see nothing."

should we sport with it?" Read *Grace Abounding* along with Sir Thomas Browne's *Religio Medici*, written about 1635, and published in 1642,—the one "plain and simple," the other the most brilliant masterpiece of deliberate art. "Surely," says Browne, "though we place Hell under Earth, the Devil's walk and purlue is about it: men speak too popularly who place it in those flaming mountains, which to grosser apprehensions represent Hell. The heart of man is the place the Devils dwell in; I feel sometimes a Hell within myself; *Lucifer* keeps his Court in my breast; *Legion* is revived in me."[1] Bunyan tells us how, talking once with an "ancient Christian," "I found him, though a good man, a stranger to much conflict with the Devil." So, one feels, he might have said of Sir Thomas, despite Lucifer and Legion. Augustine's *Confessions* would have been more intelligible to him—a book in many ways like his own.

Bunyan's book is a record of conflict with the Devil— he would himself have said. He tells how fear of hell came over him intermittently when he was young, and then ceased to come. "In these days the thoughts of Religion were very grievous to me." But God did not leave him, for once he was saved from drowning in "a crick of the Sea," and once by a strange chance from death, "when I was a Soldier." For long it was unknown on which side he fought in the Civil War. There is now documentary evidence that it was for the Parliament.[2] This is his only allusion to it. "One of the Company desired to go in my room; to which, when I had consented, he took my place; and coming to the Siege, as he stood Sentinel, he was shot into the head with a Musket-bullet, and died."

His wife's account of her father waked in him some desires to Religion, and he changed his way of life. He "fell in with the Religion of the times"—church-going,

---
[1] *Religio Medici*, § 51.
[2] It would be in 1644, when he was sixteen.

singing, "the spirit of Superstition . . . Vestments, Service and what else." Then came a sermon about the Sabbath, and that afternoon, "as I was in the midst of a game at Cat, and having struck it one blow from the hole, just as I was about to strike it the second time, a voice did suddenly dart from Heaven, into my Soul, which said, *Wilt thou leave thy sins and go to Heaven; or have thy sins and go to Hell?*" (*G. A.* § 22). It was his first experience of conviction of sin; and concluding at once that he had already sinned beyond hope, "I went on in sin with great greediness of mind." One day, a woman, "a very loose and ungodly wretch," told him that he was "the ungodliest fellow, for swearing, that ever she heard in her life." This rebuke struck home. "How it came to pass, I know not; I did, from this time forward, so leave my swearing, that it was a great wonder to my self to observe it" (*G. A.* § 28). From now on, his neighbours began to take him for "a new and religious man." But "as yet I was nothing but a poor painted Hypocrite, yet I loved to be talked of, as one that was truly Godly. I was proud of my Godliness." This, he says, went on for a year.

Then came that day in Bedford, when he overheard three or four poor women talking, as they sat at a door in the sun, and being now "a brisk Talker also my self in the matters of Religion,"[1] he drew near to hear. But "they were far above, out of my reach: Their talk was about a new birth, the work of God on their hearts." They also spoke of "their own Righteousness, as filthy and insufficient to do them any good. And methought they spake, as if joy did make them speak; they spake with such pleasantness of Scripture-language." Bunyan felt his heart begin to shake; he knew he had not the new birth (*G. A.* §§ 37-39). He made it his business to be going again and again into the company of these poor people, "for I could not stay away; and the more

[1] Compare *Ignorance*, "a very brisk lad" from the Country of *Conceit*.

I went amongst them, the more I did question my condition."

While his mind still worked with this impulse, new questions began to trouble him. Was he one of the elect? Was the Day of Grace gone? "I cannot now express with what longings and breathings in my Soul, I cried to Christ to call me. Thus I continued for a time, all on a flame to be converted to Jesus Christ" (*G. A.* § 74). Many months passed, with the sense of his sin heavy upon him—"My Conscience now was sore and would smart at every touch." "I saw that I wanted a perfect Righteousness, to present me without fault before God; and this Righteousness was no where to be found, but in the Person of Jesus Christ" (*G. A.* §§ 83, 84). Much of all this is reproduced in the account which Hopeful gives of his conversion while he talks with Christian on the Enchanted Ground.

He began by and by to find comfort and hope in the thought that his sins should be forgiven, and he was "so taken with the love and mercy of God that . . . I thought I could have spoken of his Love, and have told of his mercy to me, even to the very Crows that sat upon the plowed lands before me, had they been capable to have understood me" (*G. A.* § 93). But about a week or fortnight after this, "I was much followed by this Scripture; *Simon, Simon, behold, Satan hath desired to have you*, Luk. 22. 31, and sometimes it would sound so loud within me, yea, and, as it were, call so strongly after me, that once, above all the rest, I turned my head over my shoulder, thinking verily that some man had, behind me, called me . . . and although that was not my name, yet it made me suddainly look behind me; believing that he that called so loud, meant me" (*G. A.* §§ 94, 95). Afterwards he thought it a warning from Heaven of what was coming.

For now he began to wonder whether there were in truth a God, or Christ, and whether the Scriptures were not rather fable. "*Every one doth think his own Religion rightest; both Jews, and Moors, and Pagans; and how if all our Faith and Christ, and Scriptures should be but a Think so too?*" (*G. A.* § 98). He next began to fancy he might be possessed of the devil, and to wonder about the sin against the Holy Ghost, to "be daunted with such conceits as these" that God mocked at his prayers. The Tempter, too, whispered that he would cool him insensibly—"*What care I*," saith he, "*though I be seven years chilling your heart, if I can do it at last?*" (*G. A.* § 111).

But, afterwards, "the Lord did more fully and graciously discover himself unto me" (*G. A.* § 115), and he "saw that the Justice of God, and my sinful Soul could embrace and kiss each other through [Christ's] blood" (*G. A.* § 116). He was led from truth to truth by God. "Methought I was as if I had seen him [Christ] born, as if I had seen him grow up, as if I had seen him walk through this World, from the Cradle to the Cross; to which also, when he came, I saw how gently he gave himself to be hanged, and nailed on it, for my sins and wicked doings" (*G. A.* § 121). This passage may serve as commentary on those in the *Pilgrim's Progress* where Christian sees the Cross, and afterwards tells how he saw it—and it may be noted that this is one of the things he saw for himself, no man showing it to him.

But now came the tempter "with a more grievous and dreadful temptation than before. And that was to sell and part with this most blessed Christ, to exchange him for the things of this life, for any thing" (*G. A.* § 134). Nothing could stop the thought. "Sometimes it would run in my thoughts, not so little as an hundred times together; *Sell him, sell him, sell him.* . . . By the very force of my mind, in labouring to gainsay and resist this wickedness, my very body would be put into action, or motion, by way of pushing or thrusting with my hands or elbows; still answering, as fast as the destroyer said, *Sell him; I will not, I will not, I will not; no, not for thousands, thousands, thousands of Worlds"* (*G. A.* §§ 137, 138). "At last, after much striving, even until I was almost out of breath, I felt this thought pass through my heart, *Let him go, if he will*" (*G. A.* § 140). And then for years he was haunted by the text about Esau selling his birthright and finding no place for repentance—over and over again it "would be set at my heart, even like a flaming Sword" (*G. A.* § 179). Satan "strongly suggested" that "*God hath been weary of you for these several years already because you are none of his*" (*G. A.* §§ 177, 178).

All this is very like what we read in Cowper's letters to Samuel Teedon, the Olney schoolmaster, but it is not really a parallel case. Bunyan had voices of two kinds; he had days and sometimes weeks when he was under the influence of voices of comfort. Texts, with grace and encouragement overflowing in them, were suggested to him—he believed from another quarter. At last "I remember one day, as I was in divers frames of spirit, and considering that these frames were still according to the nature of the several Scriptures that came in upon my mind; if this of Grace, then was I quiet; but if that of *Esau*, then tormented; *Lord*, thought I, *if both those Scriptures would meet in my heart at once, I wonder which of them would get the better of me*" (*G. A.* § 213). This thought is proof of sanity, as Cowper's thoughts are unmistakable evidence of insanity. One great difference between sane and insane lies in this power of seeing two things at once, of responding to the thought or impulse and its corrective. Bunyan is never quite swept out of himself by any voice or impulse, though we can believe him when he says that "all those tumultuous thoughts did use, like masterless hell-hounds, to roar and bellow, and make an hideous noise within me" (*G. A.* § 175).

Peace came to him at last in the realization that Christ was his Righteousness, and that this did not depend on

BUNYAN

"the good frame of his Heart" or on its bad frame—or, as we should say, on his feelings—Christ was the same yesterday, to-day and forever. "Now did the Chains fall off my legs indeed" (*G. A.* § 231). "'Twas glorious to me to see his exaltation and the worth and prevalency of all his benefits, and that because now I could look from myself to him" (*G. A.* § 233). He began now to realize that he had gained from his temptation "a very wonderful sense both of the Being and Glory of God, and of his beloved Son," and he was "made to see more into the Nature of the Promises than ever I was before" (*G. A.* §§ 245 ff.) and into "heights and depths in Grace, and Love, and Mercy" (*G. A.* § 253).

If it be asked how Bunyan came to have such an experience, which is (perhaps not unhappily) not given to most men, that is bound up with the temperament which enabled him to write as he did. Imagination is the most priceless of gifts, but Fancy is apt to come with it. Imagination is the faculty in virtue of which the artist sees what he describes, and *is* the man whom he paints or of whom he tells—sees as he sees, feels as he feels, thinks as he thinks. It is the gift by which reality is interpreted, while Fancy, on the other hand, sweeps away beyond reality, and makes impossible groupings of the real. For the work he has to do the poet or artist must feel more than any other men.

> A primrose by a river's brim,
> A yellow primrose was to him,
> And it was nothing more—

so says Wordsworth of Peter Bell—and the reviewer asked, what more was it? Which had the true view? Which knew best what a primrose is? Who has the true view of the spiritual life—Bunyan, with his wrestlings with Satan, with texts dinned into his ears that spoke of the enormity of sin, with his extraordinarily sensitive conscience, sensitive as a painter's eye for colour—or the common man who could have told him, and with justice (as Froude and Macaulay have since done), that he was nothing like as bad as he fancied? Does the one see a great deal more than is real, or the other a great deal less?

It is established, in any case, that good work in any sphere of art comes from men of the sensitive type, who have that intensity of imagination for which everything stands clear in its outlines and colours — not merely stands, but is, acts, and moves in a world of similar realities;—men who have also the power of co-ordinating and of checking imagination by reality, as Bunyan does. For his common sense is one of his strongest features. Thus, before the magistrates in November, 1660, "I was as sparing of my speech as I could, without prejudice to truth," and again, "As I was going forth of the doors, I had much ado to forbear saying to them, that I carried the peace of God along with me: But I held my peace, and blessed be the Lord went away to prison with God's comfort in my poor soul." And there, when he wrote *Grace Abounding*, he still was.

III

Bunyan tells us that he wrote *The Pilgrim's Progress* almost involuntarily. In prison in 1675, he began some literary work about "the way and race of Saints in this our Gospel day," and then "fell suddenly into an Allegory about their Journey and the way to Glory." Thoughts multiplied in his head like sparks, till he surrendered to the unsought inspiration. He wrote his book, as living books are written, under an impulse so powerful and so unexpected that it seemed to come from without, with an unusually full and happy flow of thoughts. He had no intention at first to publish it—

no not I,
I did it mine own self to Gratifie.

*Neither did I but vacant seasons spend
In this my Scribble; Nor did I intend
But to divert my self in doing this,
From worser thoughts, which make me do amiss.
Thus I set Pen to Paper with delight,
And quickly had my thoughts in black and white.*

The poets from Euripides to Wordsworth would tell him that he worked in the one right spirit—there must be joy in creation,—and there was joy in the creation of the Pilgrim. "Some there be that say he laughs too loud," we read in the verse prefixed to the Second Part, and we can guess who they were. There is in the Second Part a Mr Feeblemind, whom the Pilgrims meet and whom Old Honest thinks very like an old acquaintance, and so it proves. For he is nephew of Mr Fearing, and comes like him "from the Town of Stupidity, which lieth *four Degrees* to the Northward of the City of Destruction"; and he has his uncle's "whitely look and a cast like his with his Eye." It is remarkable how Bunyan visualizes his characters, and then (as if he had read Lessing) contrives to tell us what they were like with no halt in the story; for it is not he, but Old Honest, who thus bluntly describes the features of his old fellow-citizen and his nephew. Feeblemind is not as bad as he looks; he has the fixed resolve and the dour courage that stupid men sometimes have; but when he confesses his ways of thinking, they are distressing. "*I am a man of weak and feeble Mind. . . . I shall like no Laughing, I shall like no gay Attire, I shall like no unprofitable Questions. Nay, I am so weak a Man, as to be offended with that which others have a liberty to do.*" He is one of the few Pilgrims who seem not to have read the adventures of Christian. He must have been drawn from life; and how Bunyan must have enjoyed drawing him! Yet how kindly he does it! It is one of his characteristics—a common feature of fine humour—to have no antipathies, and Bunyan's books are singularly free from any trace of irritations—if he felt them.

Much has been written of the literary antecedents of the Pilgrim.[1] "Some say the Pilgrim's Progress is not mine," he wrote in a metrical advertisement to the reader, at the end of the *Holy War*; but, he says, "It came from mine own heart"—"Manner and matter too was all mine own." Many allegories of pilgrimage are now known to have existed before his day, but it is supremely unlikely that he could ever have heard of many of them. And, if he did? Who hears of them now, unless some curious antiquary here or there? Shakespeare borrowed almost all his plots; "he only gave the spirit (*Geist*), which put life into them," as Heine said. No allegory known to Europe has any hint of such life as those of Bunyan. There was in the Epistle to the Hebrews—an epistle much in Bunyan's mind, as the Esau text shows—a passage, in which the Christian life is compared to a pilgrimage in search of a heavenly country. This once granted, and the idea of allegory, no wonder thoughts came "like sparks" to such a mind, so full of life and humour, so rich in experience. And the mode enabled him to give the fullest expression to the whole of himself, gaiety and seriousness at once. Some people will not realize that the highest humour is serious,—that Shakespeare was serious when he drew the Fool in *Lear*,—that, as Plato said, tragedy and comedy come from the same hand, or that, in Bunyan's own words,

> Some things are of that Nature as to make
> One's fancie Checkle while his heart doth ake.

Allegory is the hardest of all literary modes, harder than Tragedy, with less range and more pitfalls. There

---

[1] Do Giant Despair and the Vision from the Delectable Mountains owe anything to cantos ix and x of the First Book of the *Faerie Queene*? It is a very attractive idea and very doubtful.

BUNYAN

are inconsistencies and improbabilities in the *Pilgrim's Progress* as there are in the *Odyssey*, and still more in *Don Quixote*—perhaps even in *Robinson Crusoe*.[1] Some of them are accidents; others are inherent in the scheme. Of these some are "outside the tragedy," as Aristotle put it in criticizing Sophocles' *Œdipus*; but, the improbabilities once thus admitted, the rest follows. Others are lost sight of in the general impression; the charm of the whole thing is too great. From the moment when we see "a Man cloathed with Rags, standing in a certain place, with his Face from his own House, a Book in his hand, and a great Burden upon his Back," we accept everything as probable, we believe everything, with all the emotion that attends such belief—just as we believe the *Ancient Mariner*, an even more improbable story.

But what of the part "outside the Tragedy"? Are the adventures of a soul stirred by the fear of hell a theme of enough nobility for a great story? Is the motive either noble, or true?

It depends on the value we set on the human soul. If we hold with Plato that this life is the "study of death," or, in plainer terms, a preparation for another life of more moment; or if we hold with Kant that God, freedom, and immortality are the postulates of the practical reason—the preconceptions involved in every act, much as the law of gravitation is subconsciously assumed in all our actions which relate to matter;—then, whether hell is eternal, as Bunyan thought, or not, sin becomes a thing of real and enduring significance, and the pilgrimage of the soul toward "the higher regions" is no idle or light theme. To-day, under the influence of a rather unreflective charity and of scientific conceptions, lightly seized and ill understood, there is a tendency for men to underestimate the power of evil as a force in human affairs.

---

[1] A biologist friend of mine has remarked on the quite improbable freedom of Crusoe from insect parasites in the Tropics, but perhaps two centuries ago Englishmen noticed these things less.

In the endeavour to reach some sort of monism, evil is viewed from a distance which permits pleasant talk of its being a necessary condition for good, and so forth. But, when, in practice there results an easier ideal of conduct and a more genial tolerance of evil, so long as it is not physical pain,—can we say that it is sound thinking?

But, we are asked, can a work stand as a picture of the Christian life, in which the family and the city are discarded? The question implies some failure to realize the limitations of Allegory and some misrepresentation of what we read in the book. In the second edition Bunyan added the conversation with Charity, in which Christian with tears explains that he did all he could to bring his family with him and they refused to come; and in the Second Part we see that he had really done a great deal for them and for the people of his city. For a man's own inward state is the measure of all he does for men, is, in fact,—in a sense,—his chief contribution to society. His estimate of his own spiritual, intellectual and moral needs and possibilities sets a limit to what he will suppose other men to need and to what he will attempt for them. And even if the criticism were true, that family and city are abandoned, Bunyan knew, as we have seen, that sometimes a family has to be forsaken—and he knew the pain of it. If these views are right—and there seems to be historical as well as philosophic reason for supposing them so—Bunyan or any man might look far for a nobler motive for story or allegory, a truer or a more vital.

With the warrant of Scripture under his eyes, and with his own indelible memories of "strong suggestions," it is not surprising that Bunyan does not speak of evil in the impersonal way, but personifies it. An illustration may help at this point. Christian, at one awful stage, goes through Bunyan's own experience; and, in looking back, Bunyan's sense enables him to clear things. He makes a free use of italics in printing his books, and this whole passage is italicized by him. "*One thing I would not let slip, I took notice that now poor* Christian *was so confounded, that he did not know his own voice; and thus I perceived it; Just when he was come over against the mouth of the burning Pit, one of the wicked ones got behind him, and stept up softly to him, and whisperingly suggested many grievous blasphemies to him, which he verily thought had proceeded from his own mind. This put* Christian *more to it than anything that he met with before, even to think that he should now blaspheme him, that he loved so much before; yet if he could have helped it, he would not have done it; but he had not the discretion neither to stop his Ears, nor to know from whence those blasphemies came."* Now, whether evil is to be regarded or not as a personal force or a series of such forces, this episode of Christian's journey through the Valley of the Shadow of Death is true to the human mind and its experience; and if Bunyan's language is not what we somewhat crudely call scientific, it lies close alongside of the experience it is intended to describe. The horrible complications of the mind at variance with itself, the co-existence within it of *velle* and *nolle*, its subjection to a yoke which it feels to be foreign, which it hates and yet rather likes and so much the more detests—through all this Bunyan had been, like Augustine before him; and really, if the experience is to be put at all into words, none seem adequate to express its horror but those which attribute personality to the element or elements of evil. The error in such an attribution is less than the opposite error, which overtakes us, when, for the pedantry of a scientific dialect, we sacrifice something of the truth of an experience, blunting its edges to make it symmetrical with theory.

In any case Satan and Apollyon were among the necessary preconceptions of a writer in Bunyan's day, and the terms, however grotesquely they may strike a modern ear, corresponded with what he felt he had experienced; so that it seems fairer to accept them as "outside the tragedy," as "given," and then without prejudice consider what Bunyan makes of his story as he works within his limitations, as every artist must.

No one will suggest that Bunyan read Aristotle, yet the curious coincidence of his method in story-telling with a famous dictum in the *Poetics* may help us to understand something of his genius. "The poet should speak as little as possible in his own person. . . . Homer, after a few prefatory words, at once brings in a man, or woman, or other personage; none of them wanting in characteristic qualities but each with a character of his own."

Let us take Mr *Worldly Wiseman* as an example. We are only told his name and that he comes from *Carnal Policy*, a very great town; and, Christian happening to cross his way, he had "some guess of him" and spoke. He at once begins to reveal himself. "How now, good fellow, whither away after this burdened manner?" The question has a superficial look of sympathy, and a suggestion of some want of it. Christian explains his errand, and Wiseman abruptly asks, "Hast thou a wife and Children?"—a practical common-sense sort of thing to ask, though not very obviously his affair.[1] Then he has a happy idea—the originality of this kind of man is generally rather threadbare. He offers a practical suggestion. "I would advise thee then that thou with all speed get thy self rid of thy Burden; for thou wilt never be settled in thy mind till then: nor canst thou enjoy the benefits of the blessing which God hath bestowed upon thee till then." We need not follow the conversation; it is full of common-sense; but we do not yet know what Worldly Wiseman looked like. That we learn when Evangelist asks Christian about the man who advised him to leave the way—"What was he?" "He looked like a Gentleman, and talked much to me."

Earle, in his *Microcosmographie*, also drew a "World's Wise Man," whose "tush! is greatest at religion." There

---

[1] Charity, of course, asks the same question, but after they have invited him to stay in the Palace Beautiful.

was much drawing of "characters" about this period, and Earle's are full of humour and point—perhaps a little too full to be quite true. At any rate the archetypal wise man of this world would probably own Bunyan's as the better likeness, and no doubt would wonder that Bunyan, with so much wits about him as to understand the common-sense he puts into Worldly Wiseman's mouth, should yet reject it.

Let us take another instance, where verification comes from an unexpected source to confirm Bunyan's truth in portraiture. *Atheist* " fell into a very great laughter," when Christian and Hopeful explained to him the purpose of their pilgrimage—they would only have their travel for their pains.

Chr. Why, man? Do you think we shall not be received?

Atheist. Received! There is no such place as you dream of in all this World!

Chr. But there is in the World to come.

Atheist. When I was at home in mine own Country, I heard as you now affirm, and from that hearing went out to see, and have been seeking this City twenty years, but find no more of it than I did the first day I set out.

Chr. We have both heard, and believe that there is such a place to be found.

Atheist. Had I not when at home believed, I had not come thus far to seek ; but finding none, (and yet I should, had there been such a place to be found, for I have gone to seek it further than you) I am going back again and will seek to refresh my self with the things that I then cast away for hopes of that which I see not.

Fourteen centuries earlier Lucian had written his account of his argument with Hermotimus. " I conceive Virtue," he said to his friend, " under the figure of a City, whose citizens are happy, absolutely wise, all of them brave, hardly distinguishable from Gods. Their relations are all peace and unity. Their life is serene and blissful in the enjoyment of all good things." Should not men seek such a city, asks Hermotimus, and never count the toil nor lose heart? "Certainly above all things else we should devote ourselves to it and let the rest go, nor pay any great heed to our country that is here; nor, though our children or parents (if we have any) cling to us and cry, ought we to yield, but, if we can, urge them also to take the same journey; and, if they won't or can't, then shake them off and go straight to that all-happy City—letting even one's coat go, if they lay hold of it to keep us back, and press on thitherward. For there is no fear that they will shut you out there, even if you come without a coat. I remember hearing a description of it all once before from an old man, who urged me to go with him to the City; he would show me the way, and on my arrival, he would enroll me, and make me one of his own tribe and kin, so that I should share the universal happiness. But I would not hearken—through folly and youth—it was fifteen years ago; or by now I might have reached the suburbs and been at the gates.... If the city had been near at hand and plain for all to see, long ago (you may be sure) with never a doubt I would have gone to it and been a citizen long since. But as the City (as you say) lies far away, it is necessary to seek the road to take you there and the best guide." And then Lucian proves at great length how impossible it is to find either road or guide, and how absurd is the quest, and his elderly friend gives up a life-time's endeavour, resolved henceforth "to live like an ordinary person without eccentric or vain hopes." Lucian's antagonists, unlike Bunyan's, are generally puppets, easily bowled over. Bunyan's men, like Plato's Callicles in the *Gorgias*, walk away (on feet of their own) convinced that they are right and the Pilgrim wrong.

It is interesting to note that the city which Christian seeks is the same as that at which Lucian laughs. Lucian had read Plato, and Bunyan the Epistle to the Hebrews.

The writer of that epistle was a man of Hellenistic culture—"the most cultured Greek of them all"[1]—and he too as he wrote had his eye with Plato upon "the place above the heavens." If the glimpse of the Celestial City from the Delectable Mountains owes anything to the *Faerie Queene* (i. 10)—and there is resemblance—then we might say that Bunyan's City is connected with Plato's by a second line of ancestry, In any case Atheist and Lucian could change places. Atheist's words would fit the Greek story, and Lucian could have said nothing else to Christian.

Bunyan does not "play" in writing his allegory, any more than when he wrote *Grace Abounding*, though he has of course more scope here for humour. He will not under-estimate the Christian's foes; the cost shall be faithfully counted, and no Pliable can accuse Bunyan of telling him only half the story as poor Christian did. But this is not all. As he wrote, he fairly saw his men and identified himself with them. Such a faculty is the outcome of experience and imagination. He had himself been Ignorance, for he too was "a brisk talker." He had looked down the street where Atheist lived (*cf. G. A.* §§ 97, 98). Worldly Wiseman had tried to let him a house in the village of Morality, where (as he very justly remarked in 1678) houses stood empty and were to be had at reasonable rates.[2] *By-Ends*—and that half-brother of his mother's, the Mr *Two-Tongues*, who was "the parson of our Parish," holding on in spite of the Uniformity Act, like his much-harassed contemporary the Vicar of Bray, who was probably connected with that honourable family—the old gentleman Mr Legality, and the "pretty young Man," his son Civility, with the "simpering looks"—Bunyan had known them all. And

[1] J. H. Moulton in *Cambridge Biblical Essays*, p. 472.
[2] Pepys' Diary is a commentary on the gradual depopulation of this village. The place has looked up a good deal of late years, and, like Ottawa, Toronto, and other great towns, has changed its name. It is now called Social Righteousness.

now Imagination breathed upon them, and they lived and looked and spoke with their native accents. Dialogue is instinctive with Bunyan. Even in other works, where it is less obvious, he falls naturally into it. It is one of the most charming features of his Allegories—so full of ease is it, so free and natural and close to life. Its spontaneity and its homely phrase are not to be allegorized. When Christian "snibbeth his fellow" and tells him he talks "like one upon whose head is the shell," this is not allegory, it is character. It is such unstudied words, that bring us face to face with men as they talk. Austere and relevant persons delete such things; the man of genius puts them in—or rather, finds them in and cannot cut them out, and in consequence he is reproached for laughing too loud.

The *Pilgrim's Progress* is one of those permanent books which survive their own theories. Paul, Augustine, à Kempis, and Bunyan had their views of the world natural and spiritual, and many of these views are no longer held. But they put more into their books than views—they worked life and experience into them in such a way that no re-modelling of Theology or Philosophy will take away their value. They stand as part of the great inheritance of our race—the living records of lives that were lived in the fullest sense of the word, lives of which no fraction was lost, but all was realised and turned to account by minds specially gifted for living and for telling what life is.

Like all such books, Bunyan's *Pilgrim* takes us into new regions and opens up new avenues of experience. For many of us it is now the one great type of the Christian life,—begun with a burden and moving on to freedom and ever higher happiness—but hard and dangerous, full of Doubting Castles and Sloughs of Despond, with much of the Valley of Humiliation and the Shadow of Death. It gives us the unspeakable feeling which pulsed through Christian's mind, when " he thought

he heard the Voice of a man, going before him," and
gathered from that " That some who feared God were in
this Valley as well as himself." Above all it is a book
of Victory. There is the Celestial City, with its bells
ringing,[1] at the end, but, what is more to the point for us
just now, we see Christian wounded, shamed and fallen
" with a dreadful fall," with Apollyon "sure of him " at
last—and yet there and then consciously "more than
conquerour through him that loved us." As Christian
said elsewhere (with a smile), " I think verily I know the
meaning of this." And, when the last page is read, how
often has the word of the " Man of a very stout Countenance" come to the reader's lips—" Set down my name,
Sir " ?

IV

The *Holy War*, which followed the First Part of the
Pilgrim's Progress and preceded the *Second*, must here
have its usual fate, and be obscured by the greater book.
It is a more elaborate allegory, carefully worked out at
great length. When the reader is a third of the way
through, he wonders what there is to fill the pages before
him—will the interest of the story last so long? It does
last. If it hurts the allegory as a work of art (though
this is a questionable suggestion), that there is no end to
the history of Mansoul as there is to the life of Christian,
yet Bunyan here is true to fact. Emmanuel recaptures
Mansoul, but war still hangs about its coasts, and the
story of that prolonged war might fascinate not merely
those who are interested in the spiritual life, but any
man who loves a good story. For as a piece of mere
narrative it is admirable. Many and many a historic
siege is less real ; Bunyan had learnt something even in
those days of the Civil War, of which he says so little.
The characters, too, though here they must inevitably be

---

[1] It is perhaps worth while remarking how readily Bunyan sets the bells
ringing in his books—the bells he gave up in real life.

more lightly sketched than in the story of an individual, are yet drawn by the same hand, some faintly, others, who are more in the centre of things, more strongly and clearly. In short, the whole book is so natural and human that we are startled to find the Diabolonian prisoners being crucified by the Mansoulians—it seems too horrible to be true, until we notice in the margin "Rom. 8, 13, and 6, 12, 13, 14." The marginalia in Bunyan are not to be ignored.

The sights and sounds of the siege, the glittering lines of the troops, the fluxes and refluxes of feeling within the city—it is all the record of an eye-witness, as indeed Bunyan claims in his preface—

> *I saw the* Princes *armed men come down*
> *By troops, by thousands, to besiege the Town.*
> *I saw the* Captains, *heard the* Trumpets *sound,*
> *And how his forces cover'd all the ground.*
> *Yea, how they set themselves in battel-ray*
> *I shall remember to my dying day.*
>   *I saw the* Colours *waving in the wind* . . .[1]
>   *I saw the* Mounts *cast up against the Town,*
> *And how the slings were plac'd to beat it down.*
> *I heard the stones fly whizzing by mine ears* . . .
>   *I saw the Battering Rams and how they play'd* . . .
>   *I saw the Fights and heard the Captains shout* . . .
>   *I heard the cries of those that wounded were* . . .
>   *I was there when the* Gates *were broken ope* . . .
> *I heard the groans, and saw the joy of many ;*
> *Tell you of all, I neither will, nor can I.*
> *But by what here I say, you well may see*
> *That* Mansouls *matchless Wars no Fables be.*

Every word of this is borne out by the story.

But the book is not all strain and stress. There is the relief about it that Bunyan's humour could so well

---

[1] Repetition of "I saw" in *Faerie Queene*, iv. 1, 49.

give. The despatches between Diabolus and his "horribly beloved" in Mansoul are excellent. The passing talk between Mr *Profane*, who carries these state-papers, and Cerberus on duty at *Hellgate-hill*, who swears by St Mary; the conversation at Mr *Carnal Security's* feast; the identification of *Falsepeace* on trial, are as good as any of the dialogues in the *Pilgrim's Progress*. "I was his play-fellow," says *Search-Truth*, "only I was somewhat older than he; and when his mother did use to call him home from his play, she used to say, *Falsepeace, Falsepeace*, come home quick, or I'le fetch you. Yea, I knew him when he sucked; and though I was then but little, yet I can remember that when his mother did use to sit at the door with him, or did play with him in her arms, she would call him twenty times together, My little *Falsepeace*, my pretty *Falsepeace*, and O my sweet Rogue, *Falsepeace*; and again, O my little bird *Falsepeace*; and how I do love my child! The Gossips also know it is thus, though he has had the face to deny it in open Court." Did all this actually take place in Mansoul? Or had the imagination that saw *Falsepeace* on trial carried Bunyan away, till the abstraction became a man, a real man with a real childhood behind him, which he instantly realized, as if he remembered it all to have happened at a door in Bedford fifty years before, when as a little boy he first noticed how a mother talks to a baby?

It is not fair to a book so true, so vivid, so profound, and so amusing as the *Holy War* to dismiss it in a page or two. It must be read; and a quiet attention to its large outlines and (not less) to its detail will reveal the author on more sides of his character than one.

While Bunyan was busy with *Badman* and the *Holy War*, some one else saw and seized the chance of continuing the *Pilgrim's Progress*. And, just as Cervantes was driven into completing *Don Quixote* by a spurious Don, Bunyan himself took in hand the story of Christiana at first perforce, though he soon fell in love with his task.

It is commonly said that the Second Part is not as good as the First. Froude was all but contemptuous of it. Certainly to the historian and to such as must have consistency at all costs, it is a disquieting book. How old are Christiana's sons? They begin as "sweet babes," though of course they are obviously long past the cradle. At the beginning of the First Part they are old enough to argue against their father's purpose, but most parents will realize that they do not need to be very old to do that. On the hill *Difficulty*, James (the youngest) is a "little boy," and the whole four of them stept back, and "were glad to cringe behind" when they came to the lions on the hill-top. This was outside the Palace Beautiful, where they stayed a month. From thence they passed through the two Valleys, and came to the house of Gaius (a day's journey from Vanity Fair), and there James married. There are too many marriages altogether to please Froude, to say nothing of needless giants.

But, allowing for all this, the book is full of fine characters. It is perhaps impossible to make much of the four boys, but Christiana and Mercy are women indeed, and very different women. Mercy is as charming a character as any in fiction. The episode of her Suitor, Mr *Brisk*, is admirable. She was always sewing when he came—" I will warrant her a good Huswife, quoth he to himself." But he finds she gives away all she makes, and he leaves off coming. Mercy is not troubled; " I might a had Husbands afore now, tho' I spake not of it to any; but they were such as did not like my Conditions, though never did any of them find fault with my Person: So they and I could not agree."

Greatheart is one of Bunyan's great figures—a development of the excellent (but rather dim) Ironside captains in the *Holy War*, who could fight and preach as need required.[1] "Truly," said Cromwell (25 Dec. 1650), "I think he that prays and preaches best will fight best." We have only one of *Greatheart's* sermons, and though Christiana ejaculates "This is brave," it is more than enough. But, apart from his sermon, he is a character that appeals to the reader, as do Old *Honest*, "a Cock of the right kind" ("Not Honesty in the *Abstract*, but *Honest* is my name")—and the weaker brethren, *Ready-to-Halt* and *Feeblemind*, and the stalwart men at the book's end, *Valiant* and *Standfast*.

Perhaps as typical an incident as any in the Second Part is the sickness of Matthew. "One Mr *Skill*, an Ancient, and well approved Physician," was sent for and quickly diagnosed the case—"he concluded he was sick of the Gripes. Then he said to his Mother, *What Diet has* Matthew *of late fed upon?* Diet, said *Christiana*, nothing but that which is wholsom." A good deal, by the way, is said of diet in the Second Part; over and over again we are told what the Pilgrims had to eat; now it is "a *Heave-shoulder* and a *Wave-breast*," or a feeble Pilgrim is given "a Bottle of Spirits, and some comfortable things to eat," while Christiana and Mercy have each "a Bottle of Wine, and also some parched Corn, together with a couple of Pomgranates," and some Figs and Raisins for the boys. But *Skill* will not be put off, and it proves that he is right; for Samuel reminds them how Matthew ate some fruit overhanging the way near the gate. *Skill* recognizes that this belonged to Beelzebub's orchard, and adds that many have died of it. "Then *Christiana* began to cry, and she said, O naughty boy, and O careless Mother, what shall I do for my Son?

Skill. *Come do not be too much dejected; the Boy may do well again; but he must purge and Vomit.*

Christiana. Pray Sir try the utmost of your Skill with him whatever it costs.

[1] Professor Firth (*Cromwell*, p. 369) says he "is but an allegorical representation of what Cromwell was to the Puritans."

Skill. Nay I hope I shall be reasonable : So he made him a Purge; but it was too weak. 'Twas said, it was made of the Blood of a Goat, the Ashes of a Heifer, and with some of the Juice of Hyssop, *etc.*[1] When Mr Skill had seen that that Purge was too weak, he made him one to the purpose. 'Twas made *ex Carne et Sanguine Christi.* (You know Physicians give strange Medicines to their Patients) [in the margin Bunyan adds *The Lattine I borrow*], and it was made up into Pills with a Promise or two, and a proportionable quantity of Salt. Now he was to take them three at a time fasting in half a quarter of a Pint of the Tears of Repentance." It wrought kindly with him, after he was prevailed on to take it, and quite rid him of his trouble.

So the family moves on together to the Celestial City, meeting kindly faces and leaving pleasant memories. We even read how *Christiana* took leave of the Porter at the Palace Beautiful, and "put a Gold Angel into his Hand, and he made her a low obeisance." They do not have Christian's troubles, and that again is true to fact, for such troubles belong chiefly to spiritual solitude, and here was a group of people, bound by ties of blood, and a common purpose and experience.

One of the features of seventeenth century England was the music on the roads. Justice Shallow as a young man "sung those tunes that he heard the carmen whistle and sware they were his fancies and his good-nights." The carmen, it seems, composed them, songs and airs. Autolycus, in the *Winter's Tale*, and Christian, in the First Part, alike sing as they go. But the songs in the Second Part are in other metres than the rhyming ten-syllable lines which contented Christian—in easier rhythms and more musical. The song, which follows the talk with *Valiant*, has a lyric note—a note disappearing at that time from English verse for a while.

[1] For prescriptions even in the 18th century, see H. Grey Graham, *Social Life in Scotland*, vol. i. pp. 50-52.

> Who would true Valour see,
>   Let him come hither;
> One here will constant be
>   Come Wind, come Weather.

In the Valley of Humiliation they hear the shepherd boy, "in very mean clothes but of a very fresh and well-favoured Countenance," singing as he sits by himself—"He that is down, needs fear no fall." The birds about the Palace Beautiful, too, are all singing—"you may hear them all day long. ... They are very fine Company for us when we are *Melancholy*." This Valley and its descent had no music for poor Christian.

The Pilgrims even demolished *Doubting Castle*, as they went by, and slew its owner, but it seems that the property passed to another of the family who rebuilt it, for it certainly stands to-day, an imposing structure with much science in the building of it, but the guest rooms are as ill-furnished as of old. Vanity Fair itself they found "much more moderate now than formerly." "I think," says Mr *Contrite* of that place, "the Blood of *Faithful* lieth with load upon them till now; for since they burned him, they have been ashamed to burn any more: In *those* days we were afraid to walk the Streets, but *now* we can shew our Heads."

Thus Bunyan wrote in 1685, and it looks as if he had "the *Brittan* Row" in his mind—as if the twelve years of his imprisonment in Bedford had been not merely "an awakening to the Saints in the country," but some kind of enlightenment even to others of his neighbours. Twelve years in "a stinking Dungeon," and a spirit unbroken by it,—good humour, good temper, and faith triumphant, and no grudge felt—and then the wonderful books; no wonder things were "more moderate." Nonconformity was not yet clear of dungeon and court; the locks of the last gates "went *damnable* hard," as Bunyan puts it, but the key called Promise was to open them in time.

It is difficult to reckon what a great book does. What did the *Pilgrim's Progress* do for England? What has been its effect on our language? Could we say that it has done for English Prose what Burns did for Poetry—"showed how it may build a princely throne on humble truth?" What has been its influence as the most widely read and translated work of the imagination in English—a book accessible to millions who never read Shakespeare, where they may meet a world of men, men outside their ordinary range and yet intelligible and individual, knowable as one's next-door neighbours are not? What again has the book meant in the religious history of England? What did the eleven editions in cheap type and paper,[1] issued before Bunyan's death and William III.'s arrival in 1688, do to keep alive the Puritan spirit in this country, and to keep it happy and bright in places where there was no tinker-preacher with his "sparkling eyes"[2] and his patience to make things "more moderate?" What has been done for English liberty by the book and its writer together? Those twelve stubborn years in prison, the separation from wife and children and the blind little girl, and the sturdy thinking of it all out, so as not to be taken unawares by whip, pillory, banishment or death (*G. A.* § 327)—what did these do to nerve men then and thereafter to bear what they could not alter? "Where I cannot obey actively, there I am willing to lie down, and to suffer what they shall do unto me."

And supposing he had been talked round and had agreed no longer "devilishly and perniciously to abstain from coming to church to hear divine service," and to be no longer "an upholder of several unlawful meetings and conventicles to the great disturbance and distraction of

---

[1] Dr Brown says it is computed that 100,000 copies were sold in Bunyan's own lifetime.

[2] We learn from a contemporary that Bunyan was "tall of stature, strong-boned, though not corpulent, somewhat of a ruddy face, with sparkling eyes"; J. Brown, *Bunyan*, p. 399.

the good subjects of the kingdom, contrary to the laws of our sovereign lord, the King, etc."? Bedford might have kept a tinker the more—and possibly none of the best at that, for there is nothing to show that renegades make good tinkers—and what would England have lost?

COWPER

IN 1763 the positions of Reading Clerk and Clerk of Committees in the House of Lords became vacant. They were patent offices in the patronage of Major William Cowper, a member of a family brilliant in law and letters. The Major had a first cousin of the same house and the same name, a young barrister, in chambers in the Inner Temple, who had been at the bar for nine years without gaining much celebrity in his profession. He was a young man of great personal charm and a certain natural gaiety. Like nearly all the other members of the family, men and women, he wrote verse, but in a lighter vein than most of them, though his father, the Rev. John Cowper, had set him the example of writing ballads (4 Dec. '81, 4 Aug. '83).[1] Again, like the rest of his family, he was a Whig, and "the son of a staunch Whig" (4 Dec. '81). "How the deuce you came to be a Tory," he wrote in later days to another cousin, "is best known to yourself; you have to answer for this novelty to the shades of your ancestors, who were always Whigs, ever since we had any" (10 Feb. '93).

It was obviously appropriate for the Major to appoint a young man of such claims to both the vacant offices, and he did. Something of the kind had long been the young lawyer's wish, and now he had attained it. Unfortunately he changed his mind, and asked to have instead the Clerkship of the Journals of the House of Lords, an office of less pay but less publicity, which was also vacant and in the Major's gift. With some reluctance

[1] Dates given in brackets refer to letters of Cowper written on the days indicated.

the patentee consented, and the transference was made. But now difficulties appeared. The Major's right to present was questioned, and an order was made that the Clerk presented should be examined at the Bar of the House as to his qualifications. To be able to meet this ordeal, William began to attend the office daily and to read the Journals of the House. "My days are spent in reading the Journals," he wrote, "and my nights in dreaming of them" (9 Aug. '63).

Law, poetry, and melancholy ran in his family, and the last had now laid hold upon him. The strain continued until, in November, to escape from the examination and the enmity of men, he made three attempts to destroy himself. The Major, for whom he sent on the third of these occasions, realized the state of the case, asked for the "deputation," and took it away with him; "thus ended all my connection with the Parliament Office."

The poor man was on the verge of insanity. His brother John Cowper, a Fellow of Corpus College, Cambridge, came to him at once, but failed to comfort him. He then asked to see his cousin, the Rev. Martin Madan, an Evangelical clergyman in high repute as a leader of his party and a popular preacher—hitherto suspected by his young relatives of being an "enthusiast." Madan spoke to him of the Gospel and of Christ's righteousness, and he was comforted. But the disease was upon him, and there was nothing for it but to send him to the house of Dr Nathaniel Cotton at St Albans—the Collegium Insanorum, where for a year and a half he remained.

So in humiliation and distress a career was ended. There was no more thought of the bar or of public life. Cowper left his physician's house sane and happy, and full of a new Christian conviction, but in all else a broken man, incapable of action, whose utmost hope might be to reach his grave without relapse. Of more than this there was no prospect. Separated from all his old friends, his only connexions with the world were through the post.

Cowper was a Whig of the eighteenth century and of the great Whig tradition—a man of aristocratic descent and popular sympathies, who had that ease and lightness of touch which is the peculiar privilege of those in whom culture and humour are finely compounded. The exquisite playfulness of his later years shows itself early; the tenderness and sensibility that invariably go with the profoundest humour are there also, but in this case, as in others, it is not in youth that they reach their perfection. He had at Westminster school, under Vincent Bourne, a sound Classical training, and perhaps, as has been suggested, learnt other things from "Vinny" Bourne beside Latin verse.[1] There is an affinity between them in their gifts of observation and fondness for animals, and the pupil amused himself in later years by rendering the master into English—with a certain freedom which stamps the personality of the translator on the rendering. Humour, and the early accomplishment of Latin verse, are his initial equipment; and it has been remarked by John Conington that, in his original poems, Cowper is perhaps the greatest master we have in English of the Horatian style. His ease in metre, and his ease and terseness in thought, suggest the comparison, while the critic goes on to add that he has a deeper and more sustained gravity in his serious poems than Horace ever reached, and, in his lighter verses, as in the *Epistle to Joseph Hill*, a sprightliness and ease seldom equalled by the Latin poet, who, however, never wrote anything so prosaic as the *Colubriad*.

Very few of his letters survive from before the first attack of insanity. Those of the time of his recovery have little enough of the quality that tempted his friends later on to preserve whatever he wrote. They are all

---

[1] "Bless him," wrote Lamb of Vincent Bourne, "Latin wasn't good enough for him, why wasn't he content with the language which Gay and Prior wrote in?" (Letter to Wordsworth, 7 April 1815. Lucas, No. 206. The punctuation in Canon Ainger's edition differs. The text of Lamb's letters seems as difficult as their collection). See Cowper, 23 May '81.

but sermons—earnest, eager and monotonous. But, as he gained in health and happiness, his letters show more and more of his charm.

Wishful to be near his brother, he established himself in Huntingdon, with a manservant, Sam Roberts, who attended him for thirty years, and a disastrous waif, Dick Coleman, rescued from a drunken cobbler, and destined to be a life-long source of trouble. He lived in lodgings for a while, and there "in three months . . . by the help of good management and a clear notion of economical matters, I contrived to spend the income of a twelvemonth" (9 Nov. '85). As he wrote to his friend Joseph Hill at the time, "a man cannot always live upon sheep's heads, and liver and lights, like the lions in the Tower; and a joint of meat, in so small a family, is an endless encumbrance. My butcher's bill for last week amounted to four shillings and tenpence. I set off with a leg of lamb, and was forced to give part of it away to my washerwoman. Then I made an experiment upon a sheep's heart, and that was too little. Next I put three pounds of beef into a pie, and this had like to have been too much, for it lasted three days, though my landlord was admitted to a share in it. Then as to small beer, I am puzzled to pieces about it. I have bought as much for a shilling as will serve us at least a month, and it is grown sour already" (3 July '65).

A little later he writes: "I am become a professed horseman, and do hereby assume to myself the style and title of the Knight of the Bloody Spur. It has cost me much to bring this point to bear; but I think I have at last accomplished it" (14 Aug. '65). Again: "My distance from Cambridge has made a horseman of me at last, or at least is likely to do so. My brother and I meet every week, by an alternate reciprocation of intercourse, as Sam Johnson would express it; sometimes I get a lift in a neighbour's chaise, but generally ride" (18 Oct. '65).

It was now that he made the acquaintance of the family of the non-resident rector of a parish near King's Lynn. The friendship was due to the son, William, who accosted the stranger one day after morning service, and it quickly developed.

"Their name is Unwin," he writes to Hill, "the most agreeable people imaginable; quite sociable and as free from the ceremonious civility of country gentlefolks as any I ever met with. They treat me more like a near relation than a stranger, and their house is always open to me. The old gentleman carries me to Cambridge in his chaise. He is a man of learning and good sense, and as simple as parson Adams. His wife has a very uncommon understanding, has read much to excellent purpose, and is more polite than a duchess. The son who belongs to Cambridge, is a most amiable young man, and the daughter quite of a piece with the rest of the family. . . . You remember Rousseau's description of an English morning; such are the mornings I spend with these good people; and the evenings differ from them in nothing, except that they are still more snug and quieter" (25 Oct. '65).

The Rev. Morley Unwin was perhaps all Cowper says, but hardly an energetic clergyman, if contemporary complaints may be trusted. The daughter, Susanna, is a dim figure—"Your poor sister!" Cowper wrote fifteen years later to William, "she has many good qualities, and upon some occasions gives proof of a good understanding; but as some people have no ear for music, so she has none for humour. Well, if she cannot laugh at our jokes, we can, however, at her mistakes, and in this way she makes us ample amends for the disappointment. Mr Powley is much like herself; if his wife overlooks the jest, he will never be able to find it. They were neither of them born to write epigrams or ballads, and I ought to be less mortified at the coldness with which they entertain my small sallies in the way of drollery, when I reflect that if Swift himself had had no other judges he would never have found one admirer" (24 Dec. '80). William Unwin, however, became and remained one of his most intimate and valued friends. Cowper's correspondence with him survives—a hundred and twenty-eight letters, and few better.

Mrs Unwin, the mother, lives in the history of English literature, as his intimate throughout life. He solved his early difficulties of housekeeping by moving into the Unwins' house, and except when he went to see his brother John in his last illness, it appears that he and Mrs Unwin never parted again for twenty-four consecutive hours. "Your mother," he wrote to William after twenty years of intimacy, "comforts me by her approbation, and I steer myself in all that I produce by her judgment. If she does not understand me at the first reading, I am sure the lines are obscure, and always alter them; if she laughs, I know it is not without reason, and if she says, 'that's well, it will do'—I have no fear that anybody else should find fault with it. She is my lady chamberlain who licenses all I write" (n.d., probably Aug. 1786). The only extant picture of Mrs Unwin is a characterless affair that conveys no notion to the mind. There are no letters of her own that survive, and those of Lady Hesketh that speak of her belong to the period when her health had already given way. Lady Hesketh did not care for her, and rather wickedly nicknames her "the Enchantress." But to the poet himself she was everything. "That I am happy in my situation is true; I live, and have lived these twenty years with Mrs Unwin, to whose affectionate care of me, during the far greater part of that time, it is, under Providence, owing that I live at all" (12 Oct. '85). The sonnet, "Mary! I want a lyre with other strings," and the famous lines "To Mary," are evidence more familiar.

In July 1767 Mr Unwin was thrown from his horse and died. His widow and Cowper left Huntingdon and settled at Olney in September—in a house still standing and but little changed, on the base of the triangular market-place, looking up the broad main street—a house of great interest to every student of Cowper. The choice was not altogether a good one.

"Seven months in the year," he writes to Hill, "I have been imprisoned by dirty and impassable ways, till both my health and Mrs Unwin's have suffered materially" (19 June '86). He complained (when deliverance was now in sight, though not before) of the "bad air in winter, impregnated with the fishy smelling fumes of the marsh miasma" (3 July '86), which may be less a fair account of Olney than a generalization from the cellar full of water, over which he and Mrs Unwin had to sit sometimes for months together (5 Aug. '86). He kept no horse now, the roads were bad, and in 1791 he wrote that he had not been "more than thirteen miles from home these twenty years, and so far very seldom" (6 Mar. '91).

The attraction in Olney was the ministry of John Newton — famous among evangelical divines of the eighteenth century. An ill-spent youth, redeemed by long devotion to the girl with whom, when she was thirteen, he fell in love, and who, after seven years' of faithful affection on his part, became his wife; adventures in the navy and on board a slave-ship; private study and conversion, produced at last a minister of force and tenderness, hard with the hardness of an idealist and a self-made man, gentle in virtue of a great capacity for love and friendship, not always wise and sympathetic, but always conscientious, always ready to be his best for his friend's sake. His *Letters to a Wife* won Edward Fitzgerald's admiration, as containing "some of the most beautiful things I ever read: fine feeling in fine English." Nor is it without light upon character, that one of the authors of the *Olney Hymns* could write thus to the other: "If I walked the streets with a fiddle under my arm, I should never think of performing before the window of a Privy Counsellor, or a Chief Justice, but should rather make free with ears more likely to be open to such amusement. . . . This has been one reason why I have so long delayed the riddle. But lest I should seem to set a value upon it that I do not, by making it an object of still further inquiry, here it is :

> I am just two and two, I am warm, I am cold,
> And the parent of numbers that cannot be told ;
> I am lawful, unlawful—a duty, a fault ;
> I am often sold dear, good for nothing when bought,
> An extraordinary boon, and a matter of course,
> And yielded with pleasure—when taken by force."
>
> (30 July '80.)

To the *Olney Hymns* Cowper contributed sixty-seven —and one wonders whether it was he or Newton who chose the motto from Virgil for the title-page—" perhaps the most extreme instance of the eighteenth century passion for Virgilian quotation," it has been called.

> Cantabitis, Arcades, inquit
> Montibus hæc vestris ; soli cantare periti
> Arcades. O mihi tum quam molliter ossa quiescant
> Vestra meos olim si fistula dicat amores.

The reference was faithfully added and two texts from the New Testament.

Cowper is one of the few English poets who have much influenced the hymnary. Still in common use, in one religious community and another, his hymns are his best-known works, and it is impossible to estimate how much they have done to advance in the English speaking world that Evangelical religion of which they are the outcome. In form and phrase they are simple and direct—obvious, it might be said, in every aspect of them—the outcome of intense feeling and deep conviction—and " the spontaneous overflow of powerful feeling" was one of Wordsworth's descriptions of poetry. The same precision and delicacy of touch that are in his other poetry are here; but as there is little scope for humour in the hymn-book, they do not give the same impression of the complete Cowper. But it would be a half Cowper, at best, if they were left out of the account.

So William Cowper, Esquire, of the Inner Temple, had successfully isolated himself from all his early friends and relatives, and lived in an obscure little country town with a clergyman and a clergyman's widow as his only intimates, and church-going and prayer meetings as his daily round. "We have," he writes,

> "One parson, one poet, one belman, one crier,
> And the poor poet is our only 'squire"
>
> (3 Jan. '84).

The Olney people called him "Sir Cowper" (31 July '69). He gardened, as the third book of *The Task* tells us in its title, and more faithfully in its minutely realistic account of the raising of the early cucumber—from the "stercorarious heap" to its artificial fertilization (462-543). His letters, with constant allusions to exchange of seeds and fruits, show that his plants grew, and that he was so far more successful than some gardeners. He kept birds and animals as pets. His last thought on leaving London for St Albans had been to entrust his cat to Joseph Hill—he forgot his books, and they were lost for ever, and he lived the rest of his days on borrowed volumes. At one time at Olney he seems to have had as many as twenty pets, and he made their cages himself. Of these his three hares, Bess, Puss and Tiney, are the most famous—hares with histories and characters—"old Tiney surliest of his kind."

> I kept him for his humour's sake,
>   For he would oft beguile
> My heart of thoughts that made it ache,
>   And force me to a smile.

> But now beneath this walnut shade
>   He finds his long last home,
> And waits, in snug concealment laid,
>   Till gentler Puss shall come.

There is a feeling about the lines that suggests Wordsworth.

For a while Cowper amused himself with drawing (3 May '80), but it tried his eyes, and he fell back upon poetry as a last resort. For want of a theme Mrs Unwin suggested to him *The Progress of Error*. The title has an interesting likeness to others chosen by the poets of his family. His aunt Judith (Mrs Madan) had written a *Progress of Poetry*, and his uncle Ashley Cowper (Lady Hesketh's father) a *Progress of Physick*, and each had achieved several editions. The idea of Error seems due to Mrs Unwin. The poem was the germ of his first volume, published in March 1782, with the title, *Poems by William Cowper of the Inner Temple, Esq.*

The publisher was Joseph Johnson, to whom later on he gave a testimonial that shows character and illustrates the times—" I verily believe that, though a bookseller, he has in him the soul of a gentleman. Such strange combinations sometimes happen." (26 June '91).

By May, Cowper sends William Unwin a transcript of a letter from no less a person than Benjamin Franklin.

" The relish for reading of poetry," says Franklin, " had long since left me, but there is something so new in the manner, so easy and yet so correct in the language, so clear in the expression yet concise, and so just in the sentiments, that I have read the whole with great pleasure, and some of the pieces more than once ";

and he desires his respects to the author. In a letter sent next month to Unwin, the author owns to being particularly gratified " by the plaudit of Dr Franklin."

The praise, limited as it may seem, is just. There is a newness in the work of the poet, unobscured by some indebtedness for the form to Churchill, whom he admired. When Franklin praises the language, the modern critic will be with him. It has Cowper's touch throughout—it is light, easy, and graceful, and is clearly written by a man who is master of his instrument. The rhyming decasyllabics, while more or less modelled on the conventional standard, begin to show more freedom. The description of the poet in *Table Talk* (700-15), the panegyric on Chatham in the same poem (340 ff.), the defence of Whitefield, under the thin disguise of Leuconomus, and the quick, vivid, and apt dialogue on faith in *Hope* (347-438), and many other things in the volume have a stamp which we recognize in all his work as Cowper's own. The dialogue on faith is particularly happy—Horatian in its ease, its naturalness and brightness, if its subject is one which Horace never touched. It is not parody—the characters in it, Vinoso, the colonel, the ensign, and "the church-bred youth" would, like Callicles in Plato's *Gorgias*, admit the justice of the views attributed to them (if rhyme and metre be conceded), and might wonder what was wrong with them, while the reader revels in the situation just as he does in the *Gorgias*. *Retirement* is generally recognized as the happiest of the poems. For there the poet was on his own ground.

> The calm retreat, the silent shade
> With prayer and praise agree;
> And seem by Thy sweet bounty made
> For those who follow Thee.

So he had written in one of the *Olney Hymns*, and here he comes nearer the silent shade and the quiet retreat. The Satires and *Retirement* end with a Virgilian touch—*Illo Vergilium me tempore*—which yet is Cowper:

> Me poetry (or rather notes that aim
> Feebly and faintly at poetic fame)
> Employs, shut out from more important views,
> Fast by the banks of the slow-winding Ouse;
> Content if thus sequestered I may raise
> A monitor's, though not a poet's praise,
> And while I teach an art too little known,
> To close life wisely may not waste my own.

The poems win Cowper a monitor's, though not a poet's, praise, and they fell flat. They lack construction; they are, as Coleridge called them, "divine chit-chat," at best; and they are hopelessly misdirected. They live to-day in virtue of quotations and on the strength of *The Task*, and for the sake of their author. Nature never built him for a satirist. Satire calls for wit, and Cowper had humour; for hate, and Cowper was incapable of it—he would forgive anything to a friend, tobacco as to William Bull, fiddling in a parson as to Johnny Johnson, Roman Catholicism as to "Lady Frog" and her husband, and even their chaplain "Griggy." "I believe no man was ever scolded out of his sins," he wrote to Newton (17 June, '83); and what else does a satirist set before him? Cowper is too gentle for his *rôle*, too playful. What is more, the poems are too like his letters of the 1764 period; they preach and do it flagrantly.

While he was still awaiting reviews, Cowper wrote a delightful letter to Unwin, in which he explained why he attached importance to them. "Alas," he says, referring to *The Monthly Review*, "when I wish for a favourable sentence from that quarter (to confess a weakness that I should not confess at all), I feel myself not a little influenced by a tender regard to my reputation here, even among my neighbours at Olney. Here are watchmakers, who themselves are wits, and who at present perhaps think me one. Here is a carpenter, and a baker, and not to mention others, here is your idol Mr Teedon, whose smile is fame. All these read *The Monthly Review*, and all these will set me down for a dunce, if those terrible critics show them the example. But oh! wherever else I am accounted dull, dear Mr Griffiths [editor of the *M. R.*], let me pass for a genius at Olney!" (12 June '82).

Mr Teedon did recognize his greatness. Writing to Unwin, Cowper speaks of "a certain Lord Archibald Hamilton" wishing to make his acquaintance, "from motives which my great modesty will not suffer me to particularize," and he proceeds: "'And is that all?' say you. Now, were I to hear you say so, I should look foolish and say 'Yes.'—But having you at a distance, I snap my fingers at you, and say—'No, that is not all'— Mr Teedon who favours us now and then with his company in an evening, as usual, was not long since discoursing with that eloquence which is so peculiar to himself"—here let us interrupt the story with another quotation on Mr Teedon's eloquence. "At Olney," Cowper writes to Hill, "I have a Mr Teedon to dread. . . . He is the most obsequious, the most formal, the most pedantic of all creatures, so civil that it would be cruel to affront him, and so troublesome that it is impossible to bear him. Being possessed of a little Latin, he seldom uses a word that is not derived from that language, and, being a bigot to propriety of pronunciation, studiously and constantly lays the accent upon the wrong syllable. I think that Sheridan would adore him. He has formed his style (he told me so himself) by the pattern that Mr Hervey has furnished him with in his *Theron and Aspasio*; accordingly, he never says that my garden is gay, but that the flowery tribe are finely variegated and extremely fragrant. . . . If he cannot recollect a thing, he tells me it is not within his recognizance, convincing me at the same time that the orthography of the word is quite familiar to him by laying a particular stress on the *g*. In short he surfeits me" (29 June '85; quoted in J. C. Bailey's *Cowper*, p. xxvii.). Mr Teedon then was "discoursing with that eloquence, which is so peculiar to himself, on the many providential interpositions that had taken place in his favour. 'He had wished for many things,' he said, 'which, at the time when he formed those wishes, seemed distant and improbable, some of them indeed impossible. Among other wishes that he had indulged, one was, that he might be connected with men of genius and ability;—' and in my connection with this worthy gentleman,' said he, turning to me, 'that wish, I am sure, is amply gratified.' You may suppose that I felt the sweat gush out upon my forehead, when I heard this speech; and if you do, you will not be at all mistaken. So much was I delighted with the delicacy of that incense" (7 Feb. '85).

But now a new influence came into the poet's life. One day in July 1781, Cowper saw a strange lady going into the shop of Mr Ashburner, the draper, at the apex of the market-place, which his windows commanded. She was with a friend of their household, and he asked Mrs Unwin to invite them both to tea at once. They came, and the poet in a fit of shyness would hardly enter the room, but he did, and his shyness was very quickly dissolved. A new and close intimacy sprang up; Lady Austen became "Sister Anne"—"by her own desire I wrote to her under the assumed relation of a brother, and she to me as my sister" (9 Feb. '82). The friendship lasted about three years. She came and settled near them in Olney, and virtually lived with them. "She has many features in her character which you will admire," he writes to Unwin. . . . "Discover but a wish to please her, and she never forgets it; not only thanks you, but the tears will start into her eyes at the recollection of the smallest service. With these fine feelings she has the most, and the most harmless vivacity you can imagine" (26 Sept. '81). He speaks of her "sense of religion and seriousness of mind, for with all that gaiety she is a great thinker" (9 Feb. '82).

It is clear that she brought a new element into the narrow round of Olney. She appealed to the poet's humour, and she called it out into his poetry—it was evident enough in his letters. She told him the story of John Gilpin, and his ballad upon it was the first piece from his pen to capture the English world. She admired blank verse, and set him to write upon "the sofa," and *The Task* came into being.

The Task was the keystone of his fame during his lifetime. Some of it, by now, shows the touch of time, but it stands all the same as a great landmark in English literature. Like its predecessors it is slight of structure, but that was here of less consequence. It is full of sound morals, but they do not now obscure the force and freshness of the poet's new experience of living nature. The freedom of blank verse rid him of one element of monotony, and, while it shows Milton's influence, modified by Thomson, still

> So nice his ear, so delicate his touch,

that influence has not, like Pope's (satirized in *Table Talk*), "made poetry a mere mechanic art." The poetry is a free, a living, an original thing here, past all possibility of mistake, and England felt it. The "return to nature," which every generation makes when it throws over the tradition of its parents, was made in earnest. The poem has hardly proceeded a hundred lines before the poet is out of doors, and not in a conventional country of bards and swains and groves, but in his own, where

> Ouse, slow winding through a level plain
> Of spacious meads with cattle sprinkled o'er
> Conducts the eye along his sinuous course
> Delighted . . .
> Scenes must be beautiful which, daily viewed,
> Please daily, and whose novelty survives
> Long knowledge and the scrutiny of years.

It was just that; there is nothing very novel about "lanes of grassy swarth" or "the elastic spring of the unwearied foot" or the fresh air, until you notice that they are always new; and now, in language at once intelligible, near enough to common speech and yet above it, because "the spontaneous overflow of powerful feelings," he took his countrymen, the poets and the Evangelicals pre-eminently, into the fresh air for good and all, and they escaped into a real world. Cowper meant all he wrote—it flows over in his letters, too—witness the letter to Lady Hesketh (6 Dec. 1785) in which he discusses the scent in the fields of Olney, and the endeavours he has made to account for it.

"I had a strong poetical desire to describe it when I was writing the Commonscene in *The Task*, but feared lest the unfrequency of such a singular property in the earth should have tempted the reader to ascribe it to a fanciful nose, at least to have suspected it for a deliberate fiction."

The confession illustrates his methods in more ways than one. None of his descriptions, he says elsewhere, is second-hand.

He gave his age what it needed, what it was seeking and moving toward—freedom and truth in poetry, and a new touch with nature. In other ways, also, he stood near his contemporaries, and his poem bore witness to his strong sympathies with the oppressed, his love of freedom and his affection for his native land.

Freedom and nature, these are two of his great notes; and his affinities with Wordsworth are perceptible in both directions. There are long passages in *The Task* that, by sheer length, suggest *The Prelude* or *The Excursion*, but the poem also suggests them in other ways.

> But trees and rivulets whose rapid course
> Defies the check of winter, haunts of deer,
> And sheepwalks populous with bleating lambs,

And lanes in which the primrose ere her time
Peeps through the moss that clothes the hawthorn root,
Deceive no student. Wisdom there and truth,
Not shy as in the world and to be won
By slow solicitation, seize at once
The roving thought and fix it on themselves.
(vi. 109.)

Such a passage is Wordsworthian, one might say, alike in thought and movement.

Mr Teedon duly read *The Task*. Within a month of its publication he waited on its author, "and, as if fearful that I had overlooked some of them myself, has pointed out to me all its beauties" (27 July '85). But others read it, whose approval meant more. For Lady Hesketh, his cousin, read it, and wrote to him after some eighteen years' cessation of their correspondence. They had exchanged letters for about two years after he left St Albans, but when one reads the sort of thing she wrote in her old age (dashing off her ideas with no time for punctuation), it ceases to be surprising that she did not in her youth care to keep up a correspondence with an invalid whose letters were sermons of the most unblushing type. After his death she writes vigorously to John Johnson to vindicate his memory from any charge of "Enthusiasm or Calvinism" (Lady Hesketh, 22 Oct. 1801). If her letters ceased, the family provision for "the stricken deer that left the herd" had not ceased. And now when the restoration of all the qualities which she had loved in him as a youth was proved, she wrote again; and everything that could be done for his bodily comfort and mental happiness, from this time onward she did. His letters to her are many and they are charming.

It is in his letters that we see Cowper most freely. He "loved talking letters dearly" (24 Apr. '86). Talking letters are very well, if it is the right person talking, and here it is; and one mark, at least, of good conversation is to be found in them. For, after a while, the reader can almost tell, without looking at the heading, to whom the letter is addressed, Unwin, Newton, or (later) Lady Hesketh or Johnny Johnson. They have, too, something of that strange gift one finds in Plato's dialogue—they are close to conversation and yet are not conversation, they are natural talk, but natural talk sublimated, or raised somehow to a higher power, and yet natural still. They have nothing of the deliberate cleverness of Horace Walpole, and they are much simpler even than Lamb's letters. Lamb, for instance, in four letters between November 1800 and March 1801, writes the same panegyric of London; the words are not identical, but it is substantially the same thing, and Wordsworth gets it and Robert Lloyd, and Manning twice—an elaborated passage, like others that came first in letters, stayed in Lamb's head and reappeared long after in essays. Nothing of the kind comes in Cowper. His language is much more rapid, his taste is surer, than Lamb's. He does not use slang—hardly half a dozen words could be collected from his correspondence that have dropped out of the language. Yet, using an English singularly pure and high, he never loses his ease and mastery. The thing is luminously clear, whatever it is. It has been well remarked that even the letters written in madness to Teedon about his dreadful "wakings" are lucid and logical, and perfect in sobriety and clearness of expression. "Cowper's letters," Wordsworth said, "are everything that letters can be."[1]

If there is not in the poet's life at Olney the variety of outward event or of literary and philosophic discussion that make the letters of other poets and literary men fascinating, still it is surprising how much variety there can be in a monotonous little town. We watch the whole population from the window, till we come to know their names, and where they are going, at what hour or on what errand—and they cease to be tiresome as no

[1] Knight, *Life of Wordsworth*, iii. p. 376.

doubt they really were in life. Cowper often speaks of the great poverty of the place. Robert Smith, Pittite M.P. for Nottingham, entrusted him with money for its relief, and in this way he came into close quarters with it.

"Mon Ami," he writes to Joseph Hill, "If you ever take the tip of the Chancellor's ear between your finger and thumb, you can hardly improve the opportunity to better purpose than if you should whisper into it the voice of compassion and lenity to the lace-makers. I am an eye-witness of their poverty.... There are very near one thousand two hundred lace-makers in this beggarly town, the most of whom had reason enough, while the bill was in agitation, to look upon every loaf they bought as the last they should ever be able to earn" (8 July '80). When "our new tax-maker" proposes to tax candles, he writes thus: "I wish he would visit the miserable huts of our lacemakers at Olney, and see them working in the winter-months, by the light of a farthing candle, from four in the afternoon till midnight" (3 July '84). "When ministers talk of resources, that word never fails to send my imagination into the mud-wall cottages of our poor at Olney. There I find assembled in one individual, the miseries of age, sickness, and the extremest penury.... The budget will be opened soon, and soon we shall hear of resources. But I could conduct the statesman, who rolls down to the House in a chariot as splendid as that of Phaeton, into scenes that, if he had any sensibility for the woes of others, would make him tremble at the mention of the word" (19 Feb. '85).

Here are one or two of the scenes Cowper knew. "You never said a better thing in your life," he writes to Unwin, "than when you assured Mr Smith of the expediency of a gift of bedding to the poor of Olney. There is no one article of this world's comforts with which, as Falstaff says, they are so heinously unprovided. When a poor woman, and an honest one, whom we know well, carried home two pair of blankets, a pair for herself and husband, and a pair for her six children ; as soon as the children saw them, they jumped out of their straw, caught them in their arms, kissed them, blessed them, and danced for joy. An old woman, a very old one, the first night that she found herself so comfortably covered, could not sleep a wink, being kept awake by the contrary emotions, of transport on the one hand, and the fear of not being thankful enough on the other" (31 Dec. '85).

A Sunday School is proposed in 1785, and Cowper is in favour of it. " I know not indeed, while the spread of the gospel continues so limited as it is, how a reformation of manners, in the lower class of mankind, can be brought to pass ; or by what other means the utter abolition of all principle among them, moral as well as religious, can possibly be prevented. Heathenish parents can only bring up heathenish children; an assertion no where oftener or more clearly illustrated than at Olney; where children, seven years of age, infest the streets every evening with curses and with songs, to which it would be unseemly to give their proper epithet" (24 Sept. '85). There were too many public-houses and too much drinking, though we read of Mr Bean getting five of these houses suppressed (2 Sept. '88). Not all the clergy, Cowper says, were of Mr Bean's and Mr Unwin's mind (23 May '81), and the Government "is too much interested in the consumption of malt liquors to reduce the number of vendors" (24 Dec. 80).

Olney had its relaxations. We hear of a lion at the Cherry Fair held every 29th of June—" seventy years of age and as tame as a goose" (18 July '78). Again, "a drum announces the arrival of a giant" (5 Jan. '85), or a strolling company performs in a barn (8 Feb. '83). There was the public whipping of a thief behind a cart (17 Nov. '83)—the stocks (24 June '88)—the fifth of November. There was the *Monthly Review*. There were politics. Thus, when the war with America was nearing an end,

Cowper writes, "It is reported among persons of the best intelligence at Olney—the barber, the schoolmaster, and the drummer of a corps quartered at this place, that the belligerent powers are at last reconciled, the articles of the treaty adjusted, and that peace is at the door. I saw this morning at nine o'clock, a group of about twelve figures very closely engaged in a conference, as I suppose, upon the same subject. The scene of consultation was a blacksmith's shed, very comfortably screened from the wind, and directly opposed to the morning sun. Some held their hands behind them, some had them folded across their bosom, and others had thrust them into their breeches pockets. Every man's posture bespoke a pacific turn of mind" (26 Jan. '83).

There were general elections, and here I cannot resist a long quotation. "We were sitting yesterday after dinner, the two ladies and myself, very composedly, and without the least apprehension of any such intrusion in our snug parlour, one lady knitting, the other netting, and the gentleman winding worsted, when to our unspeakable surprise a mob appeared before the window; a smart rap was heard at the door, the boys halloo'd, and the maid announced Mr Grenville. Puss was unfortunately let out of her box, so that the candidate was refused admittance at the grand entry, and referred to the back door, as the only way of approach. Candidates are creatures not very susceptible of affronts, and would rather, I suppose, climb in at a window than be absolutely excluded. In a minute the yard, the kitchen and the parlour were filled. Mr Grenville advancing toward me shook me by the hand with a degree of cordiality that was extremely seducing. As soon as he and as many more as could find chairs were seated, he began to open the intent of his visit. I told him I had no vote, for which he readily gave me credit. I assured him I had no influence, which he was not equally inclined to believe, and the less, no doubt, because Mr Ashburner, the draper, addressing himself to me at this moment, informed me that I had a great deal. Supposing that I could not be possessed of such a treasure without knowing it, I ventured to confirm my first assertion by saying that if I had any I was utterly at a loss to imagine where it could be, or wherein it consisted. Thus ended the conference. Mr Grenville squeezed me by the hand again, kissed the ladies, and withdrew. He kissed likewise the maid in the kitchen, and seemed upon the whole a most loving, kissing, kind-hearted gentleman. He is very young, genteel and handsome. He has a pair of very good eyes in his head, which not being sufficient as it should seem for the many nice and difficult purposes of a senator, he has a third also, which he wore suspended by a ribband from his buttonhole. The boys halloo'd, the dogs barked, Puss scampered, the hero, with his long train of obsequious followers, withdrew. We made ourselves very merry with the adventure, and in a short time settled into our former tranquillity, never probably to be thus interrupted more. I thought myself, however, happy in being able to affirm truly that I had not that influence for which he sued; and which, had I been possessed of it, with my present views of the dispute between the Crown and the Commons, I must have refused him, for he is on the side of the former" (29 March '84). Mr Grenville, however, was elected at the top of the poll.

Mr Grenville might be "a most loving, kissing, kind-hearted gentleman," but Cowper had for some years back been under no delusions as to the attitude of George III. toward British liberty. He might call himself "an unconcerned spectator" (31 Jan. '82), but he watched. He discussed in letters to Unwin the likeness and unlikeness of the King to Charles I. (13 Feb., 18 May '80). A few months before this election he wrote: "We say, the King can do no wrong; and it is well for poor George the Third that he cannot. In my opinion, however, he has lately been within a hair's-breadth of that predicament.

"... It is not a time of day for a King to take liberties with the people; there is a spirit in the Commons that will not endure it" (27 Dec. '81). "I am the King's most loyal subject and most obedient humble servant. But by his Majesty's leave, I must acknowledge that I am not altogether convinced of the rectitude even of his own measures or the simplicity of his views; and if I were satisfied that he himself is to be trusted, it is nevertheless palpable that he cannot answer for his successors" (25 Jan. '84). "Stuartism, in my mind, has been the characteristic of the present reign; and being and having always been somewhat of an enthusiast on the subject of British liberty, I am not able to withhold my reverence and good wishes from the man, whoever he be, that exerts himself in a constitutional way to oppose it. The son of Lord Chatham seems to me to have abandoned his father's principles" (to Newton, Feb. '84).

Years later he wrote to Lady Hesketh during the French Revolution: "The French are a vain and childish people, and conduct themselves on this grand occasion with a levity and extravagance nearly akin to madness; but it would have been better for Austria and Prussia to let them alone. All nations have a right to choose their own mode of government, and the sovereignty of the people is a doctrine that evinces itself; for whenever the people choose to be masters they always are so, and none can hinder them. God grant that we may have no revolution here, but unless we have a reform, we certainly shall. Depend upon it, my dear, the hour is come when power founded on patronage and corrupt majorities must govern this land no longer. Concessions too must be made to dissenters of every denomination. They have a right to them, a right to all the privileges of Englishmen, and sooner or later, by fair means or by force, they will have them" (1 Dec. '92, *cf.* 16 Dec. '92). The recluse of Olney was no bad political prophet. Most people will agree to-day that he was right about France and about England.

When the Birmingham mob sacked Priestley's house on 14 July 1791, Cowper wrote to his friend Bull, the Independent minister of Newport Pagnell: "I have blest myself on your account that you are at Brighton and not at Birmingham, where it seems they are so loyal and so pious that they show no mercy to dissenters. How can you continue in a persuasion so offensive to the wise and good! Do you not yet perceive that the Bishops themselves hate you not more than the very blacksmith of the establishment, and will you not endeavour to get the better of your aversion to red-nosed singing men and organs? Come—be received into the bosom of mother-church, so shall you never want a jig for your amusement on Sundays, and shall save perhaps your academy from a conflagration" (26 July '91). Point is added to this when we find that Newport Pagnell had had similar experiences, when the Middlesex Militia were there in 1781. "Yesterday, being Sunday, was distinguished by a riot, raised at the Bull Inn by some of the officers, whose avowed purpose in doing it was to mortify a town which they understood was inhabited by Methodists" (27 Feb. '81).

William Bull, to whom Cowper wrote in this easy strain, he describes in a letter to Unwin. "A dissenter, but a liberal one; a man of letters and of genius; master of a fine imagination, or rather not master of it—an imagination which, when he finds himself in the company he loves, and can confide in, runs away with him into such fields of speculation as amuse and enliven every other imagination that has the happiness to be of the party. At other times he has a tender and delicate sort of melancholy in his disposition, not less agreeable in its way. No men are better qualified for companions in such a world as this, than men of such a temperament. Every scene of life has two sides, a dark and a bright one, and the mind that has an equal mixture of melancholy and vivacity is best of all qualified for the con-temptation of either; it can be lively without levity, and pensive without dejection. Such a man is Mr Bull. But—he smokes tobacco. Nothing is perfect—

> *Nihil est ab omni*
> *Parte beatum*" (8 June '83).

Bull indeed smoked tobacco, and for his sake Cowper wrote a gay palinode to the nymph of the plant, which, as he observed, supplied himself with snuff—and Mrs Unwin too.[1] At least five different snuff-boxes occur in his letters. His cousin Theodora sent him one; he inherited his uncle Ashley's; and he commissioned Mrs John Newton to buy one. "We admired it," he wrote to her, "even when we supposed the price of it two guineas; guess then with what raptures we contemplated it when we found that it cost but one. It was genteel before, but then it became a perfect model of elegance and worthy to be the desire of all noses" (14 Mch. '82).

A month after writing the poem on tobacco, Cowper visited Bull, who gave him Mme Guyon's poems—"a quietist, say you, and a fanatic, I will have nothing to do with her.—[He is writing to Unwin.] It is very well, you are welcome to have nothing to do with her, but in the meantime her verse is the only French verse I ever read that I found agreeable; there is a neatness in it equal to that which we applaud with so much reason in the compositions of Prior. I have translated several of them, and shall proceed in my translations, till I have filled a Lilliputian paper-book I happen to have by me, which, when filled, I shall present to Mr Bull. He is her passionate admirer, rode twenty miles to see her picture in the house of a stranger, which stranger politely insisted on his acceptance of it, and it now hangs over his parlour chimney" (3 Aug. '82).

---

[1] Letter of 22 June, 1782. "Tobacco was not known in the golden age. So much the worse for the golden age" (3 June '83, to Wm. Bull).

These versions of Mme Guyon Cowper gave to Bull—
"they are yours to serve you as you please"—and Bull
published them in 1801 in a neat little volume, printed
at Newport Pagnell, as Lilliputian as the manuscript.

Bull continued to be his friend—"my Delphic oracle,"
he calls him (to Lady Hesketh, undated, probably Jan. '86).
Cowper was a man of friendships. "You must know,"
he says to Lady Hesketh, "that I should not love you
half so well, if I did not believe you would be my friend
to eternity. There is not room enough for friendship to
unfold itself in full bloom, in such a nook of life as this"
(25 May '86).

The snuff-boxes are a reminder that we have not yet
looked into the daily round of Orchard Side, which is
faithfully chronicled in the letters. Many things in
daily use had to come from London, so Cowper is
constantly writing to John Newton, William Unwin, or
Hill, to buy and despatch to them the necessities of life.
The articles come down by waggon—"the Windmill
in St John St. is that [inn] from which ours sets out,
and the best time to send is Tuesday night or Wednesday morning, else the waggon is loaded and the parcel
left to another opportunity" (14 Apr. '88; 24 Dec. '90).
The appeals for fish are constant. "Among other deplorable effects of the war, the scarcity of fish which it
occasioned was severely felt at Olney" (14 Mch. '82).
His friends, however, did their best to relieve this
scarcity. "The salmon you sent us arrived safe, and
was remarkably fresh," he says to Unwin. "What a
comfort it is to have a friend who knows we love
salmon, and who cannot pass by a fishmonger's shop
without finding his desire to send us some, a temptation
too strong to be resisted!" (24 Nov. '81). "Your
mother wishes you to add a handful of prawns, not
only because she likes them, but because they agree
with her so well that she even finds them medicinal"
(26 Nov. '81). Next he is thanking Newton for "a

barrel of oysters, exceeding good," and begging Mrs Newton's acceptance of a couple of chickens (17 Dec. '81), for they requited their London friends with country poultry of their own rearing. "Mrs Unwin sends her love, and will be much obliged to Mrs Newton if she will order her down a loaf of sugar, from ninepence to tenpence a pound, for the use of my sweet self at breakfast" (21 Dec. '81). Cocoa-nuts, Elliott's medicines, snuff, Bohea, tooth-powder, English muslin "with cross stripes," "ell and nail long" (24 Dec. '87), "eight blue, deep-blue water-glasses" at "three shillings a pair" (5 Ap. '84), tallow fats, "another keg of Geneva, that excellent liquor of which we both take a tablespoonful every day after dinner" (11 Apr. '93), sponge-biscuits, "a pound of the best pins" (3 May '84), a cuckoo-clock "made in Germany" (5 June '89)—all sorts of things appear in turn at the ends of these familiar letters.

We learn all about the poet's wardrobe too. "I am a very smart youth of my years," he wrote to Lady Hesketh when he was fifty-four; borrowed hair "continues to me the charms of my youth, even on the verge of age" (9 Nov. '85). He writes to Unwin for a hat. "The depth of the crown must be four inches and one-eighth. Let it not be a round slouch, which I abhor, but a smart well-cocked fashionable affair. A fashionable hat likewise for your mother; a black one if they are worn, otherwise chip" (21 Mch. '84). "We have to trouble you yet once again in the marketing way. I want a yard of green satin, to front a winter under waistcoat, and your mother a pound of prepared hartshorn. Being tolerably honest folks, it is probable that we shall some time or other pay you all our debts" (20 Oct. '84). "My neck-cloths being all worn out, I intend to wear stocks, but not unless they are more fashionable than the former. In that case I shall be obliged to you, if you will buy me a handsome stock-buckle for a very little money; for twenty or twenty-five shillings perhaps a second-hand affair may be purchased that will make a figure at Olney" (23 May '81). "Thanks to your choice," he writes Lady Hesketh, "I wear the most elegant buttons in all this country; they have been much admired at the Hall. When my waistcoat is made I shall be quite accomplished" (8 Sept. '87)—and in his next letter we learn that the waistcoat fulfilled the prophecy. Referring to Abbott's portrait of him in the archery uniform of his friends, the Throckmortons, he writes: "Green and buff are the colours in which I am oftener seen than in any others, and are become almost as natural to me as to a parrot, and the dress was chosen indeed principally for that reason" (29 Aug. '92). There are other curious touches here and there. We gather that he never wore trousers, but when as a young man he went yachting with Sir Thomas and Lady Hesketh (24 Sept. '85). Romney, who painted the wonderful portrait of him— more striking the longer one studies it—gave him a strop (8 Sept. '93). Most amazing of all, there was a time when Mrs Unwin wore her poet's shoes (27 June '92). But the difficulty in writing of Cowper's letters is the regret, which increases with every page, that so much must be left out.

In autumn 1786 Lady Hesketh moved the poet's household to Weston Underwood—a very happy change. It brought him nearer to the Throckmortons and their park and gardens, and the closer proximity to this delightful young couple was an added happiness to a life that needed it. Mrs Frog, as he came to call her—a pleasant variant upon Mrs Throck—(polysyllabic names have to be abridged in the interest of friendship)—Mrs Frog made fair copies of his Homer for him; she was "my lady of the inkbottle. . . . She solicited herself that office" (24 Aug. '86); and she enlisted her brother-in-law, George, and their domestic chaplain.

Her picture survives, and shows us a lady not unlike the portraits of Marie Antoinette; her hair is a great structure, beyond masculine description, presumably in the style of the day; she has a little waist, cheeks with a high colour, and full and rather pouting lips. Wherever we meet her in the letters, she is a figure of gaiety and kindness.

In 1773 Cowper had a long attack of madness which left him with a permanent delusion — that God had required him to kill himself, and that his failure to obey had finally stamped him God's enemy. The seventy letters to Teedon, which Mr Thomas Wright has printed, and others to more reasonable friends, form a terrible record of insanity. With years the disease gained strength, and he sought refuge from himself in translating Homer. Homer is the easiest and the most difficult of Greek authors to render; and Cowper tripped, as Charles Lamb pointed out, over Homer's swiftness.[1] He was too much under Milton's influence. His letters are full of references to Homer, and his criticisms and comments are fresh and interesting. Every kindness that Lady Hesketh, and Johnson, and Hayley could minister to a mind diseased, he had. Hayley's services were surely the most ingenious poet ever devised for poet, but they were in vain.[2] Deeper and deeper in misery Cowper sank. Mrs Unwin's health gave way and she died, and her poet unhappily survived her for four years. Even now, in an interlude of his disease, he could write with the extraordinary power and pathos of the *Castaway*, and he did a good deal of miscellaneous translation, Milton's Latin poems and Virgil's *Moretum*.

His last piece of original composition, a poem written in a lucid interval in March 1799, is the *Castaway*. It tells of a sailor of Anson's who fell overboard on a night of storm when rescue was impossible, and how he

---

[1] Letter to Charles Lloyd, 31 July 1809. Thirteen years before he had praised Cowper's *Odyssey* as "very Homeric"; letter to Coleridge, 14 June 1796.

[2] See *Atlantic Monthly*, July 1907.

COWPER

> Waged with death a lasting strife
> Supported by despair of life.

Verse after verse gives the vivid sense of his long struggle, till

> By toil subdued he drank
> The stifling wave, and then he sank.

> No poet wept him ; but the page
> Of narrative sincere,
> That tells his name, his worth, his age,
> Is wet with Anson's tear :
> And tears by bards or heroes shed
> Alike immortalize the dead.

> I therefore purpose not, or dream,
> Descanting on his fate,
> To give the melancholy theme
> A more enduring date :
> But misery still delights to trace
> Its semblance in another's case.

> No voice divine the storm allayed,
> No light propitious shone,
> When, snatched from all effectual aid,
> We perished, each alone :
> But I beneath a rougher sea
> And whelmed in deeper gulfs than he.

On the 25 April 1800 he died, still feeling "unutterable despair."

England had already living others of greater poetic power who were to eclipse him in poetry. But some three years after his death Hayley published a quarto *Life of Cowper*, the real feature of which was a number of the poet's letters—somewhat cut about, it is true, to please Lady Hesketh, who was charmed with the result.

"Johnny" Johnson followed with his familiar correspondence, and Grimshaw and Southey in turn republished in rival editions all the letters they could get. Others have since been added. By now it is possible to maintain that it is rather as a letter-writer than as a poet that Cowper will live, or at least that the letters will be read more than the poems. Yet one writes it with reluctance. In any case, letters and poems together give us such a picture as we have nowhere in English, save in Boswell and Lockhart—and one which, it is possible to maintain, surpasses both in charm.

BOSWELL

"WHO is this Scotch cur at Johnson's heels?" some one asked Goldsmith in 1763. "He is not a cur," said Goldsmith; "he is only a bur. Tom Davies flung him at Johnson in sport, and he has the faculty of sticking."[1]

The bur was James Boswell, Esquire, eldest son of a Scottish Judge, Lord Auchinleck. He was twenty-two years old, and had already begun to pack his life with vivid interests. Johnson, he says,[2] "used to tell with great humour, from my relation to him, the following little story of my early years, which was literally true: 'Boswell, in the year 1745, was a fine boy, wore a white cockade, and prayed for King James, till one of his uncles (General Cochran) gave him a shilling on condition that he should pray for King George, which he accordingly did. So you see (says Boswell) that *Whigs of all ages are made the same way.*'" The delicate way in which he transfers his autobiography to Johnson's lips is characteristic. When rather older, he went to Edinburgh University, and there made the friendship of W. J. Temple, who soon went on to Cambridge, and with whom he kept up a correspondence through life. In 1759 he went to Glasgow to attend Adam Smith's lectures. It is something to captivate one's professors, and Boswell did it; for Adam Smith gave him a testimonial to the effect that he was "happily possessed of a facility of manners."[3]

"Some days ago," writes Boswell (29 July 1758), "I

---

[1] *Life*, i. 417. Throughout references are made to Dr Birkbeck Hill's six-volume edition.
[2] *Life*, i. 431.   [3] Rae, *Adam Smith*, p. 58.

was introduced to your friend Mr Hume; he is a most discreet, affable man, and has really a great deal of learning and a choice collection of books. He is indeed an extraordinary man,—few such people are to be met with nowadays. . . . Mr Hume, I think, is a very proper person for a young man to cultivate acquaintance with. Though he has not perhaps the most delicate taste, yet he has applied himself with great attention to the study of the ancients, and is likewise a great historian, so that you are not only entertained in his company, but may reap a great deal of useful instruction." David Hume was nearly thirty years older than his critic of eighteen, and had already published most of his more notable books. So early did Boswell consider with whom a young man might profitably cultivate acquaintance, and conclude to aim at the best.[1] He goes on to tell Temple that "your grave, sedate, philosophic friend"—it is not Hume that is meant—has been "violently in love with" Miss W——t, but now "it is changed to a rational esteem of her good qualities, so that I should be extremely happy to pass my life with her; but if she does not incline to it, I can bear it *æquo animo*, and retire into the calm regions of philosophy. She is indeed extremely pretty . . . at the same time she has a just regard for true piety and religion, and behaves in the most easy, affable way. She is just such a young lady as I could wish for the partner of my soul; and you know that is not every one; for you and I have often talked how nice we would be in such a choice. I own I can have but little hopes, as she is a fortune of thirty thousand pounds." Temple was to receive such confidences for many years about many "charmers" and "princesses."

In Glasgow Boswell fell in with Roman Catholics and decided to become one; but, according to the anecdote

---

[1] Years later we find Hume still entertaining him—"an elegant supper, three sorts of ice-creams. What think you of the northern Epicurus style?" *Letter to Temple*, 19 June 1775.

flippantly told, the family lawyer represented that it was no gentleman's act to save his soul at the cost of such annoyance to his relatives, and he gave up the notion. His parents' distress was exactly the reason to reach and touch his imagination. He compacted however that he should enter the army. His father took him to London in March 1760, and asked the Duke of Argyle for a commission in the Guards. The Duke got out of it very happily: "I like your son; that boy must not be shot at for three-and-sixpence a day."

He seems to have visited Cambridge, for years later he reminds Temple of the days "when you and I sat up all night and read Gray with a noble enthusiasm; when we first used to read Mason's *Elfrida* and when we talked of that elegant knot of worthies Gray, Mason and Walpole, etc."[1] Temple was at Trinity Hall, and Gray was the great poet of the day, in residence half a mile away at Pembroke.

He returned to Scotland, and now began to plunge into literature, prose and verse. *The Cub at Newmarket* has an autobiographical suggestion intended by the author. About the same time (1761) Boswell received the honour of a dedication. An *Ode to Tragedy* appeared, from the hand of one who had,—like most young persons,—

> A soul by nature formed to feel
> Grief sharper than the tyrant's steel,
> And bosom big with swelling thought
> From ancient lore's remembrance brought.

The dedicator in his preface says: "I should be sorry to contribute in any degree to your acquiring an excess of self-sufficiency. . . . I own indeed that when . . . to display my extensive erudition, I have quoted Greek, Latin and French sentences one after another with astonishing celerity; or have got into my *Old-hock humour* and fallen a-raving about princes and lords,

[1] *Letter to Temple*, 4 April 1775.

knights and geniuses, ladies of quality and harpsichords; you, with a peculiar comic smile, have gently reminded me of the *importance of a man to himself* and slily left the room with the witty Dean lying open at—P.P. *clerk of this parish.*" The author evidently knew himself and was aware of his weaknesses, for he lays them out frankly enough; and he knew Boswell. Who was he?

That question was put to Boswell by the Hon. Andrew Erskine, who was carrying on a very lively correspondence with him—each with his eye on the press, for these gay letters were written for the world, every line of them. "The author of the *Ode to Tragedy*," replies Boswell, "is a most excellent man: he is of an ancient family in the west of Scotland, upon which he values himself not a little. At his nativity there appeared omens of his future greatness; his parts are bright, and his education has been good; he has travelled in post-chaises miles without number; he is fond of seeing much of the world; he eats of every good dish, especially apple pie; he drinks old hock; he has a very fine temper; he is somewhat of a humourist, and a little tinctured with pride; he has a good, manly countenance, and he owns himself to be amorous; he has infinite vivacity, yet is observed at times to have a melancholy cast; he is fat rather than lean, rather short than tall, rather young than old; his shoes are neatly made, and he never wears spectacles. The length of his walking stick is not as yet ascertained, but we hope soon to favour the republic of letters with a solution of this difficulty, as several able mathematicians are employed in its investigation, and for that purpose have posted themselves at different given points in the Canongate; so that when the gentleman saunters down to the Abbey of Holyrood House, in order to think of ancient days, on King James the Fifth and Queen Mary, they may compute its altitude above the street according to the rules of geometry."[1]

[1] *Letter to Erskine*, 17 Dec. 1761.

It ought not to be hard to identify this young man of ancient family in the West of Scotland. Such little feats are easy to every historical critic.

Literature mattered a great deal to Boswell. "Many years ago," said he to Johnson in 1778,[1] "when my imagination was warm, and I happened to be in a melancholy mood, it distressed me to think of going into a state of being in which Shakespeare's poetry did not exist. A lady, whom I then much admired, a very amiable woman, humoured my fancy, and relieved me by saying, 'The first thing you will meet in the other world, will be an elegant copy of Shakespeare's works presented to you.'"[2] Dr Johnson smiled benignantly at this, and did not appear to disapprove of the notion.

With this interest in literature, and a recommendation from Lord Hailes to make the acquaintance of Johnson, Boswell revisited London in 1763. The advice jumped with the young Scot's inclination. Carlyle, in his true and sympathetic essay, has not perhaps emphasized how clearly Johnson by now stood at the head of the world of letters. Smollett had already (1759) described him as "that great CHAM of literature."[3] Even so Carlyle is very right in saying that not every young gentleman of family would have cared to know him, much less to subordinate himself to him.[4]

"I," writes Horace Walpole (26 May 1791), "never would be in the least acquainted with Dr Johnson. . . . Johnson's blind Toryism and known brutality kept me aloof; nor did I ever exchange a syllable with him. . . . Sir Joshua said 'Let me present Dr Goldsmith to you'; he did. 'Now I will present Dr Johnson to you.' 'No,' said I, 'Sir Joshua, for Dr Goldsmith, pass—but you shall *not* present Dr Johnson to me.'" Goldsmith, he explains elsewhere, "was an idiot with once or twice a

---

[1] *Life*, iii. 312. [2] *Life*, iii. 312. [3] *Life*, i. 348.
[4] Cf. *Life*, iv. 117. "Strange, however, it is, to consider how few of the great sought his society."

fit of parts" (8 Oct. 1776), but for Johnson he had nothing but contempt. There was Johnson's pension—one-sixth of his own, for which so far no reason so tangible as Johnson's Dictionary could be offered, though it may fairly be urged that the nation has often had far poorer equivalents for £100,000 than the letters of Horace Walpole.

Even Johnson's appearance wakes the sneers of Walpole. "I have no patience with an unfortunate monster trusting to his helpless deformity for indemnity for any impertinence that his arrogance suggests" (27 Dec. 1775). It was lucky perhaps that he did not presume on the helpless deformity. Osborne the bookseller could have warned him—"Sir," said Johnson, "he was impertinent to me, and I beat him."[1] In 1773 at Iona, when the boat could not be brought close in shore, the old man of sixty-four would not submit to be carried ashore on some one's shoulders—"he sprang into the sea and waded vigorously out."[2] Foote the actor thought it safer in 1775 not to mimic him on the stage.[3] But this is by the way. Boswell meant to meet Johnson, and he did.

"On Monday the 16th of May [1763] when I was sitting in Mr Davies' back-parlour, after having drunk tea with him and Mrs Davies, Johnson unexpectedly came into the shop."

What manner of man he was, Boswell himself elsewhere describes—apologizing for such minute particulars, by recalling that "Dr Adam Smith, in his rhetorical lectures at Glasgow, told us he was glad to know that Milton wore latchets in his shoes instead of buckles."[4] Later on he tells us how Johnson sought his aid in choosing silver buckles—"not the ridiculous large ones now in fashion."[5]

Of Johnson, then, he writes[6] that "he had a loud

---

[1] *Life*, i. 154. [2] *Hebrides*, 368. [3] *Life*, ii. 299.
[4] *Hebrides*, 19. [5] *Life*, iii. 325. [6] *Hebrides*, 18.

voice and a slow deliberate utterance, which no doubt gave some additional weight to the sterling metal of his conversation. [Lord Pembroke called this his bow-wow way.[1]] His person was large, robust, I may say approaching to the gigantick, and grown unwieldy from corpulency. His countenance was naturally of the cast of an ancient statue, but somewhat disfigured by the scars of that *evil*, which, it was formerly imagined, the *royal touch* could cure.[2] . . . His head, and sometimes also his body, shook with a kind of motion like the effect of a palsy; he appeared to be frequently disturbed by cramps, or convulsive contractions, of the nature of that distemper called *St Vitus's Dance.*" Miss Reynolds tells of his "antics" and "straddles," and how "he whirled and twisted about to perform his gesticulations" in entering a door, and how "as soon as he had finish'd, he would give a sudden spring, and make such an extensive stride over the threshold, as if he was trying for a wager how far he could stride."[3] Boswell talks of his counting his steps and going back to retrace them if they came wrong, and another observer of his touching posts as he passed, deliberately laying his hand on them and going back in like manner to rectify an omission.[4]

"Mr Davies mentioned my name, and respectfully introduced me to him. I was much agitated; and recollecting his prejudice against the Scotch, of which I had heard much, I said to Davies, 'Don't tell where I come from'—'From Scotland,' cried Davies roguishly. 'Mr Johnson, (said I) I do indeed come from Scotland,

---

[1] *Life*, ii. 326 n.

[2] "We had Johnson, the Author of the Dictionary, etc., to dine with us to-day. He seems to be a Man of very strong sense and deep judgment, but not remarkably bright or of quick apprehension. He is also fond of sarcasm, which has a double portion of Gall flowing from the most disgusting Voice and person you ever beheld."—Walter Spencer-Stanhope ("Annals of a Yorkshire House, from the Papers of a Macaroni and his Kindred," 1911). Johnson was then visiting Oxford.

[3] *Johnsonian Miscellanies*, ii. 273.   [4] *Life*, i. 485.

but I cannot help it.'" Johnson at once caught at the phrase—so many people came from Scotland just then—"*droves* of Scotchmen,"[1] he said. "The noblest prospect which a Scotchman sees is the high road that leads him to England";[2] "Sir, it is not so much to be lamented that Old England is lost as that the Scotch have found it."[3] This was a favourite vein of his, so now he "stunned" the last man who came from Scotland with: "That, Sir, I find, is what a very great many of your countrymen cannot help."

He now turned to Davies and began to grumble at Garrick, which he did from time to time, though he would allow no one else to say a word against him. Boswell recovered his spirits and ventured a gentle protest. "Sir, (said he, with a stern look) I have known David Garrick longer than you have done: and I know no right you have to talk to me on the subject."

"I now felt myself much mortified," says Boswell, "and began to think that the hope which I had long indulged of obtaining his acquaintance was blasted." But he had a "faculty of sticking"—or as he puts it "his ardour was uncommonly strong"—and he did not go, but stayed and listened and remembered and noted all down immediately after. "Don't be uneasy," said Davies, "I can see he likes you very well."[4]

Some days later, encouraged by Davies, and "enlivened by the witty sallies of Messieurs Thornton, Wilkes, Churchill and Lloyd, with whom I had passed the morning," Boswell called on Johnson at his chambers in the Temple. "He received me very courteously; but it must be confessed, that his apartment, and furniture, and morning dress, were sufficiently uncouth. His brown suit of clothes looked very rusty; he had on

---

[1] *Life*, ii. 311.   [2] *Life*, i. 425.
[3] *Life*, iii. 78; cf. *Journal of Fanny Burney*, Aug. 23, 1778. "My dear, what makes you so fond of the Scotch? I don't like you for that."
[4] *Life*, i. 391-395.

a little old, shrivelled, unpowdered wig, which was too small for his head; his shirt-neck and knees of his breeches were loose; his black worsted stockings ill drawn up; and he had a pair of unbuckled shoes by way of slippers. But all these slovenly particularities were forgotten the moment that he began to talk."[1]

So began the great intimacy which has been the delight of a century already. It was not so strange as it seems. Johnson was a solitary man, without wife or child. His house was full of people who were there because "if I did not shelter them no one else would, and they would be lost for want." But he had other reasons. He said to Sir Joshua Reynolds: "If a man does not make new acquaintance as he advances through life, he will soon find himself left alone. A man, Sir, should keep his friendship *in constant repair*."[2] "Sir," he said to Boswell, "I love the acquaintance of young people; because, in the first place, I don't like to think myself growing old ... and then, Sir, young men have more virtue than old men; they have more generous sentiments in every respect. I love the young dogs of this age."[3] "I am always on the young people's side," he said to Mrs Thrale;[4] and Miss Reynolds tells how once in Devonshire he ran a race with a young lady, kicking his shoes off as he went, and leaving her far behind.[5] "Dr Johnson," wrote Fanny Burney, "has more fun, and comical humour, and love of nonsense about him, than almost anybody I ever saw."[6]

To Boswell Johnson took amazingly. "I opened my mind to him ingenuously,"[7] wrote Boswell, and they talked freely of the Christian religion, of ghosts, of books, of "the paternal estate," and of going abroad, and all sorts of things. They constantly met, and Boswell had

---

[1] *Life*, 395, 396. [2] *Life*, i. 300. [3] *Life*, i. 445.
[4] *Johns. Misc.* i. 317. [5] *Johns. Misc.*, ii. 278.
[6] Letter to Mr Crisp, Mch. 1779; Diary and Letters (A. Dobson), i. 211.
[7] *Life*, i. 404.

the honour of having tea with the blind Miss Williams, the first of Johnson's permanent residents. "Am I not fortunate," Boswell once wrote to Temple (8 May 1779), "in having something about me that interests most people at first sight in my favour?" So it proved. "Come to me as often as you can," said Johnson to him on 13 June; and again on 25 June, "Give me your hand, I have taken a liking to you." And as it began in 1763 it went on to the end. "Never, my dear Sir," he wrote (27 Aug. 1775), "do you take it into your head to think that I do not love you; you may settle yourself in full confidence both of my love and my esteem; I love you as a kind man, I value you as a worthy man and hope in time to reverence you as a man of exemplary piety. I hold you as Hamlet has it, 'in my heart of hearts.'"[1] "My regard for you," he said, "is greater almost than I have words to express; but I do not choose to be always repeating it; write it down in the first leaf of your pocket-book, and never doubt of it again."[2]

It is easy to laugh at Boswell—Johnson did it frequently, snubbed him and sometimes humiliated him. "Why treat me so," Boswell once asked, "before people who neither love you nor me?" JOHNSON. "Well, I am sorry for it I'll make it up to you twenty different ways, as you please." BOSWELL. "I said to-day to Sir Joshua, when he observed that you *tossed* me sometimes—I don't care how often, or how high he tosses me, when only friends are present, for then I fall on soft ground; but I do not like falling on stones, which is the case when enemies are present.—I think this is a pretty good image, Sir." JOHNSON. "Sir, it is one of the happiest I have ever heard."[3]

Boswell's image is indeed a happy one. Carlyle was right when he spoke of him as having an open, loving heart. Boswell is available for his friends in every way, —if in no other, then they can laugh at him—as long as

[1] *Life*, ii. 383.   [2] *Life*, iii. 198.   [3] *Life*, iii. 338.

they like him, let them laugh as much as they please. So he says in a song he wrote on himself:—

> Boswell is pleasant and gay,
>   For frolic by nature design'd ;
> He heedlessly rattles away
>   When the company is to his mind.
> This maxim, he says, you may see,
>   We can never have corn without chaff ;
> So not a bent sixpence cares he
>   Whether *with* him or *at* him you laugh.

So he owns to being " desirous of calling Johnson forth to talk and exercise his wit, though I should myself be the object of it."[1] " Mr Gibbon with his usual sneer" was another matter[2] —" he is an ugly, affected, disgusting fellow, and poisons our literary Club to me."[3]

Boswell was ridiculous from the cradle to the grave, and he knew it, for he too had a sense of humour. He knew he was telling stories against himself, and Johnson warned him against it—happily in vain. Gray spoke of him as a " fool," and Walpole called him " the quintessence of busy bodies,"[4] a generation before Macaulay explained his greatness in literature as due to the fact that he was such a fool. His contemporaries and his readers have laughed at him for being ridiculous, but he was not so ridiculous as they have thought. Kindness, tenderness, unfailing good humour, indomitable devotion were not things that Gibbon or Walpole could afford to ridicule. These things made Boswell. He had faults—even vices —of the sort we associate with selfishness, but he was not a selfish man. He said extraordinarily silly things, and

---

[1] *Life*, ii. 187. [2] *Life*, iv. 73.
[3] *Letter to Temple*, 8 May 1779. The Club was founded in Febry. 1764. "Damn sneerers," wrote Wm. Blake, in his copy of Lavater, against Aphorism 59.
[4] Letter of 22 May 1781.

did them, and he was very vain.[1] But if we analyse, the ridiculous is very often merely the unfamiliar or the unconventional—anything that runs counter to our preconceptions. A black man is to some minds a highly ludicrous object, especially if he has ideals right enough in a white man. Similarly a white man was once—before they knew us too well—a ridiculous sight in Africa. But "Cambyses," said Herodotus, "must have been mad, or he would not have laughed at other people's customs." One day Boswell owned to Johnson that he "was occasionally troubled with a fit of *narrowness*." It cannot have been often, for he is quite right in confessing to romantic enthusiasms, and they carry a man into generosity. But mark Johnson's reply—"Why, Sir (said he) so am I. *But I do not tell it*." That is the difference between being ridiculous and not being ridiculous—"so am I, but I do not tell it." It is the frankness that leaps over the bounds of conventional caution that makes a man ridiculous. Goldsmith was in a way another of the same kind. Boswell often speaks of him as "talking away carelessly."

Here lies Nolly Goldsmith, for shortness called Noll,
Who wrote like an angel and talk'd like poor Poll;

wrote Garrick.[2] Anything that came into their heads, Goldsmith and Boswell would talk of at once. Not they! An immense fund of shrewd and serious observation they kept in reserve, and men who saw less, felt less, thought less, were less and did less, laughed at them. And perhaps, if one excepts Sir Joshua, they were the kindliest natures in the wonderful group.

[1] Baretti wrote: "He makes more noise than anybody in company, talking and laughing loud;" and: "Boswell is not quite right-headed in my humble opinion."—*Life*, iii. 136 note. "All the time I myself am *pars magna*, for my exuberant spirits will not let me listen enough."—Boswell to Temple, 17 April 1775.
[2] *Cf.* Johnson's remark, *Life*, iv. 29.

It may further be remarked that the "open loving heart" of Boswell led him more surely aright than the clever heads round him led their owners. He always knew who were the real great men and the good men. Walpole said he had "a rage of knowing anybody that ever was talked of. He forced himself on me in Paris. . . . He then took an antipathy to me on Rousseau's account, abused me in the newspapers, and exhorted Rousseau to do so too." How Walpole knew what Boswell exhorted Rousseau to do, I do not know. But, while Walpole has touched off Boswell's foible here, we may remark how unadvisedly he has given away the fact that Boswell knew the better man of the two at once. So it always is with Boswell—he knows the real greatness; and, what is more, the really good and great man quickly saw the worth of Boswell. The greatest men of the age were—Boswell's intimates; in art Sir Joshua Reynolds, in literature Oliver Goldsmith and Samuel Johnson, in statesmanship Edmund Burke and Pascal Paoli. *Principibus placuisse viris non ultima laus est*, wrote Horace long ago, and he was right, if by the "first men" we may mean men indeed and the first of them. And that is Boswell's praise.

One episode of this visit to London deserves to be recalled. "One evening . . . when Dr Hugh Blair and I were sitting together in the pit of Drury-lane playhouse, in a wild freak of youthful extravagance, I entertained the audience *prodigiously* by imitating the lowing of a cow. . . . I was so successful in this boyish frolick, that the universal cry of the galleries was '*Encore* the cow! *Encore* the cow!' In the pride of my heart I attempted imitations of some other animals, but with very inferior effect. My reverend friend, anxious for my *fame*, with an air of the utmost gravity and earnestness, addressed me thus: 'My dear sir, I would *confine* myself to the *cow*.'"[1] Blair, it is interesting to remember, was an Edinburgh professor and a great preacher of the

[1] *Hebrides*, p. 396.

Moderate school. He had recently been introduced to Johnson. "I love Blair's sermons," said Johnson in 1781. "Though the dog is a Scotchman, and a Presbyterian, and every thing he should not be, I was the first to praise them."[1]

But we are keeping Boswell too long in London, which was after all a stage on his journey to Holland, where he was to study law. It is something to remember what happened here. A young Scotsman, unknown, very young and foolish, comes to London, and is introduced to Samuel Johnson; and when he goes, Johnson takes a four days' coaching journey to see him off at Harwich. "As the vessel put out to sea, I kept my eyes upon him for a considerable time, while he remained rolling his majestick[2] frame in his usual manner: and at last I perceived him walk back into the town, and he disappeared."[3]

In Utrecht Boswell studied, perhaps not exactactly, for we find that on his return to Edinburgh he kept up a correspondence with a lady whom he called Zelide (an anagram, it is suggested, for De Zeyl), and thought of marrying. He travelled in Europe,—in Germany and in Italy. He visited Voltaire at Ferney in 1764 and told him how Johnson and he were some day to visit the Hebrides. "He looked at me, as if I had talked of going to the North Pole, and said, 'You do not insist on my accompanying you?'—'No, sir.'—'Then I am very willing you should go.'"[4] Boswell also saw Rousseau, whom he later on aided in his migration to England in

---

[1] *Life*, iv. 98.
[2] "Of late it has become the fashion to render our language more neat and trim by leaving out k after c, and u in the last syllable of words which used to end in our. The illustrious Mr Samuel Johnson . . . has been careful in his Dictionary to preserve the k as a mark of Saxon original . . . I have retained the k . . . An attention to this may seem trivial. But I own I am one of those who are curious in the formation of language in its various modes. . . . If this work should at any future period be reprinted, I hope that care will be taken of my orthography."—Preface to *Corsica*.
[3] *Life*, i. 473.   [4] *Hebrides*, p. 2.

1766, when, as Hume says, Thérèse was escorted "by a friend of mine"—"very good-humoured, very agreeable, and very mad."[1] It was apparently Rousseau who set him off on the greatest expedition of all.

The story of Corsica's wars of independence against Genoa, which ended in the sale of the island to France, in its subjugation by France, in Napoleon Bonaparte and the identification of the island at last with the Republic—all this may be left on one side for our present purpose. Boswell went to see Paoli, the hero and statesman of the island. He was perhaps the first English visitor to the island, and had to risk being caught by Barbary corsairs on his voyage in 1765. But once landed he enjoyed himself to the full. Adventure, enthusiasm and imagination—the sense of the great scene, the great struggle and the hero—all set him in the seventh heaven.

"My journey over the mountains was very entertaining. I past some immense ridges and vast woods. I was in great health and spirits and fully able to enter into the ideas of the brave rude men." At Bastelica, happening "to have an unusual flow of spirits," he harangued the men of the place, "with great fluency," expatiating on the bravery of the Corsicans, the proper cultivation of the island, and the possibility of "engaging a little in commerce. But I bid them remember, that they were much happier in their present state than in a state of refinement and vice, and that therefore they should beware of luxury."[2]

Johnson used to tell Boswell he was "the most *unscottified*" of his countrymen,[3] that his pronunciation was "not offensive,"[4] and so forth, and Boswell had a wild preference for England. "Were my daughters," he wrote to Temple (3 July 1789), "to be Edinburgh-mannered girls, I could have no satisfaction in their company." He did not recognize that the Scotsman is

---

[1] Morley, *Rousseau*, ii. 101 n. [2] *Corsica*, p. 313.
[3] *Life*, ii. 242. [4] *Life*, ii. 159.

in the nature of things, unless depraved, the inevitable superior of the Englishman, as every candid and informed mind will own. They are Nature's aristocracy, but he did not see this and he tried to be English. But race was too strong for him, as the conclusion of his harangue with the moral note effectively proves.

At last he met Paoli. "I had stood in the presence of many a prince, but I never had such a trial as in the presence of Paoli. I have already said, that he is a great physiognomist.... For ten minutes we walked backwards and forwards through the room, hardly saying a word, while he looked at me, with a steadfast, keen and penetrating eye, as if he searched my very soul. This interview was for a while very severe upon me. I was much relieved when his reserve wore off and he began to speak more."[1] And then they became great friends, as they remained through life. "My timidity wore off,"[2] Boswell writes, and we can see that it did. "He smiled a good deal, when I told him that I was much surprised to find him so amiable, accomplished and polite; for although I knew I was to see a great man, I expected to find a rude character, an Attila King of the Goths, or a Luitprand King of the Lombards."[3] No, Paoli was not an Attila nor a Goth. How could he bear to be confined to an island yet in a rude uncivilized state, when in Italy and elsewhere he could enjoy *noctes cœnæque Deûm*? "He replied in one line of Virgil:

Vincet amor patriæ laudumque immensa cupido."[4]

In fact "my flow of gay ideas relaxed his severity and brightened up his humour."[5]

They talked as Johnson and Boswell had talked at the Mitre. Boswell told him "how much I had suffered from anxious speculations,"[6] of his metaphysical researches and his reasoning beyond his depth; and Paoli listened and

[1] *Corsica*, p. 315. [2] *Corsica*, p. 317.
[3] *Corsica*, p. 324. [4] *Corsica*, p. 320.
[5] *Corsica*, p. 343. [6] *Corsica*, p. 349.

sympathized and counselled. He read his guest clearly enough. There was no need for Boswell to tell him, as he did "The People of Scotland," that he is "a very universal man," that "I can drink, I can laugh, I can converse in perfect humour with Whigs, with republicans, with dissenters, with Independents, with Quakers, with Moravians, with Jews. But I would vote (he concluded) with Tories and pray with a Dean and Chapter."[1] Paoli, like Johnson, felt the charm of a man so friendly and sympathetic. They both saw the weakness—the great flaw that spoiled so much of his life. "Sir," said Johnson to him, "a man may be so much of every thing, that he is nothing of any thing."[2] Paoli put the same thought to him and offered him a cure for the melancholy which was partly constitutional—the reverse side to his gaiety and sensibility—and partly cultivated. "I hold always firm one great object," said Paoli, "I never feel a moment of depression."[3] Of course Boswell did not take the advice. To the end he had his moods. "Of the exaltations and depressions of your mind you delight to talk, and I hate to hear," wrote Johnson in 1783.[4]

Paoli was one of those great men of simple mind and simple taste. It is not surprising he recommended Boswell to read Plutarch and Livy rather than modern memoirs [5]—"Je ne puis souffrir long temps les diseurs de bons mots," he said.[6] He owned to visions and dreams,[7] to belief. "'I never lost courage, trusting as I did in Providence.' I ventured to object: 'But why has not Providence interposed sooner?' He replied with a noble, serious and devout air, 'Because his ways are unsearchable. I adore him for what he hath done. I revere him in what he hath not done.'"[8] How this might have

[1] *Life*, iii. 375 n. [2] *Life*, iv. 176. [3] *Corsica*, p. 350.
[4] *Life*, iv. 249. [5] *Corsica*, p. 354. [6] *Corsica*, p. 351.
[7] *Corsica*, p. 361. Compare the very singular story of the dream which Abraham Lincoln told his cabinet on the day when he was shot.—John G. Nicolay, *Short Life of Abraham Lincoln*, p. 531.
[8] *Corsica*, p. 355.

amused Horace Walpole or Gibbon! Boswell's comments shew how clear his recognition of goodness is, if his resolution is unstable.

"The contemplation of such a character really existing, was of more service to me than all I had been able to draw from books, from conversation, or from the exertions of my own mind. I had often enough formed the idea of a man continually such, as I could conceive in my best moments. But this idea appeared like the ideas we are taught in the schools to form of things which may exist, but do not; of seas of milk and ships of amber. But I saw my highest idea realized in Paoli. It was impossible for me, speculate as I pleased, to have a little opinion of human nature in him."[1] "Never," he writes, "was I so thoroughly sensible of my own defects as while I was in Corsica."[2]

But there was gaiety in this Corsican life as well as serious thought. "Every day I felt myself happier. . . . One day when I rode out, I was mounted on Paoli's own horse, with rich furniture of crimson velvet, with broad gold lace, and had my guards marching along with me. I allowed myself to indulge a momentary pride in this parade, as I was curious to experience what could really be the pleasure of state and distinction with which mankind are so strangely intoxicated. . . . I enjoyed a sort of luxury of noble sentiment." "I got a Corsican dress made, in which I walked about with an air of true satisfaction"—and not only in Corsica, for he wore it at the Shakespeare Jubilee at Stratford-on-Avon and when he called on Lord Chatham.[3] He played to his friends on his German flute "some of our beautiful old Scots tunes, Gilderoy, the Lass of Patie's Mill, Corn riggs are bonny,"

---

[1] *Corsica*, p. 350.   [2] *Corsica*, p. 370.
[3] "Could your Lordship," he wrote to Chatham, 8 April 1767, "find time to honour me now and then with a letter? I have been told how favourably your Lordship has spoken of me. To correspond with a Paoli and a Chatham is enough to keep a young man ever ardent in the pursuit of virtuous fame."—*Life*, ii. 59 n.

and then sang an English song. "Never did I see men so delighted with a song as the Corsicans were with the Hearts of oak. 'Cuore di quercia,' cried they, 'bravo Inglese.' It was quite a joyous riot. I fancied myself to be a recruiting sea officer. I fancied all my chorus of Corsicans aboard the British fleet."[1]

"You are longer a boy than others,"[2] said Johnson to him when they were embarking for Mull. Of course he was,—not the English public-school boy, however, who is a great deal more self-conscious,—but the natural boy of adventures, fancying himself this and that, keen in his enjoyment of every glimpse into the romantic and heroic. Grown men of course grow out of such moods—such things are childish and they do not have them, or if they do, "I do not tell it." Boswell went on "fancying" all his life and wrote his fancies in his books, and men read and enjoyed them thoroughly and said what a fool he was. It would be rather delightful to be such a fool now and then, all the same.

Boswell came back to England in 1766, with his head full of Corsica, and in 1768 he got his book out—"An Account of Corsica, The Journal of a Tour to that Island, and Memoirs of Pascal Paoli, by James Boswell, Esq." It went quickly through two editions and reached a third inside a year, and it produced an enormous effect. Sympathy—effective sympathy—with Corsica by now would mean war with France, and many felt it would be a righteous war for such a cause. Lord Mansfield however held that the Ministry was too weak, and the nation too wise, for war. "Foolish as we are," wrote Lord Holland, "we cannot be so foolish as to go to war because Mr Boswell has been in Corsica; and yet, believe me, no better reason can be given for siding with the vile inhabitants of one of the vilest islands in the world."[3]

[1] *Corsica*, pp. 340, 341.   [2] *Hebrides*, p. 308.
[3] *Cf.* Trevelyan, *Early History of C. J. Fox*, pp. 144, 145.

Everybody read the book. "Mr Boswell's book," wrote Gray, "has pleased and moved me strangely; all, I mean, that relates to Paoli. He is a man born two thousand years after his time! The pamphlet proves, what I have always maintained, that any fool may write a most valuable book by chance, if he will only tell us what he heard and saw with veracity." As if a fool really knew what to hear and see; as if veracity and perspective were within a fool's range! "A dialogue between a green goose and a hero," said Gray ungratefully. Hume, who saw it in MS., told Boswell, "he imagined my account of Corsica would be a book that will stand."[1] John Wesley wrote in his Journal: "Fri. 11 [November 1768] I returned to London. The next week I visited the Classes, and at intervals read Mr Boswell's 'Account of Corsica.' But what a scene is opened therein! How little did we know of that brave people! How much less were we acquainted with the character of their General, Paschal Paoli! As great a lover of his country as Epaminondas, and as great a general as Hannibal." John Wesley read interminably, as his Journal shows, and he praised with discrimination. The likeness to Hannibal proved too true, for the French drove Paoli out of Corsica, and he was for twenty years a refugee in England. Then for some years following the Revolution he was in his country again, but between the tyranny of Napoleon and the fumbling of England Corsica was no place for him, and he came back to London, where he died in 1802. George III gave him a pension in 1769—£1200 a year—another outcome of Boswell's book, Walpole said. Paoli's house in London became Boswell's headquarters there,—he entertained him "in an elegant hospitality," as he puts it;[2] and in the dismal years that followed the deaths of Johnson and Mrs Boswell,—when Johnson's prophecy was fulfilled only too

[1] *Letter to Temple*, Febr. 1767.   [2] *Life*, iii. 324.

literally: "In losing her you would lose your anchor and be tost without stability by the waves of life,"—Paoli was a wise and strong friend to the weak, loveable and unhappy lawyer.

One point more in connexion with the book may be noted, the classical learning in the earlier part, when Boswell summarizes the history of Corsica, with quotations from Greek and Latin authors from Herodotus and Strabo to Petrus Cyrnæus. It was still the age of the Classics. Perhaps the *Life of Johnson* is the landmark between that age and ours. After that came the French Revolution, the *Lyrical Ballads*, the Waverley Novels, and the Reform Bill; and the Classics passed out of the House of Commons and the life of England, to be no more the enjoyment and inspiration of a Carteret and a Fox, but to welter in the hands of lexicographers and grammarians—*inutile lignum*. But we may recognize that Boswell read them and knew them—especially the Latins.[1] When Johnson and he landed on Inch Keith (18 Aug. 1773) and saw the ruined fort with its inscription "Maria Re 1564"—"when we got into our boat again, he called to me, 'Come, now, pay a classical compliment to the island on quitting it,'" and Boswell rejoined,

Invitus regina tuo de littore cessi.

"'Very well hit off,' said he." Johnson's feelings show the coming change. When Charles James Fox talked to him at the Club about Catiline's conspiracy, "I withdrew my attention, and thought about Tom Thumb."[2] Boswell bought an Ovid in Inverness and read it a good deal on the rest of their journey through the Hebrides.[3] In the Highlands they often talked in Latin—"such Latin as I could speak."[4]

---

[1] *Life*, iii. 407. He expresses his regret at having learnt so little Greek, "as is too generally the case in Scotland."
[2] *Johns. Misc.* i. 203.   [3] *Hebrides*, pp. 294, 321.   [4] *Hebrides*, p. 321.

Of the years between Boswell's return from Corsica and his marriage in 1769, we have a double record in the *Life of Johnson* and the letters to Temple. The latter were recovered in a curious way in 1850. An Englishman, buying something at Boulogne, found his purchase wrapped in a sheet of paper bearing the name James Boswell. He at once tracked the sheet to the store of an itinerant vendor of waste paper, and found nearly a hundred letters. They are of the most intimate type, full of Boswell — his "flights," his "Spanish stateliness," his "soul of more Southern frame," his "warm imagination"—"the candid generous Boswell," the "man of many popular and pleasant talents." He tells his friend of his projects of marriage—he had many in mind, before his cousin Margaret Montgomerie married him (1769). The recovery of the letters has also let the world see perhaps only too much of his vanities and follies. Thus, in February 1767, he wrote to Temple about his ordination—"My friend, it is your office to labour cheerfully in the vineyard, and, if possible, to leave not a tare in Mamhead." (The Scripture seems mixed, but a clergyman might be trusted to get it straight.) "In a word, my dear Temple, be a good clergyman, and you will be happy both here and hereafter," and he recommends marriage to him. "In the meantime, my friend, I am happy enough to have a dear infidel, as you say," and he tells his clerical friend his projects for her, and by and by is shocked when Temple describes his notions in plain English. There is a good deal of this in the letters, and a good deal of drinking. The drinking he never quite got over. Paoli exacted a promise from him which he kept for some time.[1] A short extract from a letter of 12 August 1775 will suffice. "My promise under the solemn yew I have observed wonderfully, having never infringed it till, the other day, a very

---

[1] Letter to Temple, 28 April 1776; three weeks before, he had pledged himself to Paoli for a year, and had so far kept his pledge.

jovial company of us dined at a tavern, and I unwarily exceeded my bottle of old Hock; and having once broke over the pale, I run wild, but I did not get drunk. I was however intoxicated, and very ill next day. I ask your forgiveness, and I shall be more strictly cautious for the future. The drunken manners of this country are very bad." Things went worse in the drinking way after his wife's death, and many stories against him are current, some perhaps true in some points. But he was always a man round whom absurd stories would gather.

In 1769 he married. "Naturally somewhat singular," he wrote years after, "independent of any additions which affectation and vanity may perhaps have made, I resolved to have a more pleasing species of marriage than common, and bargained with my bride that I should not be bound to live with her longer than I really inclined; and that whenever I tired of her domestic society I should be at liberty to give it up. Eleven years have elapsed, and I have never yet wished to take advantage of my stipulated privilege."[1] It may be added that he kept a MS. book, which he entitled *Uxoriana* and in which he entered her best remarks. She allowed him a good many visits to London.—" Sir," said Johnson, " I never knew any one who had such a *gust* for London as you have."[2] His father was not so easy about these "jaunts," even though the son pleaded that the last did not cost £20, "as I got forty-two guineas in London." Arithmetic seems to explain the father's attitude, if each jaunt ran to sixty guineas.[3]

To go to the Hebrides was in 1773 a tremendous expedition. Thirty years later the Wordsworths found the Lowlands ill supplied with the conveniences of travel. "I am really ashamed," said Johnson on their return to Edinburgh, "of the congratulations which we

---

[1] *Hebrides*, p. 24 n.   [2] *Life*, iii. 176.
[3] Letter to Temple, 19 June 1775.

receive. We are addressed as if we had made a voyage to Nova Zembla and suffered five persecutions in Japan." The roads were bad in England, as we see in Cowper's letters, and in Scotland they were worse."[1] "The highways were tracks of mire in wet weather, and marshes in winter, till the frost made them sheets of ice, covered with drifted snow. . . . Even towns were often connected only by pack-roads, on which horses stumbled perilously along and carriages could not pass at all, over unenclosed land and moorland, where, after rain, it was difficult to trace any beaten track." A stage-coach took twelve hours for the 46 miles between Glasgow and Edinburgh and ran twice a week. The inns were dirty in a degree beyond our experience.[2] There was one alleviation; there were no highwaymen, for the roads made the profession unremunerative.

Boswell for instance records how they slept on hay; how when they had "a most elegant room" once, "the pillows were made of the feathers of some sea-fowl which had to me a disagreeable smell"; and how conversely, when they had each "an elegant bed" the rain came in at a broken window and turned the clay floor into a puddle. But these things did not trouble them. Johnson had "in Mr Boswell a companion, whose gaiety of conversation and civility of manners are sufficient to counteract the inconveniences of travel, in countries less hospitable than we have passed."[3] So when luck comes their way, we find them gaily disputing "which of us had the best curtains. His were rather the best, being of linen; but I insisted that my bed had the best posts, which was undeniable.

---

[1] What follows is from H. Grey Graham, *Social Life in Scotland in 18th Century*, i. pp. 39-48. Johnson's letters from the Hebrides to Mrs Thrale confirm.

[2] *Cf.* Johnson, Letter to Mrs Thrale, 25 Aug. and foll., 1773, on the inns of Aberdeen and the barefoot housemaids. "Shoes . . . came late into this country." Again, letter of 26 Sept., on inn in Skye.

[3] Johnson's Works, *Tour in the Hebrides*.

'Well, (said he,) if you *have* the best *posts*, we will have you tied to them and whipped.'" And Boswell remembers Goldsmith adapting a line from a comedy of Cibber's, to the effect that "there is no arguing with Johnson; for if his pistol misses fire, he knocks you down with the butt end of it."[1] "I told him," on another day, "that I was diverted to hear all the people whom we had visited in our tour, say, '*Honest man!* he's pleased with every thing; he's always content!' —'Little do they know,' said I. He laughed and said 'You rogue'!" It was on that morning that Johnson waking had called "Lanky!" but corrected himself instantly and cried "Bozzy!"[2] and Boswell tells how he shortened all his friends, though "Goldy" did not like it. It adds to the pleasure of following this delightful record of travel to imagine the Doctor's "Bozzy!" Such art has Boswell in weaving in the trifling that is not trivial; it makes whatever he writes, good or bad, at least live.

"One night, in Col, he strutted about the room with a broadsword and a target, and made a formidable appearance; and, another night, I took the liberty to put a large blue bonnet on his head. His age, his size, and his bushy grey wig, with this covering on it, presented the image of a venerable *Senachi*: and, however unfavourable to the Lowland Scots, he seemed much pleased to assume the appearance of an ancient Caledonian."[3] As one of their Highland friends said: "When you see him first, you are struck with awful reverence;—then you admire him;—and then you love him cordially."[4] "It is musick to hear this man speak," said Ulinish.[5]

They were kept at Corrichatachin for some days by the weather. Their host, who bore the name of his place, insisted on a celebration of Col's visit, and they had an evening of punch. Dr Johnson had gone to bed, and it

[1] *Hebrides*, p. 292. [2] *Hebrides*, p. 308. [3] *Hebrides*, p. 324.
[4] *Hebrides*, p. 272. [5] *Hebrides*, p. 246.

was 5 A.M. on Sunday morning (26 Sept.) when Boswell followed him—" of what passed I have no recollection with any accuracy." " I awaked at noon, with a severe head-ach. I was much vexed that I should have been guilty of such a riot and afraid of a reproof from Dr Johnson. I thought it very inconsistent with that conduct which I ought to maintain, while the companion of the Rambler. About one he came into my room, and accosted me, ' What, drunk yet?' His tone of voice was not that of severe upbraiding; so I was relieved a little. ' Sir (said I) they kept me up.' He answered, ' No, you kept them up, you drunken dog;'—This he said with good-humoured *English* pleasantry."

While Boswell is dressing, we may digress to another scene. Johnson had "got into one of his fits of railing at the Scots," and speaking of the results of the Union. " ' We have taught you, (said he) and we'll do the same in time to all barbarous nations,—to the Cherokees,—and at last to the Ouran-Outangs;' laughing with as much glee as if Monboddo had been present. BOSWELL. 'We had wine before the Union.' JOHNSON. ' No, Sir; you had some weak stuff, the refuse of France, which would not make you drunk.' BOSWELL. ' I assure you, Sir, there was a great deal of drunkenness.' JOHNSON. ' No, Sir; there were people who died of dropsies, which they contracted in trying to get drunk.' " [1]

Boswell, drest and better, took up Mrs M'Kinnon's prayer-book in Johnson's room, which the ladies used as a sitting-room by day, and opened it at the passage containing the words " And be not drunk with wine wherein there is excess." " Some," he says, " would have taken this as a divine interposition." " This was another day of wind and rain; but good cheer and good society helped to beguile the time. I felt myself comfortable enough in the afternoon. I then thought my last night's riot was no more than such a social excess as may happen

[1] *Hebrides*, p. 248.

without much moral blame; and recollected that some physicians maintained, that a fever produced by it was, upon the whole, good for health; so different are our reflections on the same subject at different periods; and such the excuses with which we palliate what we know to be wrong."

Next day at tea-time in the evening "one of our married ladies, a lively pretty little woman, good-humouredly sat down on Dr Johnson's knee, and, being encouraged by some of the company, put her hands round his neck and kissed him. 'Do it again, (said he,) and let us see who will tire first.' . . . To me it was highly comick to see this grave philosopher,—the Rambler,—toying with a Highland beauty!—But what could he do? He must have been surly, and weak too, had he not behaved as he did."[1]

More than once as they rowed in the darkness among the mountainous islands, the rowers singing in Gaelic as they rowed, Boswell's imagination carried him away to America and the wild Indians,[2] with whom in canoes and among mountains Englishmen had of late had so much to do, and were soon to have more. Once they had a real storm, and Col "put into my hand a rope and told me to hold it till he bade me pull"—and so kept him stationary and pre-occupied.[3]

When they reached Iona, Boswell left others to measure, if they would, the ruins, better pleased to stroll among them at his ease and "receive the general impression of solemn antiquity." "I reflected with much satisfaction, that the solemn scenes of picty never lose their sanctity and influence, though the cares and follies of life may prevent us from visiting them, or may even make us fancy that their effects are only 'as yesterday when it is past,' and never again to be perceived. I hoped, that, ever after having been in this holy place, I should maintain

---

[1] Corrichatachin, *Hebrides*, pp. 258-262.
[2] E.g. *Hebrides*, p. 257.   [3] *Hebrides*, pp. 280-284.

an exemplary conduct. One has a strange propensity to fix upon some point of time from whence a better course of life may begin."[1]

He had had this idea before. On 9 November 1767 he had written Temple: "I am always fixing some period for my perfection as far as possible. Let it be when my account of Corsica is published; I shall then have a character which I must support."

Of the ruined chapel of Inch Kenneth Johnson wrote to Mrs Thrale: "Boswell, who is very pious, went into it by night, to perform his devotions, but came back in haste for fear of spectres."[2] Boswell revelled in feeling "exalted in piety."[3]

Back on the mainland Boswell took his friend to Auchinleck, but the visit was not quite a success. The old Judge, Whig and Presbyterian, and the old Scholar, Tory and Church of England, would not agree. To Johnson "Whiggism was the negation of all principle,"[4] and "the first Whig was the Devil."[5] Boswell would not reveal all the details of the conflict, but his father scored some points. His guest challenged him to point out any theological works of merit written by Presbyterian ministers in Scotland. The Judge's "studies did not lie much in this way," but, trusting to a vague memory, he boldly said: "Sir, have you read Mr Durham's excellent commentary on the Galatians?" "No, Sir," said Dr Johnson, which was not strange, as it is said that the book never existed; it was all a blunder of the old lawyer's and its excellence was like a bow drawn at a venture. One shot of Lord Auchinleck's Walter Scott preserved. What good had Cromwell ever done his country? "God, Doctor! he

---

[1] *Hebrides*, p. 337. [2] Johnson's letter of 24 Oct. 1773.
[3] Letter of 17 April 1775. Cf. *Life*, iv. 122. "My dear Sir, I would fain be a good man; and I am very good now," so he expressed himself "with unrestrained fervour" to Johnson.
[4] *Life*, i, 431. [5] *Life*, iii. 326.

gart kings ken that they had a *lith* in their neck."[1] Two years later the old man still harped on the enormity of his son "going over Scotland with a brute"—*Ursa Major* he called him—and thought his daughter-in-law might have stopped it—to say nothing of her poor dowry.[2]

Poor Mrs Boswell! "I know Mrs Boswell wished me well to go," wrote the Doctor. "In this," says his biographer, "he shewed a very acute penetration," and he wonders very loyally how he could have discovered it. "The truth is, that his irregular hours and uncouth habits, such as turning the candles with their heads downwards, when they did not burn bright enough, letting the wax drop upon the carpet, could not but be disagreeable to a lady. . . . She once in a little warmth, made, with more point than justice, this remark upon that subject: 'I have seen many a bear led by a man; but I never before saw a man led by a bear.'"[3] Did he quote to her Goldsmith's famous remark on Johnson: "He has nothing of the bear but the skin"?[4]

After this their meetings were in London. Boswell wrote Johnson next year of his "peculiar satisfaction in celebrating the festival of Easter in St Paul's Cathedral; that to my fancy it appeared like going up to Jerusalem at the feast of the Passover; and that the strong devotion which I felt on that occasion diffused its influence over my mind through the rest of the year." Johnson wrote him a kind and wise letter on the place of fancy in religion—"a faculty bestowed by our Creator," but still "we may take Fancy for a companion, but must follow Reason as our guide. . . . We know and ought to remember that the Universal Lord is every where present." "I love you too well," he concludes, "to be careless when you are serious." The next year (1775) Boswell

[1] *Hebrides*, p. 382 and note.
[2] Letter to Temple, 19 June 1775.
[3] *Life*, ii. 269 n.
[4] *Life*, ii. 66.

had his wish, and his letters to Temple are a curious commentary on his pious fancy.[1]

It is remarkable with what sympathy Boswell understood and interpreted the religious life of Johnson—his queer fasts on Good Friday, which Cowper thought so foolish and Walpole so ridiculous—his prayers, his sense of sin and unworthiness. "I never shall forget the tremulous earnestness with which he pronounced the awful petition in the Litany: 'In the hour of death, and at the day of judgement, good LORD deliver us.'" Johnson never liked allusions to death.

Johnson's goodness of heart is evident in all his dealings with Boswell, but he was as good to those who had nothing to offer—to the little street Arabs asleep in doorways, into whose hands he used to slip pennies that they might be able to buy breakfasts, and this in days before his pension secured himself against want—to Levett ("Levett, Madam, is a brutal fellow, but I have a good regard for him; for his brutality is in his manners, not his mind")—to Poll ("a stupid slut . . . when I talked to her tightly and closely, I could make nothing of her; she was wiggle-waggle, and I could never persuade her to be categorical")—and the rest of the "Seraglio" as Boswell called these distressed ladies—down to the poor girl he found lying in the street and lifted up and carried home on his back, and whom he had nursed into health and re-established in life.[2]

SERVIENDUM ET LAETANDUM, Johnson wrote in his pocket-book at Easter 1777.[3] And Boswell can shew how indeed he did serve—served man, in the modern sense, and served God in the older sense, with less of patronage and priggishness in it—and how he fulfilled the other duty of cheerfulness. "Sir," he said to Boswell, "I have never complained of the world; nor do I think that I have reason to complain" (1781).[4]

---

[1] Letters to Temple, 4 April, 17 April, 10 May 1775.
[2] *Life*, iv. 321. [3] *Life*, iii. 99. [4] *Life*, iv. 116.

"I cannot omit to mention," says Boswell, "that I never knew any man who was less disposed to be querulous than Johnson. Whether the subject was his own situation, or the state of the public, or the state of human nature in general, though he saw the evils, his mind was turned to resolution, and never to whining or complaint."[1] The race was *not* degenerating as Goldsmith held[2]; the world was not half as wicked as it was represented,[3] and there was *not* less religion in the nation now than formerly,[4] and when Boswell had "the black dog," he recommended him a piece of antiquarian research and some obedience to his father.[5]

"Clear your *mind* of cant," he would say.[6] "Don't, Sir, accustom yourself to use big words for little matters."[7] "Well, Madam, and you ought to be perpetually watching. It is more from carelessness about truth than from intentional lying that there is so much falsehood in the world."[8] This was what he hammered into his biographers, and one of them learnt the lesson, took notes as he went, and spent years in verifying what he wrote in the *Life of Johnson*. "The man is a kind of martyr to truthfulness," said Professor Freeman, the historian, "who can withstand the temptation of making a good story still better."[9] Boswell withstood it.

We must not forget the nonsense they enjoyed together. The friendship seems one-sided which is not a partnership in both grave and gay. "No, Sir, Warton has taken to an odd mode. For example; he'd write thus:

> Hermit hoar, in solemn cell
> Wearing out life's evening gray.

Gray evening is common enough; but *evening gray* he'd think fine,—Stay;—we'll make out the stanza:

---

[1] *Life*, ii. 357. [2] *Life*, ii. 217. [3] *Johns. Misc.*, i. 262.
[4] *Life*, ii. 96.   [5] *Life*, iii. 414. [6] *Life*, iv. 221.
[7] *Life*, i. 471.   [8] *Life*, iii. 228. [9] *Essays*, ii. 168.

> Hermit hoar, in solemn cell,
>   Wearing out life's evening gray;
> Smite thy bosom, sage, and tell,
>   What is bliss? and which the way?

BOSWELL. 'But why smite his bosom, Sir?'
JOHNSON. 'Why to shew he was in earnest,' (smiling).

—He at a later period added the following stanza:

> Thus I spoke; and speaking sigh'd;
>   —Scarce repress'd the starting tear;—
> When the smiling sage replied—
>   —Come, my lad, and drink some beer." [1]

It is to Boswell we owe the word "smiling" in the last line but one. Johnson accepted it; "he was then very pleased that I should preserve it." "Why, Sir," he once said, "the sense of ridicule is given us and may be lawfully used." [2] Boswell went further. "A good pun," he held, "may be admitted among the smaller excellencies of lively conversation." [3] Johnson held not.

They did not always agree so well, for it must not be thought that Boswell accepted all his friend's opinions. They differed as to the American War. "I am growing more and more an American," wrote Boswell to Temple (12 Aug. 1775), "I see the unreasonableness of taxing them without the consent of their Assemblies; I think our Ministry are mad in undertaking this desperate war." Johnson's view was quite as distinct: "'I am willing to love all mankind, *except an American*' ... calling them 'Rascals—Robbers—Pirates'; and exclaiming 'he'd burn and destroy them.'" [4] Miss Seward remonstrating, he "roared out another tremendous volley, which one might fancy could be heard across the Atlantic." No part of the world, he wrote in *Taxation no Tyranny*, has yet had

[1] *Life*, iii. 159. [2] *Life*, iii. 379.
[3] *Life*, iv. 316. [4] *Life*, iii. 290.

"reason to rejoice that Columbus found at last reception and employment."[1]

This was not pure Toryism. "How is it," he asked, "that we hear the loudest *yelps* for liberty among the drivers of negroes?"[2] And once "when in company with some very grave men at Oxford, his toast was, 'Here's to the next insurrection of negroes in the West Indies.'" He had a negro, Francis Barber, in his house for years, whom he educated, and who was supposed to be his servant. Boswell wishes to enter his "most solemn protest" against "the wild and dangerous attempt ... to abolish so very important and necessary a branch of commercial interest" as the Slave Trade. It would involve robbery to our fellow-subjects, and "it would be extreme cruelty to the African Savages, a portion of whom it saves from massacre, or intolerable bondage in their own country, and introduces into a much happier state of life; especially now when their passage to the West Indies and their treatment there is humanely regulated. To abolish that trade would be to

'—— Shut the gates of mercy on mankind.'

Whatever may have passed elsewhere concerning it, the HOUSE OF LORDS is wise and independent."[3] —The Lords as ever the guardians of national righteousness and the Gospel.

With the death of Johnson the history of Boswell ends for most readers, though he lived for eleven more years, and spent seven of them on his great task with the steady aid of Malone. Malone, so far a stranger to him, picked up some proofs of the *Hebrides* at the printer's, and thence came an introduction and the intimacy of common labours. Boswell's letters to Temple make a melancholy story. He never had wished to be at the Scottish bar, and in his later years tried the English. Circuit he did not like—

---

[1] *Life*, i. 455; Johnson's *Works*, viii. 167. Cf. *Life*, iv. 250.
[2] Johnson's *Works*, viii. 204.   [3] *Life*, iii. pp. 200-204.

really because he did not like lawyers. The hard, shrewd, successful type saw nothing in him but a butt, and there was nothing to check their vulgar impulse to make game of him. But there are gleams of brightness. "I was the great man (as we used to say) at the late Drawing-room, in a suit of imperial blue lined with rose-coloured silk and ornamented with rich gold wrought buttons. What a motley scene in life!"[1]

He hoped for a seat in Parliament. Johnson and his friends had doubted whether it were desirable for him, but he longed for it.[2] The first Lord Lonsdale[3] let him imagine he would give him one and kept him for months in attendance, so that in fact Mrs Boswell died alone, in spite of her husband's wild chase from London to be with her (1789). And then the blunt words: "I suppose you thought I was to bring you into Parliament; I never had any such intention," ended all.[4]

There is a curious reminder of his political activities, and his one time fancy that he might represent Ayrshire, in Burns' *Earnest Cry and Prayer to the Scotch Representatives in the House of Commons.*

> Could I like Montgomeries fight,
> Or gab like Boswell,

says the poet. It is interesting to think of these two men together, contemporaries (Burns nineteen years the younger), and both from the same region. There are things common to both—the keen sensibility, the love of men and women, the gift of being liked, the gift of expression, and the fatal gift of being all things to all men. "The writing of imaginative literature," it has been well said, "had the curious effect of disintegrating personality, and strongly individual men were incapable of it. This was really what was meant by the artistic

---

[1] Letter to Temple, 31 March 1789. [2] *Life*, iv. 267.
[3] The earl who kept the young Wordsworths out of their own.
[4] Letter to Temple, 21 June 1790.

temperament—an unstable personality moving in many worlds, and not firmly anchored in any."[1] To apply this sweepingly to men of such genius as Burns and Boswell would be rough and ready criticism at best, and yet the words are painfully suggestive, painfully near the fact, in each case. "In truth," wrote Boswell to Temple (21 July 1790), "I am sensible that I do not sufficiently 'try my ways,' as the Psalmist says, and am even almost inclined to think with you, that my great oracle Johnson did allow too much credit to good principles, without good practice."[2]

But Johnson loved Boswell, and we love him—the more as we know him better. He has given us a great book—"the most entertaining book you ever read," he promised Temple (8 Feb. 1790)—but he has given us more. He has drawn us a great man—with all the uncompromising fidelity of a whole-hearted believer in him; "he would not cut off his claws," he told Hannah More, "nor make a tiger a cat to please anybody." It is not every one who can "carry a bon-mot," as one of the great circle remarked, and the fugitive charm of talk is the hardest thing to keep on paper—if one is loyal to fact.[3] And, again, the great man may be lost in the anecdotes about him. But of Boswell's book Sir Joshua Reynolds, a great man himself and a life-long friend of Johnson, said that it might be depended upon as if delivered upon oath; and Burke, another friend of many years, said "he is greater in Boswell's books than his own." But perhaps as good a measure of what Boswell has done may be had from the curious interest with which we read the question put by Horace Walpole to Mason in a letter of 1776: "Will Dr Johnson,

---

[1] *The Comments of Bagshot*, ch. 4.   [2] Cf. *Life*, iv. 397.
[3] *Cf.* Jowett's words (Jowett's *Life*, ii. 33): "Let any one who believes that an ordinary man can write a great biography make the experiment himself ... describe the most interesting dinner party" ... and compare it with the Dilly dinner.

and I know not most of the rest by name, interest the next age like Addison, Prior, Pope, and Congreve?"[1] He had no doubt as how the question would be answered; nor have we; and the discrepancy is explained when we remember that he reckoned without Boswell.

If, as Charles Lamb suggested, we should have a "grace before books," what should we say when we have read through Boswell? What should we feel? Johnson used to say that "want of tenderness was want of parts and was no less a proof of stupidity than depravity."[2] Is he not right? What could be expected of a man who could read the *Life of Johnson* and the *Journal of a Tour to the Hebrides* and remain so incapable of tenderness as not to love the man who wrote them?

[1] Letter No. 1732 in Mrs Toynbee's edition. [2] *Life*, ii. 122.

CRABBE

ONE day at the end of February or in the beginning of March 1781 a letter of some little length was delivered to Edmund Burke. The American War was more and more clearly approaching its inevitable end, and the final struggle of the Opposition with Lord North was at its fiercest. Burke was living under the greatest pressure that a statesman can know, and one glance at the letter might, in the opinion of most men of affairs, have absolved him from further attention to it.

The first paragraph explained the situation perfectly[1] —"I am one of those outcasts on the World, who are without a Friend, without Employment and without Bread." Burke was not an ordinary English gentleman unfamiliar with want. For nine years he had lived, he best knew how, for he said little of it, a life of struggle and uncertainty in London; and the greatest of his friends could tell the same story—indeed had told it:

>Yet think what ills the scholar's life assail,
>Toil, envy, want, the Patron, and the jail.

"Having used every honest means in vain," said the writer of the letter, "I yesterday confess'd my Inabillity, and obtain'd with much entreaty and as the greatest Favor, a week's forbearance, when I am positively told, that I must pay the money or prepare for a Prison." So familar was the story; and the conclusion was the natural one. "I have no other Pretensions to your Favor than that I am an unhappy [man]. It is not easy to support the thoughts of Confinement; and I am

[1] Transcribed from fac-simile in R. Huchon, *George Crabbe and His Times*.

Coward enough to dread such an end to my suspense. Can you, Sir, in any Degree, aid me with Propriety? Will you ask any Demonstrations of my veracity? I have imposed upon myself, but I have been guilty of no other Imposition. Let me, if possible, interest your Compassion."

The writer had come to London in the previous April with three pounds, hoping that his abilities would procure him more—"of these I had the highest opinion, and a poetical vanity contributed to my delusion." "Time, Reflection, and Want, have shown me my mistake. I see my trifles in that which I think the true Light; and whilst I deem them such, have yet the Opinion that holds them superior to the common run of Poetical Publications." Some of these trifles he enclosed, concluding with a proposal to call on Burke next day.

Burke looked at the MS. poems. They were on the whole imitative and showed the influence of Pope. But amongst them were some passages, at least, of a poem on the author's native village, and one of these caught Burke's attention.

> As on their neighbouring beach yon swallows stand,
> And wait for favouring winds to leave the land,
> While still for flight the ready wing is spread:
> So waited I the favouring hour, and fled—
> Fled from these shores where guilt and famine reign,
> And cried, Ah! hapless they who still remain;
> Who still remain to hear the ocean roar,
> Whose greedy waves devour the lessening shore;
> Till some fierce tide, with more imperious sway,
> Sweeps the low hut and all it holds away;
> When the sad tenant weeps from door to door,
> And begs a poor protection from the poor.[1]

---

[1] George Crabbe, the poet's son, in his life of his father prefixed as vol. i. to the eight-volume edition of the poetical works, 1834—and as interesting a volume as any of them—(cited below as G. Crabbe), says (p. 9) that he often heard his father describe just such an occurrence which took place on 1 Jan. 1779.

CRABBE

Whatever the value of the other pieces, it was obvious that here was a voice and not an echo. This passage was never written from books—it came from life, and at no long remove. The writer had his eye well upon his object, and he wrote under the pressure of real feeling. The language was his own; it was close up to the fact —simple, strong and true. If the other poems were weaker, that was of no matter, for it is what he can do upon his highest levels that makes a poet's worth.

Next day the young man called as he had promised. He was tall and well-made, and his dress was neat, if well-worn. He had always remembered "appearance," in spite of the dread of "accompanying fashion with fasting";[1] but as long ago as the previous May his coat ("it's the vilest thing in the world to have but one coat,"[2] he wrote to his sweetheart at the time) had met with an accident and he had mended it himself. He wore a fashionable tie-wig;[3] he had lodged with a hair-dresser of some celebrity in his calling, who had recommended this piece of elegance. He spoke with a Suffolk accent —years later critical neighbours in the Midlands remarked it; he talked "through his nose," they said. But perhaps Burke looked most at his strong open face and read there the confirmation of the letter. "The night after I delivered my letter at his door," the poet said long years after to Lockhart, "I was in such a state of agitation that I walked Westminster Bridge backwards and forwards until daylight."[4]

Burke was taken with George Crabbe, gave him money to pay his debts and invited him to come and be his guest in London, and afterwards at Beaconsfield. He introduced him to his friends, to Dr Johnson, to Sir Joshua Reynolds, to Charles James Fox. He made interest for him with Dodsley, the publisher, and with the Lord Chancellor Thurlow.[5] He read and criticized his verses,

---
[1] G. Crabbe, p. 65. [2] G. Crabbe, p. 67. [3] G. Crabbe, p. 51.
[4] G. Crabbe, p. 281. [5] G. Crabbe, p. 101.

and altogether set the young poet on his feet. Such kindness and such respect from Burke went far beyond any material gift; it gave him confidence in himself and a sense of his own work, which in this case never fell away into vanity or arrogance. *Laudari a laudato viro* is a rare happiness, and it goes far to make a man. Moreover, Crabbe's son found out—though his father was not his informant[1]—that the first use he made of his new prosperity was to seek out and relieve some poor men of letters, whom he had known when sharing their wretchedness in the city; and indeed in later years whenever he went to London he took pains to find others by whom he might do the same.

The lines about the village, which impressed Burke, come from Crabbe's most significant poem—the poem in which he first definitely found himself, and which throughout bears the stamp of experience. The village was Aldeburgh, then a poor and squalid place,[2] bleak and barren on the coast of Suffolk. It was there that Crabbe was born on Christmas Eve 1754. His father had been a school-teacher, but had settled down as a deputy collector of salt-duties and warehouse-keeper in the Customs—a rough, able sort of man, the general *fac-totum* of the village.[3] He kept a boat, in which he took his boys fishing and sailing—and here the trials of the eldest began. "That boy," said his father, "must be a *fool*. John and Bob and Will are all of some use about a boat; but what will that *thing* ever be good for?"[4] For the elder Crabbe was a man of imperious temper and violent passions.[5] Later on in life, under the temptations of his office—for everybody in such a village had reasons for wishing a friend in the Custom-house, and most of them would go about getting one in the same native English way,—the collector fell into drinking habits. But there was another side to him, for he used to read Milton and Young and

[1] G. Crabbe, p. 102 [2] G. Crabbe, p. 9. [3] G. Crabbe, p. 5.
[4] G. Crabbe, p. 14. [5] G. Crabbe, p. 8.

other poets to his family, choosing his passages "with remarkable judgment and with powerful effect," his son said[1]; and, for all his rough words, he saw to it that his eldest boy had all the education he could provide,[2] and apprenticed him at last to a surgeon. This, in those easy days, was opening the door to a medical career. Crabbe's mother was a gentle creature, patient and affectionate, simple in her religious ideas and practical, but not a happy woman.[3] Her husband was eight years her junior, and as life wore on his tipsiness intensified her unhappiness, and this left a deep impression on the eldest boy, who had at times to intervene in the quarrels. This was the domestic background. There was the same poverty among the neighbours, the same struggle for existence against a barren land and an encroaching sea. Drinking and smuggling were two of the chief outlets for energy, and they produced their usual effect on character—coarseness, recklessness and suspicion.

In 1771 Crabbe was settled with a Mr Page, a surgeon at Woodbridge.[4] Like Burns he became a member of young men's discussion society. One of his friends in this club was courting a lady at Framlingham, whose bosom friend lived some two miles off at Parham, and one day he carelessly told Crabbe he would take him over with him, as "there is a young lady there, that would just suit you."[5] Crabbe was about seventeen, so of course he went. He met Miss Sarah Elmy; he fell in love and so did she; and a new life was opened for the young poet. Of course he wrote verses for her—verses of the approved style:

> My Mira, shepherds, is as fair
> As sylvan nymphs who haunt the vale,
> As sylphs who dwell in purest air,
> As fays who skim the dusky dale,

---

[1] G. Crabbe, p. 12.   [2] G. Crabbe, p. 14.   [3] G. Crabbe, p. 30.
[4] G. Crabbe, p. 20.   [5] G. Crabbe, p. 21.

> As Venus was when Venus fled
> From watery Triton's oozy bed ; etc.[1]

Probably these lines were not sent to Burke.

At Parham Crabbe found another stratum of English life from that which he had known at Aldeburgh, and here again he began to receive impressions, clear and indelible as all his impressions were. So keen an observer could not miss the contrasts between the two homes, nor the similarities beneath the contrasts. Miss Elmy's surroundings can best be described in the words of her son.[2] She lived with her uncle and aunt in those days, and twenty years later she took her little George Crabbe (the fourth of the name) to see her old home.

"I was introduced to a set of manners and customs, of which there remains, perhaps, no counterpart in the present day. My great-uncle's establishment was that of the first-rate yeoman of that period—the Yeoman that already began to be styled by courtesy an Esquire. Mr Tovell might possess an estate of some eight hundred pounds per annum, a portion of which he himself cultivated. Educated at a mercantile school, he often said of himself 'Jack will never make a gentleman'; yet he had a native dignity of mind and manners, which might have enabled him to pass muster in that character with any but very fastidious critics. His house was large, and the surrounding moat, the rookery, the ancient dovecot and the well-stored fishponds, were such as might have suited a gentleman's seat of some consequence; but one side of the house immediately overlooked a farm-yard full of all sorts of domestic animals and the scene of constant bustle and confusion."

The house had a spacious hall and some fine rooms, but all these were "*tabooed* ground, and made use of on great and solemn occasions only—such as rent-days, and an occasional visit with which Mr Tovell was honoured

---

[1] G. Crabbe, p. 24.   [2] G. Crabbe, pp. 142-144.

by a neighbouring peer. At all other times the family and their visiters lived entirely in the old-fashioned kitchen along with the servants. . . . At a very early hour in the morning the alarum called the maids, and their mistress also; and if the former were tardy, a louder alarum, and more formidable, was heard chiding the delay—not that scolding was peculiar to any occasion, it regularly ran on through all the day, like bells on harness, inspiriting the work, whether it were done ill or well. . . .

"If the sacred apartments had not been opened, the family dined on this wise;—the heads seated in the kitchen at an old table; the farm-men standing in the adjoining scullery, door open—the female servants at a side-table, called a *bouter*;—with the principals, at the table, perchance some travelling rat-catcher, or tinker, or farrier, or an occasional gardener in his shirt-sleeves, his face probably streaming with perspiration. My father well describes, in 'The Widow's Tale,' my mother's situation, when living in her younger days at Parham."

The evening entertainment deserves quotation. "The bottles (Mr Tovell's tea equipage) [were] placed on the table; and as if by instinct some old acquaintance would glide in for the evening's carousal, and then another, and another. If four or five arrived, the punch-bowl was taken down, and emptied and filled again. But, whoever came, it was comparatively a dull evening, unless two especial Knights Companions were of the party;—one was a jolly old farmer, with much of the person and humour of Falstaff, a face as rosy as brandy could make it, and an eye teeming with subdued merriment; for he had that prime quality of a joker, superficial gravity:—the other was a relative of the family, a wealthy yeoman, middle-aged, thin and muscular. He was a bachelor, and famed for his indiscriminate attachment to all who bore the name of woman—young or aged, clean or dirty, a lady or a gipsy, it mattered not to him; all were equally admired. He had peopled the village green; and it was remarked, that, whoever was the mother, the children might be recognised in an instant to belong to him. Such was the strength of his constitution, that, though he seldom went to bed sober, he retained a clear eye and stentorian voice to his eightieth year, and coursed when he was ninety. He sometimes rendered the colloquies over the bowl peculiarly piquant; and so soon as his voice began to be elevated, one or two of the inmates, my father and mother for example, withdrew with Mrs Tovell into her own *sanctum sanctorum*; but I, not being supposed capable of understanding much of what might be said, was allowed to linger on the skirts of the festive circle; and the servants, being considered much in the same point of view as the animals dozing on the hearth, remained, to have the full benefit of their wit, neither producing the slightest restraint, nor feeling it themselves."

Mr Tovell's own ways of speech were direct, and sometimes embarrassing. When his daughter died in 1778, he was deeply moved. She had been his heir, and now all would pass to Miss Elmy and her sisters, his nieces. Crabbe found him sitting "in stern silence; but the tears coursed each other over his manly face. His wife was weeping bitterly, her head reclining on the table. One or two female friends were there to offer consolation. After a long silence, Mr Tovell observed,—'She is now out of *everybody's* way, poor girl!' One of the females remarked that it was wrong, very wrong, to grieve, because she was gone to a better place. 'How do I know where she is gone?' was the bitter reply; and then there was another long silence."[1]

Inspired by Sarah Elmy, Crabbe wrote a great deal of verse. Some of it reached the poet's corner of a journal. But he had higher ambitions; and in 1775 C. Punchard,

[1] G. Crabbe, p. 40.

Bookseller in the Butter Market at Ipswich, published his poem, entitled *Inebriety*, at the price of eighteenpence. The eighteenth century was the Golden Age of impossible didactic poems with the most amazing subjects—perhaps none to eclipse this, unless Coleridge actually saw the " Oxford copy of verses on the two Suttons, commencing with

'Inoculation, heavenly maid! descend!'"[1]

Crabbe's work is frankly of the school of Pope. What is more curious, many passages of it are closely modelled on some of Pope's, line by line, the more important words and the rhymes re-appearing, though the matter is quite different. The rest of the poem is proof enough that Crabbe could write as well without a model. To make his plan of procedure still plainer, he printed as footnotes the passages from Pope which he used in this strange way.

Inebriety is the work of a young man, as yet uncertain of himself and his aims. It is confused as a whole, and often in its parts. But there are things in it that suggest his future development. The very title, and the subject which it faithfully represents, show already that habit of drawing his material from what he saw, which gives its force and veracity to all Crabbe's better work. And there are passages curiously prophetic. The quarrel of the drunkard with his wife on coming home resembles a similar scene in *The Village*, though it lacks the clear hard outline and the deeper earnestness which make that picture. He is not yet sure whether to be satirical or to paint exactly what he sees. But the Vicar, in the second part, is drawn with a more definite aim, the passage ending with the thought:

Vicars must with discretion go astray
While Bishops may be d——n'd the nearest way.

There are weak lines in the passage—a good many of

[1] *Biographia Literaria*, chap. xviii. (end).

them—but there are strong ones; and after all a picture is drawn. There the Vicar is—disorderly in dress, and in conduct. But it may be urged at the same time that he is drawn from without, and we are much less sure of his enjoyment of all he hears than we are of the tilting of his wig,—and still less sure of the motive of his retirement,[1] though there are minds more tolerant of indecency than of blasphemy. Finally, something is lost when the poet leaves the real for the conjectural, and commits himself to the damnation of bishops.

One more passage calls for quotation, for in it we find already in sufficient clearness a conviction which Crabbe held to the end. This is one of the places where he so curiously uses Pope.

> Nor think of Nature's state I make a jest:
> The state of Nature is a state undrest;
> The love of Pleasure at our birth began,
> Pleasure the aim of all things, and of Man.
> Law then was not, the swelling flame to kill,
> Man walk'd with beast, and—so he always will.

Inebriety made no fortune, and its author had to do his best at his medicine. He set up on his own account in Aldeburgh, after humiliating experiences on his father's quay. But he did not succeed. His neighbours reflected that he got most of his remedies for nothing in the ditches, for his love and knowledge of Botany could not be hid; and they decided that he could therefore have little claim on them for payment.[2] When in 1778 the Warwickshire militia were quartered in the town, he did better. He made friends among the officers, and the Colonel gave him Hudson's *Flora Anglica*, and some other text-books on Botany written in Latin. This drove him to study Latin more seriously; and from that he took

---

[1] "Rather than hear his God blasphem'd," slavish custom has taught him to retire.

[2] G. Crabbe, p. 34.

to Horace, in whom he found a congenial spirit. The pungent common-sense, the matter-of-fact thinking and the native kindliness of the Roman must have suited his temper exactly. Horace was not, however, his only classical reading. But neither Latin poetry nor Botany brought marriage nearer. So in 1780 he made his bold venture and went to London to live by literature.

Burke helped him to the publication of his *Library* (1781), but here again he is still doing other men's work. It was clear enough to Burke that he must have a profession, for he could not live on his poetry; and that profession, it was decided, was to be the Church. He was duly ordained after receiving a Lambeth degree for the purpose, and from now onward the story of his life is largely one of livings. Like the Englishmen of his day he was very frank about it all. A pluralist and an absentee, who got his work done by curates, he was honestly careful about his dues. No worse than his contemporaries, he was not much better. Religion, as we can see from early diaries, had always been a real thing with him, but there was no strong evangelic compulsion about his call to the ministry. He was much away from his parishes, and meanwhile the Methodists found stronger foothold in them. This annoyed him a great deal, and he preached and wrote against them. Yet he was no bigot—on the contrary he was a man of moderate views and kindly nature—a mild Whig, in fact, but inflexible, as the Trowbridge Tories found in the 1819 election when they tried to stop him from voting. They might kill him, he said, if they chose, but while he lived he would vote; and he did vote.[1]

Ordination was followed by marriage (Dec. 1783) and family life. His wife's health however declined after the death of one of their children in 1796, and she had long seasons of melancholia,—tenderly watched over by her husband.[2] Long after her death, their son found

[1] G. Crabbe, p. 220.   [2] G. Crabbe, p. 211.

her wedding-ring, nearly worn through before she died. It was in a paper, which bore the words:

> The ring so worn, as you behold,
> So thin, so pale, is yet of gold.
> The passion such it was to prove;
> Worn with life's cares, love yet was love.[1]

George Crabbe, the younger, leaves no doubt upon his reader's mind of what a happy childhood the poet, whose own had been so gloomy, made for his boys—"his old fellows" as he called them. The son's account of his father shows a side of him which might not have been guessed from his poetry; but once known, it fits in well.

In 1783, some months before his marriage, Crabbe brought out his *Village*. Burke had talked it over with him as he worked at it, and Dr Johnson's aid had been enlisted by Sir Joshua Reynolds. "Sir," he wrote in returning the MS. to Sir Joshua, "I have sent you back Mr Crabbe's poem; which I read with great delight. It is original, vigorous, and elegant. The alterations which I have made, I do not require him to adopt; for my lines are, perhaps, not often better than his own: but he may take mine and his own together, and, perhaps, between them, produce something better than either.—He is not to think his copy wantonly defaced; a wet sponge will wash all the red lines away, and leave the pages clean.—His Dedication will be least liked: it were better to contract it into a short, sprightly address.—I do not doubt of Mr Crabbe's success. I am, Sir, your most humble servant, Sam. Johnson." The letter is dated March 4, 1783.[2]

In particular, Johnson had rewritten lines 15-20 (as they are now numbered), and Crabbe did not use the sponge

---

[1] G. Crabbe, p. 214. *Cf.* "The wedding ring that to the finger grew," *Tales of the Hall*, xi.

[2] Printed by Crabbe himself in preface of 1807, vol ii. p. 12. A. W. Ward's edition, vol. i. 92.

but printed the red lines—the first four stronger than his own.

> On Mincio's banks, in Cæsar's bounteous reign,
> If Tityrus found the golden age again,
> Must sleepy bards the flattering dream prolong,
> Mechanick echoes of the Mantuan song?
> From Truth and Nature shall we widely stray,
> Where Virgil, not where Fancy, leads the way?

Crabbe's last couplet was better. The fifth line had no red ink. The two ran thus:

> From Truth and Nature shall we widely stray
> Where Fancy leads or Virgil led the way?

Boswell explains why the poem pleased Johnson; "Its sentiments as to the false notions of rustick happiness and rustick virtue were quite congenial with his own."[1]

Virgil was in some degree to blame for the prevalence in English poetry of easy and artificial idylls of pastoral life—so far to blame as being the author of idylls himself, which owed much of their inspiration to books. Still his debt to Theocritus was not of the same kind as that of the English pastoral-writers to himself—it was the debt of the greater poet to the less. But Crabbe was perhaps hardly thinking of the smaller poets of England so much as of Gray and Goldsmith. Gray's *Elegy* had been completed in 1750, and Goldsmith's *Deserted Village* was published in 1770. Each spoke of village life from a point aloof, in meditation and in retrospect. Crabbe looked at it in another way. His verse has the sharp edge that fresh experience gives.

> The Village Life and every care that reigns
> O'er youthful peasants and declining swains;
> What labour yields, and what, that labour past,
> Age, in its hour of languor, finds at last;

[1] *Life of Johnson* (G. Birkbeck Hill) iv. 175.

What form the real picture of the poor,
Demand a song—the Muse can give no more.

As for the amorous swains of convention, who pipe to their nymphs, they have not come within his experience. In the case of the men he knows, amorous pains are

The only pains, alas! they never feel.

Fields and flocks have their charms, but when he begins to "trace the poor laborious natives"

And see the midday sun, with fervid ray,
On their bare heads and dewy temples play;
While some, with feebler heads and fainter hearts,
Deplore their fortune, yet sustain their parts:
Then shall I dare these real ills to hide
In tinsel trappings of poetic pride?

Instead of some "cool sequester'd vale of life" he draws the actual Aldeburgh which he knew.

Lo! where the heath, with withering brake grown o'er,
Lends the light turf that warms the neighbouring poor;
From thence a length of burning sand appears,
Where the thin harvest waves its wither'd ears;
Rank weeds, that every art and care defy,
Reign o'er the land, and rob the blighted rye:

and then, steadily and relentlessly, till the poet seems forgotten in the botanist, he catalogues the weeds, every one of which heightens the sense of waste and desolation. Farming must obviously be a hard task, but perhaps sometimes a light surprises the poet as he looks over his native soil. But no! even summer and the sunshine cannot relieve the horrible impression of the earth's poverty and sterility, as the simile which follows will show—a simile as strange as any a poet ever used to tell of what sunshine can do.

With mingled tints the rocky coasts abound,
And a sad splendour vainly shines around.

CRABBE

> So looks the nymph whom wretched arts adorn,
> Betray'd by man, then left for man to scorn;
> Whose cheek in vain assumes the mimic rose,
> While her sad eyes the troubled breast disclose;
> Whose outward splendour is but folly's dress,
> Exposing most, when most it gilds distress.

And the people? How often, wrote Goldsmith,

> How often have I bless'd the coming day,
> When toil remitting lent its turn to play,
> And all the village train, from labour free,
> Led up their sports beneath the spreading tree,
> While many a pastime circled in the shade,
> The young contending as the old surveyed;
> And many a gambol frolick'd o'er the ground,
> And sleights of art and feats of strength went round.

Not so at Aldeburgh—

> Here joyless roam a wild amphibious race,
> With sullen wo display'd in every face;
> Who far from civil arts and social fly
> And scowl at strangers with suspicious eye,

There are no rural games here. The inhabitants have other uses for nightfall, for it is then that the freighted pinnace comes in and her cargo has to be unloaded and out of sight before daybreak; or else there is wrecking to be done.

> How jocund did they drive their team afield,

wrote Gray of his villagers, roused by "the breezy call of incense-breathing morn." Crabbe takes a different view of fieldwork; he had seen it in the rain—when Gray was safe and dry in his College rooms.

> See them alternate suns and showers engage,
> And hoard up aches and anguish for their age;

> Through fens and marshy moors their steps pursue,
> When their warm pores imbibe the evening dew.

But, suggests Gray, "children run to lisp their sire's return" to the blazing hearth. No, it is to other scenes that the labourer comes home, to scant fare and a comfortless hovel.

> Go, look within, and ask if peace be there:
> If peace be his—that drooping weary sire,
> Or theirs, that offspring round their feeble fire;
> Or hers, that matron pale, whose trembling hand
> Turns on the wretched hearth th' expiring brand.

He passes on to a painful picture of old age. Once the man won prizes for the straightness of his furrows. Now he is only fit to feed sheep, if fit for that—disdained by rich and poor, and the next stage must be the workhouse, with its putrid vapours, and broken families, where the happiest are the insane.

> Say ye, oppress'd by some fantastic woes,
> Some jarring nerve that baffles your repose;
> Who press the downy couch, while slaves advance
> With timid eye to read the distant glance;
> Who with sad prayers the weary doctor tease,
> To name the nameless ever-new disease;
> Who with mock patience dire complaints endure,
> Which real pain, and that alone, can cure—
> How would ye bear in real pain to lie,
> Despised, neglected, left alone to die?

And he draws another picture of such a last illness in dirt and solitude. The patient indeed is visited by the parish doctor, "a potent quack, long versed in human ills." And now, before the poor man dies,

> Fain would he ask the parish-priest to prove
> His title certain to the joys above—

the irony of the contrast here is not emphasized by Crabbe, but not unfelt.

> And doth not he, the pious man, appear,
> He, "passing rich on forty pounds a-year"?

No, it is not Goldsmith's brother, but "a shepherd of a different stock," who hunts in the morning and plays whist at night—

> A jovial youth, who thinks his Sunday's task
> As much as God or man can fairly ask.

What can he do

> To raise the hope he feels not, or with zeal
> To combat fears that e'en the pious feel?

On Sundays it is true there is a break in labour, grudged by the masters. Yet the day ends in drunkenness, and the churl goes home to "strike the bare bosom of his teeming mate"; or else in immorality, or poaching. Such is village life, man and nature alike scant of beauty and of love. But the poetry is saved by its elements of truth and pity.

An unexpected witness in support of Crabbe is John Wesley, who writes in his Journal (5 Nov. 1766): "In the little journeys which I have lately taken, I have thought much on the huge encomiums which have been for many ages bestowed on country life. How have all the learned world cried out,

> *O fortunati nimium sua si bona norint*
> *Agricolæ!*

But, after all, what a flat contradiction is this to universal experience? See that little house under the wood by the river side! There is rural life in perfection. How happy then is the farmer that lives there? Let us take a detail of his happiness." And Wesley runs over his early rising, his hurry and sweat, and asks where is his happiness in all that—or again in his fare? "Our eyes and ears may convince us, there is not a less happy body of men in all England than the country farmers. In general their life is supremely dull, and it is usually unhappy too; or of all people in the kingdom they are the most discontented, seldom satisfied either with God or man."

After *The Village* Crabbe published *The Newspaper*, a fairly obvious piece of work that any one could have done. And then for twenty-two years he printed nothing. He wrote a great deal—a treatise on Botany, for instance, a subject very dear to him for many years, though after his wife's death (21 Oct. 1813) he forsook it for Geology which had fewer memories for him.[1] But the Vice-Master of Trinity could not stomach the use of any language but Latin for a scientific treatise, and sooner than degrade Science the modest vicar burnt his book.[2] He burnt many. "I can well remember," wrote his son, "more than one grand incremation—not in the chimney, for the bulk of paper would have endangered the house—but in the open air—and with what glee his children vied in assisting him, stirring up the fire, and bringing him fresh loads of the fuel as fast as their little legs would enable them." Literature is not always so enjoyable.

At last in 1807 he published *The Parish Register*—a poem in three parts, constructed on a simple plan. A parish clergyman is represented as looking over his register, and the births, marriages and deaths of the year suggest to him the stories of the people connected with them. In 1810 he brought out *The Borough*, a series of twenty four poetical epistles, dealing with life in a small borough, its church and clergy and sects, law, physic and trade, players, inns, prisons and schools, with a number of stories about individual characters. Both these books were written, so to speak, out of his Aldeburgh experience. But by now the vein was fairly worked out, and he turned to Parham, and his remaining volumes consist of tales

[1] G. Crabbe, p. 259. [2] G. Crabbe, p. 134.

written of that class of society which he first learned to know at Mr Tovell's. These tales had a great vogue in their day, though the firm of Murray lost money on the last set, *Tales of the Hall*, for which in 1819 they paid Crabbe £3000—a great change from his first experience of London publishers. The tales have never ceased to find fit audience though few from Walter Scott to Edward FitzGerald. Jane Austen would playfully declare that, "if ever she married at all, she could fancy being Mrs Crabbe"—such was her admiration of the poetry, for she knew nothing of the man. It is Aldeburgh, however, rather than the *Tales*—the story of the poor, rather than the story of the middle-class—that forms the main interest of his work.

Time never dulled the impressions of his childhood, renewed as they were by constant contact with agricultural and other poverty in his own parishes, and in the parishes of others in which he served as curate. "The simple annals of my parish poor" are always the same. Rustic life is rough and hopeless; rustic morals are hard and bad, the poor as vicious as the rich. Marriage is rarely what we could call happy. Tale after tale suggests disappointment.

"But ever frowns your Hymen? man and maid
Are all repenting, suffering or betray'd?"
Forbid it, Love! we have our couples here
Who hail the day in each revolving year:
These are with us, as in the world around;
They are not frequent, but they may be found.

But when found they rarely exhilarate. Substantial farmers with solid comfortable wives, who fancy Wilton carpets and engravings, hardly make the pulse beat quicker—nor yet the extremely prudent Reuben and Rachel, who,

though fond as doves,
Were yet discreet and cautious in their loves,

—so cautious that they were well on in middle life, tanned and grey, and in "full autumn," before they had saved enough money and slowly picked up enough furniture to make marriage no longer a risk. The maxim of Nietzsche, "Live dangerously," comes to one with a genial warmth and wisdom after so long a course in prudence; and with it a wonder as to what would become of the race if no risks were ever taken in marriage.

Yet Crabbe owns himself,

> When from the cradle to the grave I look,
> Mine I conceive a melancholy book;

and so it is. Two pictures from it will suffice. The one is of the postponed marriage, a theme constantly repeated by Crabbe. The arrangements of English poor law gave a larger allowance for an illegitimate than for a legitimate child, and, though this was not the legislator's intention, the rule did not encourage marriage. Crabbe's pages show how efforts were made to counteract this by warrants—one man is offered by a justice of the peace the alternative of marriage or enlistment, and

> about to bear for life
> One certain evil, doubts 'twixt war and wife;
> But, while the falt'ring damsel takes her oath,
> Consents to wed, and so secures them both.

In the *Parish Register* the scene is in the church. It is painful in any case, and painful scenes lose nothing of their pain in Crabbe's poetry. But the power of the drawing is unmistakeable. At times his gift of seizing detail carries him too far. The items are faithfully co-ordinated, but they go beyond the power of the mind to combine, and the whole is lost in its parts. Here his full slow strength is felt and he moves the reader by the truth and pathos of what he draws so relentlessly.

Next at our altar stood a luckless pair,
Brought by strong passions and a warrant there;
By long rent cloak, hung loosely, strove the bride
From ev'ry eye what all perceived to hide;
While the boy-bridegroom, shuffling in his pace,
Now hid awhile and then exposed his face;
As shame alternately with anger strove
The brain confused with muddy ale to move.
In haste and stammering he perform'd his part,
And look'd the rage that rankled in his heart;
(So will each lover inly curse his fate,
Too soon made happy and made wise too late;)
I saw his features take a savage gloom,
And deeply threaten for the days to come.
Low spake the lass, and lisp'd and minced the while,
Look'd on the lad, and faintly tried to smile;
With soften'd speech and humbled tone she strove
To stir the embers of departed love:
While he, a tyrant, frowning walk'd before,
Felt the poor purse and sought the public door,
She, sadly following, in submission went,
And saw the final shilling foully spent;
Then to her father's hut the pair withdrew,
And bade to love and comfort long adieu!
  Ah! fly temptation, youth, refrain! refrain!
I preach for ever; but I preach in vain!

On the other side there is a picture of "a noble peasant," Isaac Ashford—an honest decent man. Superior to jealousy, the "bane of the poor," yet far from "Stoic pride"—from pride of any sort except in honest fame and in his "sturdy boys to virtuous labours trained." Apparently he could read, for the parish clerk agreed

 If fate should call him, Ashford might succeed.

He was an honest churchman contented with the established order in Church and State. "He had no party's rage "—which is generally the mark of a Tory. By the age of seventy he was frail, and a widower, and his children were poor. He was reluctant to go to the workhouse and eat the parish-bread, though he admitted that the laws which established it were kind and just. He was saved from it by death. In him we have, in fact, the ideal peasant of the old days in England, content to be a subject rather than a citizen, to take his ideas from squire and parson, to accept the system of the day and ask no questions—not a "village-Hampden." Crabbe has drawn him well—a likeable old man, but hardly all that a man might be, peasant or not.

Crabbe's later work deals with another rank of society, and it leaves the impression that the middle classes are no better than the lower; that their ideals are much the same; that pleasure, selfishness and greed rule them too; that life is generally an affair of disappointment, and at its best still dull. But the passages already quoted will suffice for our purpose. Their gist and emphasis admit of no mistake and need no corroboration.

M. Huchon, his careful French biographer, calls Crabbe the "poet of disillusion,"[1]—and if there can be such a poet, it is certainly Crabbe. On his monument, when he died in 1832, an inscription was carved, ending with a quotation from Byron, who is perhaps not often quoted in such places. "As a writer he is well described by a great contemporary as 'Nature's sternest painter yet her best.'" So says the monument; so said Byron; is it true?

Probably neither of Byron's adjectives is true. Crabbe was not stern—not in the popular sense, for his son's Biography reveals a character of considerable kindliness, —nor in a stricter sense. On the contrary, a good deal of what Byron means by his sternness is the repulsion which a nature of the softer type feels for ugliness. To bring this out more clearly, Wordsworth's account of

---

[1] R. Huchon, *George Crabbe and His Times*, p. 341.

himself may be cited. He is speaking of the strong shock which the French Revolution and its decline into tyranny produced in his life. He had to re-think everything; and he did it, being, as he says,

> Somewhat stern
> In temperament, withal a happy man,
> And therefore bold to look on painful things.

Painful things are the subjects of Crabbe's poetry, but he has not mastered them as Wordsworth did, for he has not penetrated them—he has left them painful as he found them, incomplete and therefore unhealed. And it is questionable whether he has not seen them rather more painful than they are. He is undone by his gift; his strong sense of fact overpowers him.

In *The Village* he clearly has Goldsmith's poem in his mind, as the quotation about the clergyman's income shows, and not that alone. In the *Register* he returns to it again.

> Is there a place, save one the poet sees,
> A land of love, of liberty and ease
> Where labour wearies not, nor cares suppress
> Th' eternal flow of rustic happiness? ...
> Vain search for scenes like these! no view appears,
> By sighs unruffled or unstain'd by tears;
> Since vice the world subdued and waters drown'd,
> Auburn and Eden can no more be found.

In fact, if Goldsmith had gone back to Lissoy,—which he had not done when he wrote his poem,—he might have found it not unlike Aldeburgh—the soil perhaps more fertile, but the people oppressed by labour, sickness, old age and poverty, and adding to the inevitable evils of life others of their own making—the products of drink and sin. "Sweet Auburn" is Eden before the fall. Goldsmith has let his imagination play upon his memory.

But if there is an imaginative element in "Sweet Auburn," is it less or more real for that? Is anything true till imagination touches and interprets it? Is not the past, so transmuted, one of the most powerful and operative things in our life? And does not this mean that imagination working upon memory has found the deeper truth? Can it not, and must it not, do the same for observation? And then, does it not give us a new perspective for our facts, which changes their value? Let us look at our facts again and make sure of them.

Here is a man who looks back to an Auburn grown to be a great city. It was a beautiful city as well,—and full of kind people, wise old men and noble old women; the younger, kind and tall and full of fun—even the servant girls good and wise. The city had great parks—a marvellous Botanic Garden with glass houses full of mysteries, wonderful plants from strange lands—a museum with an endless succession of rarities, of stuffed birds and beasts, model steam-boats, the Coolgardie nugget, and a policeman year after year the same, with his welcome for little children. The streets had great shops and tramways. It was a place by itself, full of charm and happiness. And if to-day it is a great rainy city on the Clyde, with dirty streets and smoky factories,—are we to say it never was the beautiful city of long ago? But it was, and it is; for children see things that middle-aged people miss. Crabbe was early middle-aged; and Goldsmith was a child to the end, and kept the light within him that transfigures and realizes (they are the same thing) in virtue of the least glimpse of happiness. There were, it is very likely, in Lissoy tippling husbands and quarrelsome wives,—but the young Goldsmith saw another side of them. Even very unpleasant people are kind to children, and this kindness may be every bit as real as the other features of their characters. " Little, nameless, unremembered acts of kindness and of love " are a portion even of a bad man's life. *The Village* is all

CRABBE

true, but it is not all the truth. Life may be very unhappy, hard and pinched and starved, full of labour and unkindness; but man can make himself at home everywhere, can overcome everything; and, if he does not find happiness, his unconquerable heart will often create it—for others, at any rate, and then it will be strange if he does not find it for himself.

When Crabbe's old man dies in *The Village*, neglected by doctor and parson, the village children cease to play for a little,

> To see the bier that bears their ancient friend:
> For he was one in all their idle sport,
> And like a monarch ruled their little court;
> The pliant bow he form'd, the flying ball,
> The bat, the wicket, were his labours all.

Can the old man have been an Irish immigrant from Auburn, who found Aldeburgh nearer than "wild Altama"?

But Goldsmith was not the child of a peasant, and he did not know the "cot"—or the hovel—from within.

Three years after the publication of *The Village*, there appeared in 1786 at Kilmarnock a volume entitled *Poems chiefly in the Scottish Dialect*. The first piece in it was *The Twa Dogs*. Cæsar was a gentleman's dog, a Newfoundland; Luath, a ploughman's collie—a dog to win anybody's heart. Cæsar wishes to know how "poor cot-folk" live at all. Their life appears to be "nought but toiling," and what they get to eat passes his comprehension. And then, he remarks, they have to bear with a good deal in the contempt of the rich and the tyranny of factors—

> I've notic'd, on our Laird's *court-day*,
> An' mony a time my heart's been wae,
> Poor *tenant bodies*, scant o' cash,
> How they maun thole a *factor's* snash:

> He'll stamp an' threaten, curse an' swear,
> He'll *apprehend* them, *poind* their gear;
> While they maun stan', with aspect humble,
> An' hear it a', an' fear an' tremble!
>   I see how folk live that hae riches;
> But surely poor-folk maun be wretches!

Somehow even here there is not as much misery suggested by the metre of Burns as by the long rhyming couplets of Crabbe; let us try it in prose. Years after the time Burns wrote: "My indignation yet boils at the recollection of the scoundrel factor's insolent letters, which used to set us all in tears"; and he tells us this factor was in his mind when Cæsar put the case to Luath. Luath's reply, then, may be taken as coming from experience — the answer of Burns' heart to its own question.

> They're no sae wretched's ane wad think;
> Tho' constantly on poortith's brink,
> They're sae accustom'd wi' the sight,
> The view o't gies them little fright.
>
> Then chance and fortune are sae guided
> They're ay in less or mair provided;
> An' tho' fatigu'd wi' close employment,
> A blink o' rest's a sweet enjoyment.
>
> The dearest comfort o' their lives,
> Their grushie weans an' faithfu' wives;
> The *prattling things* are just their pride
> That sweetens a' their fire-side.

Crabbe did not find much comfort at the fireside of the poor, and in Scotland things were no better, perhaps worse. Hovels with low roofs, clay floors, open hearths and sometimes no chimneys, are described by travellers. Everything was dirt, darkness and discomfort. "The 'ruffies,' or split roots of fir found in the peat moss were only lit for set purposes, such as family worship."[1] Burns has a picture of one of his homes which is memorable.

>   There, lanely, by the ingle-cheek,
>   I sat and ey'd the spewing reek,
>   That fill'd, wi' hoast-provoking smeek,
>   The auld clay biggin ;
>   An' heard the restless rattons squeak
>   About the riggin.

In such houses lived the Scottish peasantry. It was "not a beautiful world," Matthew Arnold thought. In just such a house Robert Burns himself was born—a humble dwelling, built by his father. "It was," wrote John Murdoch the schoolmaster, "with the exception of a little straw, literally a tabernacle of clay. In this mean cottage, of which I myself was at times an inhabitant, I really believe there dwelt a larger portion of content than in any palace of Europe. The 'Cottar's Saturday Night' will give some idea of the temper and manners that prevailed there."[2]

The Cottar's Saturday Night is connected by motto and more than motto with Gray's *Elegy*. It is open to criticism on various scores, but it is truer than some of its critics suppose. It is drawn from life, and generations of Scotsmen have pronounced it true to what is deepest in Scottish character. The "priest-like father" was William Burnes, the man of misfortunes. It was he, whose simple phrase "Let us worship God"—reinforced by his whole character—so strongly moved his son's imagination. "I have met with few," wrote the son, "who understood men, their manners and their ways

---

[1] Graham, *Social Life in Scotland*, vol. i. p. 183. *Cf.* also *Letters of John Keats*; 2 July 1818, at Dumfries: "There are plenty of wretched cottages whose smoke has no outlet but by the door."

[2] Scott Douglas' edition of Burns, vol. iv. p. 347.

equal to my father"—and he had seen many men by then, all the great and learned and successful of Scotland; and poor William Burnes was a struggling cotter, with a lot as hard as any to be found in Crabbe's *Village* or *Parish Register*.

Burns' own experiences of farm life were real enough and had little illusion about them. Yet what a kindly feeling he has for the poor farm on the clay soil, and for its weeds and its vermin along with it. The Daisy, of course, was a "wee modest crimson-tippèd flower"—that is intelligible. But the thistle was not different botanically from the thistles of Aldeburgh, yet he "spar'd the symbol dear." When he thinks of the tempest beating on the fox in the winter's night, he forgives him for "the blood-stain'd roost." And then there is the field-mouse,—a little thief, he expects; but he sees the ruin he has made of its "wee-bit housie," and apologizes.

"I never heard," he wrote, "the loud solitary whistle of the curlew, in a summer noon, or the wild mixing cadence of a troop of grey plover, in an autumnal morning, without feeling an elevation of soul like the enthusiasm of devotion or poetry. Tell me, my dear friend, to what can this be owing? Are we a piece of machinery, which, like the Æolian harp, passive, takes the impression of the passing accident? Or do these workings argue something within us above the trodden clod? I own myself partial to such proofs of those awful realities—a God that made all things—man's immaterial and immortal nature—and a world of weal or woe beyond death and the grave."

Burns certainly sees a great many more elements of joy in cottage life than were recognized by Crabbe—the happiness of childhood, the dignity of manhood, the beauty of Nature—and all this with no blinking of pain or of hardship. And what is his conclusion? This he gives is his *Epistle to Davie*.

Then let us chearfu' acquiesce ;
Nor make our scanty Pleasure less
    By pining at our state :
And, even should Misfortunes come,
I, here wha sit, hae met wi' some,
    An's thankfu' for them yet,
They gie the wit of *Age* to *Youth* ;
They let us ken oursel ;
They make us see the naked truth,
    The *real* guid and ill.
        Tho' losses, and crosses,
            Be lessons right severe,
        There's *wit* there, ye'll get there,
            Ye'll find nae other where.

"It was, I think," writes Gilbert Burns, "in the summer of 1784, when in the intervals of harder labour Robert and I were weeding in the garden, that he repeated to me the principal part of this *Epistle*."

But, it may be said, this is very well ; Burns so far is dealing mainly with one side of life, and there is little poetry to be found in crime and squalor such as Crabbe knew at Aldeburgh. A carousal in a low public-house is not a likely theme for true poetry. Yet Burns found poetry there, and in *Tam o' Shanter* and *The Jolly Beggars* he interpreted it. On this point Wordsworth's comment is very sound and illuminating. "The poet," he says, "trusting to primary instincts, luxuriates among the felicities of love and wine . . . nor does he shrink from the company of the passion of love though immoderate —from convivial pleasure though intemperate. . . .—I pity him who cannot perceive that, in all this, though there was no moral purpose, there is a moral effect.

    Kings may be blest, but Tam was glorious
    O'er a' the *ills* of life victorious. . . .

The poet, penetrating the unsightly and disgusting

surfaces of things, has unveiled with exquisite skill the finer ties of imagination and feeling, that often bind these beings to practices productive of so much unhappiness to themselves, and to those whom it is their duty to cherish;—and, as far as he puts the reader into possession of this intelligent sympathy, he qualifies him for exercising a salutary influence over the minds of those who are thus deplorably enslaved."[1]

The secret of this insight Wordsworth gives in his *Lines above Tintern Abbey*.

> With an eye made quiet by the power
> Of harmony, and the deep power of joy,
> We see into the life of things.

If Burns had only fitfully the power of harmony,—and perhaps no one has it always, not even Shakespeare—Crabbe obviously lacked "the deep power of joy." He was only a happy man as he got away from what he describes. He

> Fled from those shores where guilt and famine reign,
> And cried, 'Ah! hapless they who still remain!'

Wordsworth himself is also a poet of common life. Few poets have touched themes more humble than *The Old Cumberland Beggar*, *The Two Thieves*, *Beggars*, and *The Leech-Gatherer*. From early years his "favourite school" had been "the fields, the roads and rural lanes," and his chosen teachers were lowly people,—the pedlar, the old soldier on the lonely mountain road at night, little children—and the lesson he learnt was happiness.

So hold the happier poets, made of sterner stuff; and their poetry takes us deeper into human nature and opens up to us new depths of faith and happiness. "A Scottish peasant's life," says Carlyle, who knew that life from actual

[1] Some critics of Wordsworth might get a new idea of him if they would read his account of Tam o' Shanter in this *Letter to a Friend of Robert Burns*.

CRABBE

experience, " was the meanest and rudest of all lives, till Burns became a poet in it, and a poet of it; found it a *man's* life, and therefore significant to men. . . . To the ill-starred Burns was given the power of making man's life more venerable." Not altogether to Crabbe, for he is conscious chiefly of man's inadequacy; but he also touches truth on one side. We have to see it on both sides. We have to realize with Goldsmith, Burns and Wordsworth the potential beauty—yes! the actual beauty of human nature under the worst conditions, man's faculty of achieving greatness and happiness amid the worst environment of pain and sin; and then we have to realize with Crabbe the pressure of that environment,—to "expose ourselves to feel what wretches feel"; if we are to know what man indeed is. And if, as we read Crabbe, we remember that the squalor he knew in Aldeburgh a century and a half ago is intensified in the great cities of to-day, and that the inevitable development of industrialism, unaccompanied by quick social intelligence and the sense of social responsibility, has made the bad conditions of the past worse, because now on a larger scale and spread over wider areas, more depressing and more enslaving to human hearts and souls capable of all that Burns and Wordsworth have shown us,—will the contrast suggest anything to us of moment?

WORDSWORTH

TWO things stand out in the history of the criticism of Wordsworth—the high value set upon his poetry by the better minds of England, and the anticipation of the poet himself that it would inevitably be so. His poetry has been peculiarly associated with illumination and with happiness—and, again, this was anticipated by Wordsworth.

Coleridge wrote to Godwin (25th March 1801): "Have you seen the second volume of the *Lyrical Ballads* and the preface prefixed to the first? I should judge of a man's heart and intellect, precisely according to the degree and intensity of the admiration with which he read these poems." "Why," wrote Lamb to Bernard Barton, "a line of Wordsworth's is a lever to lift the immortal spirit."[1]

John Stuart Mill wrote in his *Autobiography* of the healing effect which Wordsworth's poetry had once had upon him. "What made Wordsworth's poems a medicine for my state of mind was that they expressed, not mere outward beauty, but states of feeling, and of thought coloured by feeling, under the excitement of beauty. . . . In them I seemed to draw from a source of inward joy, of sympathetic and imaginative pleasure, which could be shared in by all human beings . . . from them I seemed to learn what would be the perennial sources of happiness, when all the greater evils of life shall have been removed. And I felt myself at once better and happier as I came under their influence. . . . I needed to be made to feel that there was real, permanent happiness in tranquil con-

---

[1] Lamb's letter of 15th May 1824; edn. of E. V. Lucas, No. 328.

templation. Wordsworth taught me this, not only without turning away from, but with a greatly increased interest in, the common feelings and common destiny of human beings. . . . I found that he too had had similar experience to mine; that he also had felt that the first freshness of youthful enjoyment of life was not lasting; but that he had sought for compensation, and found it, in the way in which he was now teaching me to find it. The result was that I gradually, but completely, emerged from my habitual depression, and was never again subject to it."[1]

Mill's account of his experience in reading the poems agrees most curiously with the hope which Wordsworth expressed in a letter to Lady Beaumont after the issue of his volumes of 1807.[2] "Trouble not yourself about their present reception; of what moment is that compared with what I trust is their destiny? To console the afflicted, to add sunshine to daylight, by making the happy happier; to teach the young and the gracious of every age, to see, to think, and feel, and therefore to become more actively and securely virtuous—this is their office."

The fact stands then that Wordsworth's poetry has meant new happiness to men, and this not derivative. He has put them where they may find it themselves. For while his poetry is informed with a philosophy of life, it is still poetry—that glowing re-creation of the real, which is at once discovery and interpretation. Wordsworth foresaw, and in his strange open way he spoke of, the effect his work would have, for he had himself explored the way by which he would lead his followers from doubt and depression to a real happiness.

A long, quiet, contemplative existence among the lakes, confined within a narrow circle, which tended to become one of admiration, never much ruffled by external criticism, and with time progressively less and less open

---

[1] Mill, *Autobiography*, pp. 146-150; Knight, *Life of Wordsworth*, iii. 501.
[2] Knight, *Life*, ii. 88 f.

either to criticism or to contribution from without—such is the picture which men too commonly form to themselves of the life of Wordsworth; and they ask, as they well may, whether within such narrow and peaceful limits a poet can find the experience that may warrant him to describe himself as "a man speaking to men."

Such critics forget his youth and the French Revolution. There are times when a man of open sense and heart may crowd more experience into a decade or a single year than, in other periods, might be found in the most active life of eighty years. What is more serious, they forget that Wordsworth was a poet—"a creature of a fiery heart"— open in quite an exceptional way to impulses, a spirit for whom everything that moved was significant, not merely in itself, but in the liberty it gave to imagination. He felt with an intensity that most men never know—and insight after all is a matter of intensity of feeling. He felt, and the ordinary limitations thinned away like a mist on his native mountains, and he saw and knew. To such men the barest hint of experience is more full of revelation than a lifetime of incident and habit to most human beings. Everything in them is keener, acuter, more susceptible. They live among common scenes and common men, and nothing is common; everything is wonder:—

> By our own spirits are we deified,

he says, in speaking of poets, and he is right. The poets have insight that is almost uncanny.

But, quite apart from this, Wordsworth, between 1790 and 1798, went through an experience that no generation has since known. New ideals pulsed in furious life within him. New conceptions of human grandeur rose before his eyes not merely as ideals but as realizations. And then the glorious vision was blotted out by what was worse than he could have dreamed, and he moved in thick darkness and despair. But he came through it, and won his way at last to peace and vision. For any man such a story is one of high significance ; for such a man the value of it transcends our standards. His experience, its intensity and its issue give him a power to be found in none of our poets, except Shakespeare and Milton.

If it is to be understood at all, we have to take his life as a progression, and to read his poems with definite attention to their order. In this way we have a new series of indices to what he calls "the fluxes and refluxes" of his mind. Matthew Arnold fixed on the year 1808, John Morley on Waterloo, as the term of his really creative energy, neither denying value to the later poems, though this value depends on the earlier life. This earlier life then gives us the key to all he does.

Wordsworth, at any rate, thought it of moment to record the growth of his own mind. He began his autobiographical poem in 1799, laid it aside, and, resuming it in 1804, completed it in the next year. It was addressed to Coleridge, who prophesied that it would be a sacred roll among the archives of mankind [1]—

Dear shall it be to every human heart.

Every great poem is really more a new voyage of discovery than a record. The poet's aim in the *Prelude* is not so much self-revelation as self-discovery. His interest in himself is curiously impersonal. He has, says M. Legouis, penetrated "beneath the exterior of the individual, and has succeeded in reaching the essential feelings which make up the common heart of all mankind," and thus "his biography becomes almost an inward history of his generation." [2]

Beside the *Prelude*, one might almost say that in one sense the *Ode on Intimations of Immortality* tells the same story. It is written from no conventional standpoint—the child, the boy, the youth of the poem are the poet himself.

---

[1] Letter in Knight, *Life*, ii. 45.
[2] Legouis, *Early Life of Wordsworth* (tr.), p. 253.

In old age he dictated to Miss Isabella Fenwick at her request a series of notes relative to his poems, their occasions and purposes—curious notes full of a strange medley of reminiscences,[1] but precise and very accurate for matters removed by so wide a space of years.

In all this common minds may see vanity and want of humour. Wordsworth's vanity, Sir Henry Taylor said, was unlike that of ordinary men in being wholly undisguised.[2] For the rest, much of his work was done by turning a strong, simple gaze on common things, on things and beings with which persons of a keener sense of humour would have been shy of associating themselves. It was his way to submit his mind, without the prepossessions of the quicker wits and "self-applauding intellects," to impulses from everything that is real — the "rudest men" and "the meanest flower that blows." He was an explorer, and such men are often the butts of humorists; half in and half out of the realm of normal vision, on the very confines of common sense, they have for the time a certain look of absurdity, but in the long run they enlarge the range of the human mind.[3]

A man's birth is perhaps a reasonable enough point from which to begin his story. Wordsworth, then, was born at Cockermouth in Cumberland on 7 April 1770. His mother died when he was seven years old, his father when he was sixteen. Richard Wordsworth had been a solicitor and steward to Sir James Lowther, the first Earl of Lonsdale, who, for reasons of his own, quite other than those of poverty, insisted on borrowing the bulk of his steward's property, and refused to repay either him or his children. The second earl, about the year 1801, made

---

[1] *E.g.*, he discussed the effect of a heel galled by too tight a shoe, when he was composing *The White Doe*.

[2] Knight, *Life*, iii. 204.

[3] It has often been suggested that Wordsworth lacked humour. "I think," wrote Lamb to him (19 September 1814), "I have a wider range in buffoonery than you." The hesitation implied in "I think," is most engaging. No positive statement could be quite so convincing—"there lives more faith in honest doubt."

reparation, and did all in his power then and thereafter to make amends for the wrong. But the youth of the young Wordsworths was one of dependence upon their mother's relatives, persons of somewhat cold and narrow nature. The brothers and their sister Dorothy were generally separated, perhaps necessarily, as they were five in all.

William was educated at a school at Hawkshead. The discipline was easy. The boys, he says, might "have fed upon a fatter soil of arts and letters," but they had leisure for their own reading. Wordsworth read fairy-tales (which he defended in later life with an endearing vehemence [1]), *Robin Hood* and the *Arabian Nights;* later on Swift, Fielding, and *Don Quixote*. He rambled, bathed, and skated, and when he had enough money, he rode. It was now that he

> Whose favourite School
> Hath been the fields, the roads, and rural lanes,[2]

began his life-long series of acquaintances with tramps and wanderers. Old Daniel and his grandchild, thieving together, the old Cumberland beggar and the Pedlar of the *Excursion* belong to this period; and he describes it as one of the happiest and most fruitful of his life. His schoolmaster, William Taylor, served as model for Matthew.

Not less important than his reading and his strange acquaintances among men, was the fact that he was unconsciously learning what then he did not reckon as learning at all. He was receiving impressions — or "impulses" as he called them—from mountain and lake, tree and flower. His mind was feeding now of itself, as later on he had to train it to feed again, "in a wise passiveness" on the unnoticed, or half-noticed, beauty and grandeur of Nature. Nor, though he did not theorize much at the time upon it, was it merely of Nature that

---

[1] *Prelude*, v. 298 ff.   [2] *Excursion*, ii. 28.

he was conscious—perhaps there was Something in Nature, if we are to give real meaning to his words of later years.

> Wisdom and Spirit of the Universe!
> Thou Soul that art the eternity of thought,
> That givest to forms and images a breath
> And everlasting motion, not in vain
> By day or starlight thus from my first dawn
> Of childhood didst thou intertwine for me
> The passions that build up our human soul;
> Not with the mean and vulgar works of man,
> But with high objects, with enduring things—
> With life and nature, purifying thus
> The elements of feelings and of thought,
> And sanctifying, by such discipline,
> Both pain and fear, until we recognise
> A grandeur in the beatings of the heart.
> Nor was this fellowship vouchsafed to me
> With stinted kindness.[1]

As he says a little further on—

> The earth
> And common face of Nature spake to me
> Rememberable things.[2]

He heard and he remembered, but he did not yet perhaps notice very much.

Yet sometimes it was impossible not to notice. The most famous occasion of this kind he recalls at some length, for it was one of the earliest of those strange experiences he was to have so often, when through the usual and the calculable the utterly strange and unaccountable broke through upon him with

> Blank misgivings of a Creature
> Moving about in worlds not realiz'd.[3]

---

[1] *Prelude*, i. 401.   [2] *Prelude*, i. 586.
[3] *Ode on Intimations of Immortality.*

Something happened—he cannot exactly say what or how; but a new sense for something unknown before, something intangible but real, was left. He tells how he rowed out one summer evening in a borrowed boat ("it was an act of stealth and troubled pleasure"), dipping his oars into the silent lake—

> When, from behind that craggy steep till then
> The horizon's bound, a huge peak, black and
>   huge,
> As if with voluntary power instinct
> Upreared its head. I struck and struck again,
> And growing still in stature the grim shape
> Towered up between me and the stars, and still,
> For so it seemed, with purpose of its own
> And measured motion like a living thing,
> Strode after me. With trembling oars I turned,
> And through the silent water stole my way
> Back to the covert of the willow tree;
> There in her mooring-place, I left my bark,—
> And through the meadows homeward went, in
>   grave
> And serious mood; but after I had seen
> That spectacle, for many days, my brain
> Worked with a dim and undetermined sense
> Of unknown modes of being.[1]

These last words may be forgotten or underestimated. We may put them down as representing mere fancy, but Wordsworth did not mean that his mind played with fanciful notions. He means what he says, that he was seized and occupied with dim but powerful thoughts of something more real than he had yet dreamed of. Imagination, not fancy, woke for the time and worked upon him. But then

> Shades of the prison-house begin to close
>   Upon the growing Boy,

[1] *Prelude*, i. 377.

and the youth is "daily farther from the East." Earth,

> The homely Nurse doth all she can
> To make her Foster-child, her Inmate Man,
> Forget the glories he hath known,
> And that imperial palace whence he came.

The zest of pleasure and the sheer interest of the world absorb the growing man, and the faculties of wonder and imagination are dulled. Sometimes they die in a man altogether and he does not know it, and does not miss them. But with poets it must be otherwise.

When the time came, his uncles sent him in October 1787 to St John's College, Cambridge. Wordsworth's own account of Cambridge is in the third book of the *Prelude*—a book which will appeal very vividly to every Cambridge man. He had

> A strangeness in the mind,
> A feeling that I was not for that hour,
> Nor for that place.[1]

What that place actually was may be seen in Gunning's *Reminiscences of Cambridge*. With a particularity that an undergraduate can never quite reach, well able as he may be to seize the general characteristics of his dons, Gunning introduces us to one and another of the figures who made what Wordsworth calls

> The ring
> Of the grave elders, men unscoured, grotesque
> In character, tricked out like aged trees
> Which through the lapse of their infirmity
> Give ready place to any random seed
> That chooses to be reared upon their trunks.[2]

If there were among the dons men of intellectual outlook, who cherished any spiritual ideal, Gunning was hardly the man with whom they would share their

---
[1] *Prelude*, iii. 80. [2] *Prelude*, iii. 541.

thoughts. But he pictures a lack-lustre place, and the evidence goes to show that he was right. The studies were as uninspiring as the teachers.

> I did not love,
> Judging not ill perhaps, the timid course
> Of our scholastic studies.[1]

Wordsworth, not so free in Cambridge as at Hawkshead, managed to achieve a certain freedom—

> We sauntered, played, or rioted; we talked
> Unprofitable talk at morning hours;
> Drifted about along the streets and walks,
> Read lazily in trivial books, went forth
> To gallop through the country in blind zeal
> Of senseless horsemanship, or on the breast
> Of Cam sailed boisterously, and let the stars
> Come forth, perhaps without one quiet thought.[2]

His sister, Dorothy, as early as 26th June 1791,[3] wrote her criticism of this course of life; "William," she says, "lost the chance (indeed the certainty) of a fellowship by not combating his inclination. He gave way to his natural dislike to study as dry as many parts of mathematics, consequently could not succeed at Cambridge. He reads Italian, Spanish, French, Greek, Latin and English, but never opens a mathematical book. We promise ourselves much pleasure from reading Italian together at some time." The promise makes her look something like an accessory after the fact.

His own criticism is in the last line quoted, "Perhaps without one quiet thought." Still the interests of life are too strong for wonder. The zeal of senseless horsemanship, powdered hair, and silk stockings, had made a man of him for the time being. He had ceased to be a child and a poet.

[1] *Prelude*, iii. 493.   [2] *Prelude*, iii. 248.
[3] Knight, *Life*, i. 57.

>   Imagination slept,
> And yet not utterly. I could not print
> Ground where the grass had yielded to the step
> Of generations of illustrious men,
> Unmoved. I could not always lightly pass
> Through the same gateways, sleep where they had slept,
> Wake where they waked, range that inclosure old,
> That garden of great intellects, undisturbed.[1]

His college windows looked on Trinity Chapel

>   Where the statue stood,
> Of Newton with his prism and silent face,
> The marble index of a mind for ever
> Voyaging through strange seas of Thought, alone.[2]

He had a friend who lived in a set of rooms in Christ's, traditionally Milton's, and there Wordsworth poured libations to the poet's memory.[3] He read Spenser, the other great Cambridge poet, and called him brother; and at Trumpington he

> Laughed with Chaucer in the hawthorn shade.[4]

Two of his vacations, however, made contributions to his growth greater perhaps than those of the Cambridge terms. There was one great moment in the first of these, when, after a night spent "in dancing, gaiety and mirth," he was going homeward over his native mountains.

>   Magnificent
> The morning rose, in memorable pomp,
> Glorious as e'er I had beheld—in front,
> The sea lay laughing at a distance; near,
> The solid mountains shone, bright as the clouds,
> Grain-tinctured, drenched in empyrean light;

---

[1] *Prelude*, iii. 257. I like to think that he here describes the Second Court of St John's.
[2] *Prelude*, iii. 60. [3] *Prelude*, iii. 293-302.
[4] *Prelude*, iii. 276.

And in the meadows and the lower grounds
Was all the sweetness of a common dawn—
Dews, vapours, and the melody of birds,
And labourers going forth to till the fields.
Ah! need I say, dear Friend! that to the brim
My heart was full; I made no vows, but vows
Were then made for me; bond unknown to me
Was given, that I should be, else sinning greatly,
A dedicated Spirit. On I walked
In thankful blessedness, which yet survives.[1]

On another night he had that strange experience of finding the old soldier, alone and motionless, upon the mountain, waiting in trust upon the God of Heaven; and the scene and the man set something in motion within him. It was Imagination waking and stirring.

In the summer of 1790, he and his friend, Robert Jones, had a walking tour in France and Switzerland, and he records another of these strange experiences as occurring. They had "crossed the Alps"—the words struck a chord within him. The "lonely place," every feature of the desolate scene, "worked" upon him. Otherwise the tour was important, for it brought him under the influence of France and the Revolution. At Condrieu they met and supped with delegates returning from Paris, and after supper, "with flowing cups elate and happy thoughts," English and French joined hands, with amity and glee,

And round and round the board we danced again.[2]

He came back to Cambridge and took his B.A. degree in January 1791. It was now, his uncles thought, time to choose some calling, but he found this hard to do. He went to London, and put himself in the way of the sights and sounds of the city, yet perhaps here, too, he "was not for that hour, nor for that place." At present his proper place was France, and to France he went in November 1791.

A good part of his time in France was spent at Orleans

---

[1] *Prelude*, iv. 323.   [2] *Prelude*, vi. 386-406.

—at first chiefly among Royalist officers whose sympathies were anti-national. But now one of the great shaping influences of his life came to the poet—the French soldier Michel Beaupuy. M. Legouis has disentangled and collected the story of this brave and good man—"one of the true knights-errant of the Revolution," he calls him, and one of five brothers all worthy of that name.[1] Beaupuy belonged to the lesser nobility of Périgord, and was born in 1755—a descendant of Montaigne. Wordsworth says Beaupuy was "in service bound" to the poor, as if by the oaths of a religious order, and had for the mean and obscure,

> And all the homely in their homely works,

a courtesy that seemed a passion and a gallantry, like that he had, when a soldier, for woman.[2]

A warm friendship, and ceaseless discussion of politics with this true man,—"a meeker man than this lived never" —did much for Wordsworth. Beaupuy "to all intolerance indisposed" could discuss "old ideals in government and new," quietly and winningly.

> We added dearest themes—
> Man and his noble nature, as it is
> The gift which God has placed within his power,
> His blind desires and steady faculties
> Capable of clear truth, the one to break
> Bondage, the other to build liberty
> On firm foundations [3] . . .
> . . . and, finally, beheld
> A living confirmation of the whole
> Before us, in a people from the depth
> Of shameful imbecility uprisen,
> Fresh as the morning star.   Elate we looked
> Upon their virtues; saw, in rudest men,

---

[1] Legouis, *Wordsworth*, 201, 214-5.   [2] *Prelude*, ix. 302.
[3] *Prelude*, ix. 354.

Self-sacrifice the firmest ; generous love,
And continence of mind, and sense of right,
Uppermost in the midst of fiercest strife.[1]

M. Legouis remarks in passing upon the value of Wordsworth's evidence to Frenchmen. Excesses occurred, and "some historians have shown a tendency to lose sight of the real magnanimity and true beauty of the whole movement"—the Marseillais, in particular, have been marked out as infamous rascals—what was the impression made upon a foreigner? " It will be seen that Wordsworth is in thorough agreement with the 'legend,' and readers will conclude therefrom that upon the whole the legendary is perhaps more trustworthy than the historical version."[2]

One striking episode stands out in the story of this intercourse. It is a personal impulse given to the poet's imagination.

              We chanced
One day to meet a hunger-bitten girl,
Who crept along fitting her languid gait
Unto a heifer's motion, by a cord
Tied to her arm, and picking thus from the lane
Its sustenance, while the girl with pallid hands
Was busy knitting in a heartless mood
Of solitude, and at the sight my friend
In agitation said, "'Tis against *that*
That we are fighting."[3]

The phrase "*'Tis against that that we are fighting*," spoken simply and with feeling by his friend, with the sight before them, lodged itself in Wordsworth's mind. The words and the sight together brought home to him the meaning of the Revolution, and he entered into its spirit as he had not before. It was one of those permanent experiences, which haunt a man for ever, fresh and clear in every detail, and never lose their moving

---

[1] *Prelude*, ix. 381.
[2] Legouis, p. 200, citing *Prelude*, ix. 262-287.
[3] *Prelude*, ix. 509 ; see Legouis, p. 211-2.

power. That day his feeling for the poor and the oppressed, native to him and rooted in his fibre from early childhood, reached a new consciousness. Much that he gathered in France suffered change with time. This passion never died. Another great gain was the political intuition which political experience alone can give. His sonnets to Liberty, from 1802 to 1807, have a truth and life that speak of these earlier days.

From Orleans he went to Paris—a month after the September massacre. He walked the streets and saw the newly famous places, lived in imagination through the great scenes and the great days of the Revolution over again, thought, felt, and suffered. And then his relatives, in their cool practical way, insisted on his return to England—happily for England; for had he stayed, he might well have been guillotined with the Girondins—so impatient had he grown of being a mere spectator. In January 1793 he published his *Evening Walk* and *Descriptive Sketches* with Joseph Johnson, Cowper's publisher—to prove to his critical relatives that he "*could* do something."[1]

These poems are not, like those which came five years after them, written in "the language used by men." There are archaisms, inversions, abnormal constructions, ellipses, conceits, periphrases, personifications—everything that is antithetically opposed to the principles that he afterwards propounded—and yet there was promise in the book. At least one important result followed its publication. It brought him some years later a most significant friendship —with Coleridge.[2]

In February 1793 another book was published, which also had its effect upon Wordsworth— *An Inquiry Concerning Political Justice, and its influence on the general virtue and happiness,* by William Godwin.

The feeling which the French Revolution called forth was well described by Wordsworth in the lines often quoted—

---

[1] See letter cited by Knight, *Life*, i. 91.
[2] See *Biographia Literaria*, ch. 4.

> Europe at that time was thrilled with joy,
> France standing on the top of golden hours,
> And human nature seeming born again.[1]

In this great upheaval, it seemed that at last the incubus of the past was thrown off and that free scope had been gained for every force that worked among men for good. The power of Reason had long been a favourite tenet with thinkers—"Is it possible for us," wrote Godwin, "to contemplate what man has already done without being impressed with a strong presentiment of the improvements he has yet to accomplish?" Reason and reflection had discovered the laws that rule the physical world and had applied them to the general good; give them room, and to what height might they not raise mankind? The Revolution was the crowning application of common sense to politics, and now that the great change had been made from Tradition to Reason, the perfectibility of man, long cherished as an ideal, was to be realised. The result would be an immense increase of human happiness. After the cessation of the wars for religions and ideals, and the dull Augustan ages that followed them, the eighteenth century had seen a tide of feeling sweep over Europe—of feeling for mankind, of individual emotion, new thoughts and ideals of happiness and tenderness. The books of Rousseau and Goethe's *Werther*, the *Task*, and the *Sentimental Journey* illustrate one side of this. The religious movement led by the Wesleys and the humanitarian campaigns led, in different spheres, by Howard, Clarkson and Wilberforce, are other manifestations of the new spirit. And now in the destruction of the Bastile, which Cowper had predicted in the *Task*, men saw the symbol of a new age.[2] To contemporary France and to Europe it had stood for a system hateful to every human heart. With it privilege and caste fell, arbitrary laws and cruel taxes—

---

[1] *Prelude*, vi. 339.
[2] Cf. *Excursion*, iii. 709. Fox said: "How much the greatest event it is that ever happened in the world! and how much the best!"

all the usages that had starved and cramped mankind, heart and mind and soul. They were gone for ever. Reason had said in the clearest of voices that these things should not be. The emancipated peasants of France showed at once the soundness of all this line of thought. "Elate we looked upon their virtues." If ever a change appealed to every honest thinker, to every sweet impulse and sure conclusion, and fairly justified every hope that man could frame for his kind, for their enlargement and development on every side of their being, it was the French Revolution. And every honest-hearted man in every country of Europe could hope for nothing better than the diffusion of principles, approved beforehand by speculation and now justified in fact.

Easy and light-hearted thinking it may seem to us—too quick altogether; but we judge by the event—the immediate event—and forget the antecedents which induced these bright hopes, and the long century, which, once the power of Napoleon was broken, has seen these hopes slowly triumphing over Holy Alliances and all other forms of reaction. The immense relief from spiritual pressure which the men of that day knew, we cannot know for we have no such experience to interpret it.

> Bliss was it in that dawn to be alive
> But to be young was very Heaven! O times
> In which the meagre, stale, forbidding ways
> Of custom, law, and statute, took at once
> The attraction of a country in romance!
> When Reason seemed the most to assert her rights
> When most intent on making of herself
> A prime enchantress—to assist the work
> Which then was going forward in her name!
> Not favoured spots alone, but the whole Earth,
> The beauty were of promise.[1]

[1] *Prelude*, xi. 108. Cf. *Excursion*, ii. 212:
"The glorious opening, the unlooked-for dawn,
That promised everlasting joy to France."

It is fairly clear that this new enthusiasm carried the young Wordsworth quite away from his real sphere for the time, and took the place that should belong to Imagination and Poetry. It is not to be regretted, for it was to give him openings of another sort—to show him what intense hope and bitter grief the human heart can know,—an education indeed for one who is to help men to new happiness. He must know what has to be healed.

The young poet might be standing indeed on the top of golden hours. But men around him did not spare to suggest another view, and they too had evidence of a sort for their opinions in "the harvest that we reap from popular government and equality."[1] The time was hardly come—perhaps for some types of British mind it is not even yet come—when the poet's answer could be recognized as just—

> I clearly saw that neither these nor aught
> Of wild belief engrafted on their names
> By false philosophy had caused the woe,
> But a terrific reservoir of guilt
> And ignorance filled up from age to age,
> That could no longer hold its loathsome charge,
> But burst and spread in deluge through the land.[2]

The sunset cannon at Portsmouth he never heard, he says, without forebodings; and they were quickly fulfilled.

> In Britain ruled a panic dread of change,[3]

and in February 1793 England joined the kings of Europe in open war to oppose the liberties of France.

> This threw me first out of the pale of love;
> Soured and corrupted, upwards to the source,
> My sentiments.[4]

Alienated from the mass of his fellow-countrymen, though many felt with him, Wordsworth found his nature

---
[1] *Prelude*, x. 472.   [2] *Prelude*, x. 474.
[3] *Excursion*, iii. 827.   [4] *Prelude*, xi. 176.

torn in two. Hegel defines Tragedy as "the division of the spiritual substance against itself,"—when the spiritual forces within a man are dislocated and acting against one another—when, the stronger they are and the deeper their hold upon his nature, the more awful is their conflict. Such experience comes sooner or later to perhaps every feeling son of woman—to religious spirits and to poets most of all and most terribly. Wordsworth says that at this time he "rejoiced; yea, afterwards—truth most painful to record!—exulted" when English armies were defeated; that when, in church (to which he seems at this time and for years after to have gone somewhat rarely) prayers were offered up or praises for our country's victories, he sat silent and "fed on the day of vengeance yet to come."[1]

Meantime, reaction ruled in England. It seemed as if the Government—the shepherds of the people—thirsted "to make the guardian crook of law a tool of murder"—

> They who ruled the State—
> Though with such awful proof before their eyes
> That he, who would sow death, reaps death, or worse
> And can reap nothing better—child-like longed
> To imitate, not wise enough to avoid.[2]

Worse was yet to follow. For France also appeared in the British character of foe to liberty—

> Oppressors in their turn,
> Frenchmen had changed a war of self-defence
> For one of conquest, losing sight of all
> Which they had struggled for.[3]

---

[1] *Prelude*, x. 282-299. He probably alludes to the battle of Hondschoote, 6th and 8th September 1793, and the Duke of York's forced embarkation at Cuxhaven. So Legouis, p. 234. So C. J. Fox: "The triumph of the French Government over the English does, in fact, afford me a degree of pleasure which it is very difficult to disguise."

[2] *Prelude*, xi. 62.   [3] *Prelude*, xi. 206.

Mankind at large thus renounced the new age for the lower ideals of the past. Wordsworth fell back upon Godwin, taking refuge from fact in speculation. Godwin's defects are easy to criticise, but the inspiring thought of all his teaching will not easily be eradicated from the human mind—the supremacy of intellect. Godwin was relentlessly loyal to his mastering thought, and being a thorough-going individualist, as men of his make normally are and cannot well avoid being, he made short work of old-fashioned conditions,—gratitude, patriotism, religion, filial affection, local and social prejudices of every sort. Property gives rise to the reprehensible "system of clemency and charity"; marriage with its fixity is a danger to the unruffled calm that the understanding requires, it is "a system of fraud," a violation of individual liberty.

It is remarkable that England's two greatest poets of these two centuries came under Godwin's influence. When the world repudiated Reason, the poet clung to her the more—she was his only hope, in her alone could he find peace.

> This was the time, when, all things tending fast
> To depravation, speculative schemes—
> That promised to abstract the hopes of Man
> Out of his feelings, to be fixed thenceforth
> For ever in a purer element—
> Found ready welcome. Tempting region *that*
> For Zeal to enter and refresh herself,
> Where passions had the privilege to work,
> And never hear the sound of their own names.
> But, speaking in more charity, the dream
> Flattered the young, pleased with extremes, nor least
> With that which makes our Reason's naked self
> The object of its fervour. What delight!
> How glorious! in self-knowledge and self-rule,
> To look through all the frailties of the world,

And, with a resolute mastery shaking off
Infirmities of Nature, time and place,
Build social upon personal Liberty,
Which, to the blind restraints of general laws
Superior, magisterially adopts
One guide, the light of circumstances, flashed
Upon an independent intellect.
Thus expectation rose again ; thus hope,
From her first ground expelled, grew proud
    once more.[1]

"A strong shock," as Wordsworth says, had been "given to old opinions"—men's minds had been let loose by the Revolution and then goaded to thought by the tyrannous measures of the friends of ancient institutions. Wordsworth's was a strong head—Carlyle long after told Gavan Duffy that Wordsworth's physiognomy was that of a worker—"jaws like a crocodile," he said.[2] He was

              Somewhat stern
In temperament, withal a happy man,
And therefore bold to look on painful things;
Free likewise of the world, and thence more bold.[3]

Analysis being his present business, he would go through with it, and he cured himself of Godwinism by following it out to the end.
                      So I fared,
Dragging all precepts, judgments, maxims, creeds,
Like culprits to the bar; calling the mind
Suspiciously, to establish in plain day
Her titles and her honours ; now believing
Now disbelieving ; endlessly perplexed
With impulse, motive, right and wrong, the ground
Of obligation, what the rule and whence
The sanction ; till, demanding formal *proof*,

---

[1] *Prelude*, xi. 223.
[2] *Conversations with Carlyle.* "Neither man nor god can get on without a decent jaw-bone," Carlyle said to Tennyson, *Life of Tennyson*, ii. 234.
[3] *Prelude*, xi. 275.

And seeking it in every thing, I lost
All feeling of conviction, and, in fine,
Sick, wearied out with contrarieties,
Yielded up moral questions in despair.
   This was the crisis of that strong disease,
This the soul's last and lowest ebb.[1]

But now after a long separation from his sister, he was reunited to her. In autumn 1795 the two of them settled at Racedown in Dorset, where they lived for some two years. Her influence began to supersede that of Godwin.

Dorothy Wordsworth had suffered with her brothers from the break-up of their home. She had lived first with the maternal grandparents, and had not been happy with them. She loved an open-air life and was held closely indoors—serving, in fact, in the mercer's shop which they kept. Her grandmother had much to say on the duty of sedate behaviour, and the girl's higher life depended on the books which William lent her and which she had to make the leisure to read in secret. In 1788 a change came, for she then went to live with her uncle at Forncett Rectory, near Norwich. The Rector was also a Canon of Windsor, and in the summer of 1792, while William was discussing Republican government with Beaupuy, Dorothy was meeting King George III. and his family—the princesses at least, on the terrace at Windsor, and going to races and balls. But even so early as this year she was cherishing the dream of a cottage life with William, and it came true in 1795 —and from now onward she lived with and for her brother.

To understand her relations with him, perhaps it will be well to anticipate, and quote at once her journal for the day of her brother's marriage. It took place at Brompton in Yorkshire, and bride, bridegroom and sister drove off at once for their home at Grasmere.[2] The bride had made

[1] *Prelude*, xi. 293.
[2] The reader of *Pride and Prejudice* (written in 1796-1797) will remember the wedding of Mr Collins (ch. 26): "The bride and bridegroom set off for Kent from the church door." Mr Collins was no author of innovations, and proves a rule.

long visits to them there already. "On Monday, 4th October 1802," Dorothy writes, "my brother William was married to Mary Hutchinson. I slept a good deal of the night, and rose fresh and well in the morning. At a little after eight o'clock, I saw them go down the avenue towards the church. William had parted from me upstairs. When they were absent, my dear little Sara[1] prepared the breakfast. I kept myself as quiet as I could, but when I saw the two men running up the walk, coming to tell us it was over, I could stand it no longer, and threw myself on the bed, where I lay in stillness, neither hearing nor seeing anything till Sara came upstairs to me, and said, 'They are coming.' This forced me from my bed where I lay, and I moved, I knew not how, straight forward, faster than my strength would carry me, till I met my beloved William, and fell upon his bosom. He and John Hutchinson led me to the house, and there I stayed to welcome my dear Mary. As soon as we had breakfasted, we departed. It rained when we set off. Poor Mary was much agitated, when she parted from her brothers and sisters, and her home. Nothing particular occurred till we reached Kirby. We had sunshine and showers, pleasant talk, love and cheerfulness."[2] A passage like this enables us to understand what Wordsworth means when he speaks of human love as contributory to his spiritual restoration.

The story of this restoration is, like all stories of conversion, an extremely simple one. Wordsworth "yielded up moral questions in despair," and, after some attempt to find relief in mathematics—vain on the whole—he fell back upon the inevitable, he made that surrender which is the gist and essence of every conversion. He left off seeking and he began to accept. And accepting, he began once more to "look at the world in the spirit of love,"[3]—the poet's true work—and then the old impulses played upon him again with power. The first great

---

[1] Sara Hutchinson. [2] Knight, *Life*, i. 351.
[3] Preface to *Lyrical Ballads* (1800).

channel through which this spirit of love came to him was his sister's affection.

> Thanks to the bounteous Giver of all good!
> That the belovèd Sister in whose sight
> Those days were passed . . .
> Maintained for me a saving intercourse
> With my true self; for, though bedimmed and changed
> Much, as it seemed, I was no further changed
> Than as a clouded and a waning moon:
> She whispered still that brightness would return;
> She, in the midst of all, preserved me still
> A Poet, made me seek beneath that name,
> And that alone, my office upon earth;
> And, lastly, as hereafter will be shown,
> If willing audience fail not, Nature's self
> By all varieties of human love
> Assisted, led me back through opening day
> To those sweet counsels between head and heart
> Whence grew that genuine knowledge, fraught
>   with peace.[1]

No influence could be imagined less like Godwin's than that of Dorothy Wordsworth. "She is a woman indeed! in mind, I mean, and heart;" wrote Coleridge, "for her person is such that if you expected to see a pretty woman, you would think her rather ordinary; if you expected to see an ordinary woman, you would think her pretty! but her manners are simple, ardent, impressive. In every motion her most innocent soul outbeams so brightly, that who saw would say

> 'Guilt was a thing impossible with her.'

Her information various. Her eye watchful in minutest observation of Nature; and her taste a perfect electrometer. It bends, protrudes and draws in at subtlest beauties and most recondite faults."[2]

---

[1] *Prelude*, xi. 334-354.
[2] Letter to Cottle, June 1797, Knight, *Life*, i. 113; also in Legouis, p. 293. Coleridge is quoting his own poetry, not, it would appear, quite correctly.

Long country walks the brother and sister took together with their eyes open for Nature, and though no Racedown journals are extant, that kept at Alfoxden a little later shows the course of their interests. Here is the entry for 17th February 1798.

"The sun shone bright and clear. A deep stillness in the thickest part of the wood, undisturbed, except by occasional dropping of the snow from the holly boughs; no other sound but that of water, and the slender notes of a redbreast, which sang at intervals on the outskirts of the southern side of the wood. There the bright green moss was bare at the roots of the trees, and the little birds were upon it. The whole appearance of the wood was enchanting: and each tree, taken singly, was beautiful. The branches of the hollies pendent with their white burden, but still showing their bright red berries and their glossy green leaves. The bare branches of the oaks thickened by the snow."

> The Blessing of my later years
> Was with me when a Boy;
> She gave me eyes, she gave me ears;
> And humble cares, and delicate fears;
> A heart, the fountain of sweet tears;
> And love, and thought, and joy.[1]

So Wordsworth wrote of his sister in 1801. It was she who took him back to Nature and taught him the secret of "a heart that watches and receives." But to return to the *Prelude* and his story. "From Nature doth emotion come," he says, "and moods of calmness...."

> Hence Genius, born to thrive by interchange
> Of peace and excitation, finds in her
> His best and purest friend; from her receives
> That energy by which he seeks the truth,
> From her that happy stillness of the mind
> Which fits him to receive it when unsought... [2]

---

[1] *The Sparrow's Nest* (1807). [2] *Prelude*, xiii. 1-10.

> Long time in search of knowledge did I range
> The field of human life, in heart and mind
> Benighted; but, the dawn beginning now
> To reappear, 'twas proved that not in vain
> I had been taught to reverence a Power
> That is the visible quality and shape
> And image of right reason; that matures
> Her processes by steadfast laws; gives birth
> To no impatient or fallacious hopes,
> No heat of passion or excessive zeal,
> No vain conceits; provokes to no quick turns
> Of self-applauding intellect; but trains
> To meekness, and exalts by humble faith;
> Holds up before the mind intoxicate
> With present objects, and the busy dance
> Of things that pass away, a temperate show
> Of objects that endure . . .[1]

At leisure from theory, the poet has become content to be in contact with fact—with the true and eternal—and he finds it no dead thing, but alive, instinct with beauty, and communicative in emotion and impulse. Hence he can say in another well-known poem—

> One impulse from a vernal wood
> May teach you more of man;
> Of moral evil and of good,
> Than all the sages can.[2]

Lord Morley says this is a playful sally to a bookish friend and not to be taken literally. But two replies are open to this criticism. First, the poet in the same poem postulates "a heart that watches and receives"; and, secondly, by "impulse" he means a peculiarly intense experience not very common.[3] To one man a scene is

---
[1] *Prelude*, xiii. 16. *Cf.* (in sonnet publ. 1807, Those words were uttered):
   The immortal Mind craves objects that endure.
[2] *The Tables Turned* (text of 1798).
[3] "Impulse," "impel," and "disturb" are almost technical terms with Wordsworth, though not always. They are constantly associated with some of his very deepest experiences.

pretty or even beautiful. To the poet it speaks, when other voices are silent, speaks unutterable things that carry conviction.

> One moment now may give us more
> Than fifty years of reason;
> Our minds shall drink at every pore
> The spirit of the season.[1]

Not that sheer beauty in itself is a little matter for Wordsworth; witness such poems as *The Green Linnet*. And again take such lines as those in which he gives us the aweful suggestion of mountain solitude—

> There, sometimes doth a leaping Fish
> Send through the Tarn a lonely chear;
> The Crags repeat the Raven's croak,
> In symphony austere;
> Thither the Rainbow comes, the Cloud;
> And Mists that spread the flying shroud;
> And Sun-beams, and the sounding blast,
> That, if it could, would hurry past,
> But that enormous Barrier holds it fast.[2]

Beauty had a powerful effect upon him. Sometimes

> The breath of this corporeal frame,
> And even the motion of our human blood
> Almost suspended, we are laid asleep
> In body, and become a living soul.[3]

Thus he hears the cuckoo and becomes a boy again:

> And I can listen to thee yet;
> Can lie upon the plain
> And listen, till I do beget
> That golden time again.

---

[1] *To My Sister* (1798). [2] *Fidelity* (1807).
[3] *Lines above Tintern.*

> O blessed Bird! the earth we pace
> Again appears to be
> An unsubstantial, faery place;
> That is fit home for Thee![1]

It is when beauty has this full effect upon a poet's mind that its value grows clear; for though it speaks a language that is never quite unintelligible, yet it is too wonderful to be believed. But the poet's is a nature gifted with the faculty of wonder, and to such wonder all things are possible; and Wordsworth, like Spenser, believes what wonder catches from beauty and gives to him. And, like Spenser, he comes to hold, though he does not formulate it in quite the same way, that beauty is spiritual, or more essentially is spirit.

Thus when he has been carried by the cuckoo into the strange land of wonder, he comes back with something which we could not have expected him to bring. The little poem called *The Echo* is not very credible at first, but until we believe Wordsworth meant it, we shall not understand him.

> Yes! full surely 'twas the Echo,
> Solitary, clear, profound,
> Answering to Thee, shouting Cuckoo!
> Giving to Thee Sound for Sound. . . .
>
> Like the voice through earth and sky
> By the restless Cuckoo sent;
> Like her ordinary cry,
> Like—but oh how different!
>
> Hears not also mortal Life?
> Hear not we, unthinking Creatures!
> Slaves of Folly, Love, or Strife,
> Voices of two different Natures?
>
> Have not We too? Yes we have
> Answers, and we know not whence;

[1] *The Cuckoo* (1807)

> Echoes from beyond the grave,
> Recogniz'd intelligence?
>
> Such within ourselves we hear
> Oft-times, ours though sent from far;
> Listen, ponder, hold them dear;
> For of God, of God they are![1]

We may compare the famous passage in the *Excursion* about the shell, and the sound it gives to the ear,

> Even such a shell the Universe itself
> Is to the ear of faith:[2]

though in this later passage other ideas are suggested, which are not so clear in earlier poems, which perhaps did not yet interest the poet very much.

Thus taught by Nature, Wordsworth says he found

> Once more in Man an object of delight,
> Of pure imagination, and of love.

Indeed, without going further, we may attribute to the poet himself the experience of "the good Lord Clifford":

> Who, long compell'd in humble walks to go,
> Was softened into feeling, sooth'd and tamed.
>
> Love had he found in huts where poor Men lie,
> His daily Teachers had been Woods and Rills,
> The silence that is in the starry sky,
> The sleep that is among the lonely hills.[3]

At this point we have to reckon with the fourth great influence in Wordsworth's life—that of Coleridge, who was now at the very height of his powers. They met in the spring of 1796, and the Wordsworths left Racedown and settled at Alfoxden to be near their new friend.

---

[1] Text of 1807, omitting a stanza afterwards deleted.
[2] *Excursion*, iv. 1132-1142.
[3] *Song at the Feast of Brougham Castle* (text of 1807).

Coleridge had a very great influence on Wordsworth's thinking—he took him outside the range of Dorothy. No records of their ceaseless conversations are known to exist, but it is clear from many accounts that Coleridge was already a unique talker, with a loveable habit ot wandering at large over the wide fields of his interests— downs high as wide and wonderfully bracing. He had a great acquaintance with philosophy, ancient [1] and modern, and a great gift for relating everything to it. Perhaps even his vagueness had an emancipating effect.[2] He drove Wordsworth perforce into a larger world and compelled him to look at all things from a universal point of view. This was a great service. It secured that Wordsworth should not decline into mere impressionism or mysticism, but that with his powerful mind he should grasp Nature as a unity—always and invariably. Coleridge was a higher spirit than Godwin; he stood near Wordsworth and he admired him, and thus was able to bring back into his life in a higher and nobler form the element of Philosophy. The *Lines written above Tintern Abbey* represent in breadth, depth and beauty the new Wordsworth, born again with Dorothy into the life of nature, and with Coleridge into the life of thought, the receptive and the creative.

Pursuing the tale of his recovery, Wordsworth tells us that—

> As the horizon of my mind enlarged,
> Again I took the intellectual eye
> For my instructor, studious more to see
> Great truths, than touch and handle little ones.

---

[1] Lamb describes Coleridge at Christ's Hospital, declaiming "Jamblichus, or Plotinus."

[2] Ellis Yarnall, *Wordsworth and the Coleridges*, p. 125. Wordsworth with Rogers had spent an evening with Coleridge at Highgate. As the two poets walked away together—"I did not altogether understand the latter part of what Coleridge said," was the cautious remark of Rogers. "I did not understand any of it," was Wordsworth's hasty reply. "No more did I!" exclaimed Rogers, doubtless much relieved.

> ... I sought
> For present good in life's familiar face,
> And built thereon my hopes of good to come.[1]

And it was from life's familiar face that he caught the gleams which are the inspirations of his poems.

In 1798, an ever-memorable year, Coleridge and Wordsworth published their *Lyrical Ballads*. The volume was brought out by their friend Cottle, the Bristol bookseller. It began with *The Ancient Mariner* and ended with the *Lines written above Tintern Abbey*, to which we shall shortly return. It is a commonplace that these two poems, with some between them, mark an entirely new era in the history of English poetry.

Two years later Wordsworth reissued his poems, and wrote a preface of some length, in which he developed his views upon poetry. The essay deserves close attention. Here a few extracts must suffice—extracts rather than summary, in order to keep his own words which are significant. A Poet "is a man speaking to men: a man, it is true, endowed with more lively sensibility, more enthusiasm and tenderness, who has a greater knowledge of human nature and a more comprehensive soul, than are supposed to be common among mankind; a man pleased with his own passions and volitions, and who rejoices more than other men in the spirit of life that is in him; delighting to contemplate similar volitions and passions as manifested in the goings-on of the Universe, and habitually impelled to create them where he does not find them." "The man of science seeks truth as a remote and unknown benefactor; he cherishes and loves it in his solitude: the Poet, singing a song in which all human beings join with him, rejoices in the presence of truth as our visible friend and hourly companion. Poetry is the breath and finer spirit of all knowledge; it is the impassioned expression which is in the countenance of all Science." The poet

---

[1] *Prelude*, xiii. 51. Cf. *Excursion*, iv. 260.

writes under one restriction only, that of producing immediate pleasure, but this is not a degradation of his art, for, "it is an acknowledgment of the beauty of the universe, an acknowledgment, the more sincere because not formal, but indirect; it is a task light and easy to him who looks at the world in the spirit of love." Delight, song, passion and love—these are the constituents of poetry, he says, and a poem must come from them and reproduce them.

The condition of achieving such work is absolute truthfulness and fidelity, to the particular and to the universal; but Wordsworth does not conceive of this as a sacrifice of freedom, for the essence of poetry is life and emotion, and only life and emotion can be their own exponents. He says he will "choose incidents and situations from common life, tracing in them, truly though not ostentatiously, the primary laws of our nature: chiefly as regards the manner in which we associate ideas in a state of excitement." His aim "is to follow the fluxes and refluxes of the mind when agitated by the great and simple affections of our nature."

What he means is shown in his *Two April Mornings*. The sudden ejaculation of Matthew, "The will of God be done," is called forth by the cloud that reminds him of another April day of thirty years ago, when beneath such a sky he went out to fish, and as he passed his daughter's grave, saw another little girl, and he describes her charm, and concludes:—

> I look'd at her and look'd again:
> —And did not wish her mine.[1]

Or in *The Fountain*, where Matthew speaks of age and the need which a man of mirth has of being loved more than other men, and then, after an interval, sings his witty rhymes. Or in the story of old Timothy going hunting, and his reflection—

> "The key I must take, for my Ellen is dead."[2]

[1] Text of 1802.   [2] *The Childless Father*.

Thus does he fulfil his promise that he will try to "keep the reader in the company of flesh and blood." Finally: "I do not know how to give my reader a more exact notion of the style in which it was my wish and intention to write, than by informing him that I have at all times endeavoured to look steadily at my subject." This was to him essential: he complained, for instance, of Dryden as a translator, that "whenever Virgil can be fairly said to have his *eye* upon his object, Dryden always spoils the passage."[1]

Then as to method, Wordsworth says he will avail himself of "the charm of metrical language," the music and the associations of which "imperceptibly make up a complex feeling of delight, which is of the most important use in tempering the painful feeling always found intermingled with powerful descriptions of the deeper passions." Over all he will try "to throw a certain colouring of imagination." The style shall be manly, as befits a subject of some importance; he will use "a selection of language really used by men," and he will not "break in upon the sanctity and truth of his pictures by transitory and accidental ornaments, and endeavour to excite admiration of himself by arts, the necessity of which must manifestly depend upon the assumed meanness of his subject."

Elsewhere he says of the poet that—

> Impulses of deeper birth
> Have come to him in solitude,

and that his poetry is, in fact—

> The harvest of a quiet eye
> That broods and sleeps on his own heart.[2]

The poem is the re-creation of the "impulse"—a thing

---

[1] Letter to Scott, Knight, *Life*, ii. 28. I have hazarded the correction from "soiled." Knight's very valuable book has rather too many misprints to allow a steady confidence.

[2] *A Poet's Epitaph.*

of "sanctity and truth." Words must be used, but as soon as they begin to group themselves, they form phrases; and phrases betray. No man, who handles them with thought, but must have pulled himself up with the awful question as to his own sincerity: Is this indeed his real feeling, or has he been cheated by the sheer pleasure of the words? The poet must be sincere—above all men. No wonder Wordsworth, filled with the seriousness of the beauty he has to re-create, dreads the colour of his words—the fatal iridescences of poetic language that lead astray the writer and confuse the reader. He will, he says, himself employ the "language really used by men"—plain words that shall hide as little as words may the naked beauty of the fact. Such pieces as *A Slumber did my Spirit Seal*, the *Leech-gatherer*, the *Ode to Duty* show how great a use can be made of plain words. T. H. Green called the *Ode to Duty* "the high-water mark of modern poetry."

But does not the "certain colouring of imagination" break in upon the truth and sanctity of his pictures? There was a time, he says, in the *Stanzas on Peele Castle*, when he would have wished to

> Add the gleam,
> The light that never was, on sea or land,
> The consecration, and the Poet's dream.

But it is so no more—"a deep distress hath humanised my Soul"; he will not have "the heart that lives alone, housed in a dream, at distance from the Kind,"

> But welcome fortitude, and patient cheer,
> And frequent sights of what is to be borne.[1]

He has forgone Fancy in favour of Imagination—the steady fixing of the eye upon the object, till he sees it in the full strong light of its own essential beauty, and his soul

---

[1] Text of 1807, but with "borne" for "born." Compare the account of the wanderer (*Excursion*, i. 366) "in himself happy ... he could *afford* to suffer with those whom he saw suffer."

becomes alive to all, or to some part, of the myriad suggestions—of the truth (to be plain)—which beauty always carries with it.

On the 29th of April 1802, Dorothy Wordsworth wrote in her journal: "As I lay down on the grass, I observed the glittering silver line on the ridge of the backs of the sheep, owing to their situation respecting the sun, which made them look beautiful, but with something of strangeness, like animals of another kind, as if belonging to a more splendid world." These sheep may serve as a parable for her brother's poetry. Is it possible to ask whether they were real sheep? If they were not, we may have to make a surrender of a great deal of poetry, beside Wordsworth's. And yet Dorothy would not have seen what she did if she had not previously known what sheep were without this "certain colouring."

One reflection remains before we leave his theory of poetry. There are great poetic reputations, old and new, based on a brilliant handling of a rare or even artificial vocabulary, where a poet uses to the full the magic of vowel and consonant and strange diction. But the greatness of Wordsworth stands out when we begin to grasp with what means he produces his most wonderful effects—words precisely of the kind he describes. Longinus long before had remarked the same thing of Euripides—how he could use "quite common and vulgar words" to express the deepest and tenderest and most eternal of human feelings.

The great conclusion which Wordsworth draws from all his experience of life is the paramount duty of happiness. Among men who felt, and men who cultivated, melancholy, Wordsworth is persistently of a different mood; he is a poet who "could not but be gay in such a jocund company" as that of the daffodils dancing in the breeze,—and indeed whenever they flashed upon his inner eye. And this joy is not dependent on fancy or illusion. It was stronger as he saw deeper, and it gave him this very power of going deeper.

WORDSWORTH

> With an eye made quiet by the power
> Of harmony, and the deep power of joy,
> We see into the life of things.[1]

It is this that has given him his power of "operating changes in our way of thought." He has looked before and after, he has tasted good and evil, and his conclusion is joy. Joy is in his poetry—in the thought within it, and in the awful and austere music that the thought informs with its power and its consolation. It is strong as Nature; tells us as little and tells us as much. The *Lines written above Tintern Abbey* may sum up his work.

> I have learned
> To look on nature, not as in the hour
> Of thoughtless youth; but hearing oftentimes
> The still, sad music of humanity,
> Not harsh nor grating, though of ample power
> To chasten and subdue. And I have felt
> A presence that disturbs me with the joy
> Of elevated thoughts; a sense sublime
> Of something far more deeply interfused,
> Whose dwelling is the light of setting suns,
> And the round ocean, and the living air,
> And the blue sky, and in the mind of man,
> A motion and a spirit, that impels
> All thinking things, all objects of all thought,
> And rolls through all things. Therefore am I still
> A lover of the meadows and the woods,
> And mountains; and of all that we behold
> From this green earth; of all the mighty world
> Of eye and ear, both what they half create,
> And what perceive; well pleased to recognize
> In nature and the language of the sense,
> The anchor of my purest thoughts, the nurse,
> The guide, the guardian of my heart, and soul
> Of all my moral being.

[1] *Tintern Abbey.*

Of his later years little need be said. He lived perhaps too much alone—at least too secure from contradiction, from criticism, from the suggestion of distinct minds. With time, as happens to most men, he became closed to new impressions, and that means the gradual deadening of the old. Sometimes in the New World the forest is shorn off the side of a hill, and then rain and snow do their work and the soil is washed away; the grandeur of the rock may remain, but leaf and flower and the song of birds is gone. The old Wordsworth is well described by Henry Taylor—"a rough, grey face, full of rifts and clefts and fissures." "An object man" the village people called him,—a great figure with a great work behind him.

His age brought him bereavements, as it does to all, but it brought him honour and love and happiness in his kin. The name Mary, he once said, was to his ear the most musical and most truly English in sound of all names. He grew to be a fierce old Tory, whose vehemence against Catholic emancipation and the Reform Bill his wife and daughter would try to check, but it did not vex his Radical friends. He was "moving about in worlds not realised," they knew, and, as Mr Myers tells us, they let him be "decoyed into uttering [his diatribes] to the younger members of the family, whose time was of less importance, so as to set his mind free to return to those topics of more permanent interest, where his conversation kept all that tenderness, nobility and wisdom, which in that family, as in many others familiar with the celebrated persons of that day, won for him a regard and a reverence such as was accorded to no other man." He died on 23 April 1850.

"Here pause," as he says in one of his sonnets—and it may best be in words of his own :

> Close up these barren leaves ;
> Come forth, and bring with you a heart
> That watches and receives.

CARLYLE

AN American man of letters, Mr C. G. Leland, writes in his *Memoirs* that he bought Carlyle's *Sartor Resartus*, "first edition," and read it through forty times, of which he kept count, before he left college;[1] and there is other testimony, as striking, to the very wide influence of Carlyle in the middle of the last century. "There was the utmost avidity for his books wherever they were available, especially among the young men; phrases from them were in all young men's mouths, and were affecting the public speech."[2] Huxley, who was not one of his disciples, wrote in March 1881: "I should not yield to the most devoted of his followers in gratitude for the bracing wholesome influence of his writings, when as a young man I was essaying without rudder or compass to strike out a course for myself."[3] With Milton and Wordsworth he was one of those who most influenced T. H. Green.[4]

It is not so now. To some extent the overheightening of emphasis in some of Carlyle's later books has accentuated the reaction in fancy and fashion that always follows a great vogue, and there have not been wanting critical voices to turn the minds of the young in other directions, though not all of his critics seem destined for immortality. Nor can it be questioned that, while Froude's *Biography* revealed him in a new light to such readers as Edward Fitzgerald—"How is it," he asks, "that I did not know that Carlyle was so good, grand, and even loveable, till I

[1] C. G. Leland, *Memoirs*, i. 108. [2] Masson, *Carlyle*, p. 67.
[3] *Life of Huxley*, ii. 34. Compare E. Caird, *Essays*, i. 231; and T. E. Brown's *Letters*, 8 February 1881.
[4] Bryce, *Contemporary Biography*, 87.

read the Letters which Froude now edits?"[1]—for many the volumes went far to abolish Carlyle's influence.

None the less his works remain, and the fact stands that he was one of the formative minds of the nineteenth century. We may well ask what it was he did, and what he was; and the latter is the real question. It was, at all events, one of his own firmest convictions, a belief that lies at the heart of his best work, that in every case the man is more than his word, more than his act. The value of the book is as an index to the personality, and the personality of the great man is his real contribution to mankind. Carlyle recommends Novalis to his readers—"If they feel, with us, that the most profitable employment any book can give them, is to study honestly, some earnest, deep-minded, truth-loving Man, to work their way into his manner of thought, till they see the world with his eyes, feel as he felt and judge as he judged, neither believing, nor denying, till they can in some measure so feel and judge."[2] "Get first into the sphere of thought," he says, "by which it is so much as possible to judge of Luther, or of any man like Luther, otherwise than distractedly; we may then begin arguing with you."[3]

Carlyle was born at Ecclefechan on the 4th of December 1795. Of his father, James Carlyle, he has left an impressive memorial. The old man died in January 1832 at the age of seventy-five, and his son could not leave London to go to his burial. His mind ran upon his father and during the last days of the month he wrote down his reminiscences of him.

James Carlyle was a Scottish peasant of a type well known north of the border, bred in a school of hardship, a man "religious with the consent of his whole faculties." "Every morning and every evening, for perhaps sixty years, he had prayed to the Great Father in words which I shall

---

[1] Letter of 1 September 1882. *Cf.* letter of William Morris; Mackail, *Life of William Morris*, ii. 76. "I like him much the better for having read this book."

[2] Essay on *Novalis*, p. 50. [3] *Heroes*, Lecture iv.

now no more hear him impressively pronounce, 'Prepare us for those solemn events, death, judgment and eternity.' He would pray also, 'Forsake us not when we are old and our heads grown grey.'[1] God did not forsake him. He had an air of deepest gravity, even sternness. Yet he could laugh with his whole throat, and his whole heart. I have often seen him weep too; his voice would thicken and his lips curve while reading the Bible. He had a merciful heart to real distress, though he hated idleness, and for imbecility and fatuity had no tolerance. Once— and I think once only—I saw him in a passion of tears. It was when the remains of my mother's fever hung upon her, in 1817, and seemed to threaten the extinction of her reason. We were all of us nigh desperate, and ourselves mad. He burst at last into quite a torrent of grief, cried piteously, and threw himself on the floor and lay moaning.... It was as if a rock of granite had melted and was thawing into water....

" He seldom or never spoke except actually to convey an idea. How in a few sentences he would sketch you off an entire biography, an entire object or transaction, keen, clear, rugged, genuine, completely rounded in. . . .

" How he used to speak of death, especially in late years —or rather to be silent, and look at it! There was no feeling in him here that he cared to hide. He trembled at the really terrible; the mock terrible he cared nought for. That last act of his life, when in the last agony, with the thick, ghastly vapours of death rising round him to choke him, he burst through and called with a man's voice on the Great God to have mercy on him—that was the epitome and concluding summary of his whole life."

It is not hard to recognise some hint of James Carlyle in all his son's thoughts. Instinctively he compared men with his father.

Margaret Aitken, Carlyle's mother, was a woman of

---

[1] It is worth noting that these prayers shaped themselves in the words of Psalm lxxi. 9 and 18.

character and kindliness, of that Scottish kind who bear men, and have body and mind and soul enough to breed them. She lived to see his greatness recognized, and died when he was fifty-eight, leaving a gap in his life not to be known but by sympathetic study of the long and helpful intercourse that ceased on Christmas Day 1853, and of the sorrow that followed. She had nine children in all, of whom he was the eldest. Every volume added to his published correspondence brings further evidence to the intense love that bound the family together, the mutual support they gave to one another throughout life, the careful and tender solicitude with which brothers and sisters studied their mother and each other. No judgment upon Carlyle is adequate which does not recognize this deep tenderness. Sometimes one fancies that disappointment in other directions intensified this love of his own people, but in any case the family was one of the foundations of his being.

The world into which Carlyle was born was a difficult one. The world is never a very easy place to manage with, but the beginning of the nineteenth century was a time of peculiar trouble in Great Britain. The natural progress of the country had been dammed for a generation by the reaction against the French Revolution. The Terror and the European war had scared the governing classes of this country into a course of senseless repression —the cruelty of frightened dullness. Romilly, the reformer of the barbarous penal code, wrote in 1808: "If any person be desirous of having an adequate idea of the mischievous effects which have been produced in this country by the French Revolution and all its attendant horrors, he should attempt some legislative reform on humane and liberal principles." When he pleaded for lessening the number of offences to which the death penalty was attached, a Member of Parliament replied, "I am for hanging all,"— hanging them in public as the way was in those days,—and Lord Ellenborough and Lord Eldon were of the same mind; they were not for altering "those laws which a century had proved to be necessary, and which were now to be overturned by speculation and modern philosophy."[1] Indeed, those laws were reinforced. The *Habeas Corpus* Act was suspended. The Press was attacked; a stamp duty was imposed on newspapers to stop their circulation; five hundred writers were sentenced to more or less severe penalties between 1809 and 1822 for promoting rebellion, conspiracy or blasphemy.[2] Cobbett's stormy life is a sort of barometric record of the period, for he was at times the direct object of Government legislation. With the principles (or prejudices) that animated them, it was a vital matter for the ruling classes to keep Parliament unreformed; corruption was essential to the maintenance of the constitution. "You need not ask me, my lord, who I votes for; I always votes for Mister Most," said an independent elector to Lord Cochrane in 1806.[3]

Meantime there was an increasing amount of suffering among the people. Population had increased, and foreign trade was interrupted. A General Enclosure Act was passed in 1801,[4] and the small farmers began to disappear, pasture-rights were lost, and village industries were moving away to the towns. Harvests were bad from 1789 to 1802. Wheat was dear, but its high price benefited the landlord rather than the labourer. War and law kept the price up, and laws and wars alike were made by a Parliament of land-owners. War also meant the press-gang.

> Why would you trouble Buonaparte's reign?
> He was your great Triptolemus: his vices
> Destroy'd but realms and still maintained your
>   prices,

[1] In 1789 a woman was burnt at the stake for coining.
[2] *Cambridge Modern History*, vol. x. p. 580.
[3] E. I. Carlyle, *William Cobbett*, p. 127.
[4] A return "in chronological order of all Acts passed for the inclosure of Commons or Waste lands" was ordered to be printed by the House of Commons, 29 July 1914. It contains between 4500 and 5000 titles.

He amplified to every lord's content
The grand agrarian alchymy, high *rent*.[1]

This and much more Byron wrote in his *Age of Bronze* in 1823. Shelley's *Masque of Anarchy* was written in 1819.

In the towns, things were worse than in the country. There the new industrial conditions, heavy taxation, the closing of foreign markets and other causes led to great distress, and this to disorder. To mention merely the more outstanding disturbances of the period of Carlyle's early life, we may recall the Irish Rebellion of 1798, the Luddite riots of 1812, the Blanketeers in 1817, the Glasgow rising of 1819 (which Carlyle at the time and after attributed "with emphasis" to "grievances dreadfully real,"[2]) the Peterloo massacre of 1819 (16 August), the Cato Street conspiracy of 1820, the Bristol riots of 1831.

The rulers of the nation were not such as men would respect. Lord Melville was impeached in 1806 for frauds in the naval department, and was acquitted after a trial of fifteen days. In 1809, the King's son, the Duke of York, was accused in Parliament of permitting his mistress, Mrs Clarke, to traffic in military commissions,[3] and was forced to resign his office. George IV., as Regent and as King, had his own reputation, and the affairs of the Queen were public news. When Carlyle wrote of "Dubarrydoms," he had not to go across the sea for all his information. But as Thackeray said, "there is no stronger satire on the proud English society of that day than that they admired George [IV.]."

But even yet there is more to add. A revulsion against the French treatment of the Catholic religion, a feeling not unnatural in minds not trained to think deeply, drove the English people into vehement assertion of its own estab-

---

[1] Gladstone on this, Morley, *Life of Gladstone*, iii. p. 471 (two volume edition, ii. p. 711).

[2] *Reminiscences*, i. p. 152.

[3] See letter of Charles Lamb to Manning, 28 March 1809, "Thousands of ballads, caricatures, lives of Mrs Clarke in every blind alley."

lished religion and morality and the maintenance of their safeguards—the Test Acts and Corporation Acts. It was not till 1828 that these were repealed, even then passionately defended by Lord Eldon. Till 1836 Dissenters wishing to marry were forced by law into the parish churches where alone marriages could be celebrated. "The whole country," says M. Legouis, "caught the infection of virtuous wrath, and the English patriots easily persuaded themselves that their hatred of France and her friends was nothing more than a hatred of crime and wickedness."[1] "No period," says the Dane, Dr Brandes, "was ever more favourable to the development of hypocrisy and fanaticism than this, during which the nation was actually encouraged by its leaders to boast of its religious superiority to freethinking France."[2] Heine speaks of *ächtbrittische Beschränktheit*, and it was never so intense as then. Before the Revolution England had been far more open to the intellectual currents of Europe. Now it was patriotic to be insular. Religion suffered from this reaction. In 1819, "in spite of the need for economy," Parliament voted a million pounds sterling "for the purpose of building new churches for the Establishment, apparently in the belief that irreligion had been a prime cause of Radical outbreaks in 1816-17."[3] Lord Liverpool, in introducing the measure to the Lords, declared that its object was to "remove Dissent." When John Sterling talked of a "black dragoon in every parish,"[4] he had such facts as this in his mind. "In every village we had the Black Recruiting-Sergeant against us," said an old Radical.[5] All over Europe there was contributive evidence in the close alliance between the restored monarchies and the ecclesiastical authorities. Religion was essentially an asset of government, a substitute for police. "The English," wrote Emerson of England in 1830, "cling to the last rag of form and are dreadfully

[1] Legouis, *Youth of William Wordsworth*, p. 225.
[2] Brandes, *Naturalism in England*, p. 16.
[3] *Cambridge Modern History*, vol. x. p. 581.
[4] *Sterling*, pt. i. ch. 4. [5] G. W. E. Russell, *Collections*, ch. 10.

given to cant. . . . The Church at this moment is much to be pitied. She has nothing left but possession. If a bishop meets an intelligent gentleman and reads fatal interrogations in his eyes, he has no resource but to take wine with him." Criticism of the established religion was—apart from Dissent—still too negative to be helpful. The Liberalism of the day was doctrinaire, individualist and often atheist. Obscurantist religion and doctrinaire "philosopheism" seemed to be the spiritual alternatives —half views both.

There are other sides to the story, and the necessary corrections can be made, but without invalidating the evidence here cited.[1] There were facts enough to warrant Carlyle's question : " But of those decadent ages in which no Ideal either grows or blossoms? When Belief and Loyalty have passed away, and only the cant and false echo of them remains ; and all solemnity has become Pageantry ; and the Creed of persons in authority has become one of two things: an Imbecility or a Machiavelism ? "[2]

Thus from a home in which God was a reality, or rather *the* reality, into a world where He seemed to be little more than a simulacrum, the earnest young Carlyle passed, and there he had to find some kind of work, if he was to live. For two years he was a schoolmaster; for some further time a tutor. He had ambitions for a University chair, but they were always disappointed till he settled down to poverty and the life of letters. It was a suitable thing, he says, for Luther's function on earth, "and doubtless wisely ordered to that end by the Providence presiding over him and us and all things, that he was born poor and brought up poor. . . . No man nor no thing would put-on a false face to flatter Martin Luther. Among things, not among the shows of things, had he grown. . . . It was his task to get acquainted with *realities* and keep acquainted with them, at whatever

[1] *Sterling*, pt. ii. ch. 3. [2] *French Revolution*; Bastile, bk. i. ch. 2.

cost: his task was to bring the whole world back to reality, for it had dwelt too long with semblance."[1] Literary men, he says, are "a kind of 'involuntary monastic order.'"[2] And he accepted the conditions of his work. In later years he stimulated Monckton Milnes to get a pension for Tennyson, but he neither sought nor accepted any such thing for himself.[3]

Content to be poor, like his father, like him also, careful and thrifty, he settled down to his chosen life. It is characteristic that he abhorred Leigh Hunt's ways—"Hugger-mugger was the type of his economics, financial and other." Carlyle, says Professor Masson, "was, if I may mention such a small particular in such a context, one of the neatest-handed men I ever knew in tying up a parcel—say a book parcel to go by post—always doing it with the utmost economy of paper and string, the utmost security of knot, and yet the finest elegance of shape and general effect. A good deal of this deftness ran through his daily life. His love of order and accuracy was conspicuous even in trifles."[4] "Every Great Man, every genuine man," Carlyle says, "is by the nature of him a son of Order, not of Disorder. . . . His mission is Order; every man's is. . . . Is not all work of man in this world a *making of Order?* . . . We are all born enemies of Disorder."[5]

With this spiritual instinct for order, and a digestive apparatus that would not be ordered—subject like Oliver Cromwell, and Dr Johnson and Dr Francia, and "all great souls,"[6] to hypochondria—with an imperious Scottish conscience co-operating with his poverty to keep him,

---

[1] *Heroes*, lect. iv.

[2] *Heroes*, lect. v. Cf. *Past and Present*, bk. ii. ch. 12. "Literature . . . is not easy . . . is a quarrel and internecine duel with the whole world of Darkness that lies without one and within one ;—rather a hard fight at times, even with the three pound ten secure."

[3] Wemyss Reid, *Lord Houghton*, i. 296

[4] Masson, *Carlyle*, 110.   [5] *Heroes*, iv.

[6] *Cromwell*, vol. i. p. 44, and *Dr Francia*. So said Aristotle, citing Socrates, Plato, and Heracles, we learn from Plutarch, *Lysander*, 2.

like Luther, "a true son of Nature and fact,"[1] and as ready as Luther to fling his inkstand at any devil apparent or actual,—we find him started on a strange career. A man of unusual sensibility, he suffered greatly from depression—he was "set too nakedly *versus* the devil and all men."[2] He was undoubtedly irritable, and he knew it, and, like some other preachers, he preached to the sinner in the pulpit. "To consume your own choler," he said, "as some chimneys consume their own smoke ... is a negative yet no slight virtue, nor of the commonest in these times."[3] A master of incisive language has at times cause to regret his gift. Yet people who knew Carlyle did not judge him by his moods and words of irritation. Mrs Browning, Harriet Martineau, Professor Masson, even Benjamin Jowett (who did not altogether like him)—and others—unite in recognizing his gifts of sympathy and tender-heartedness. "Many a time," says Froude, "I have remonstrated when I saw him give a shilling to some wretch with 'Devil's elect' on his forehead. 'No doubt he is a son of Gehenna,' Carlyle would say, 'but you can see it is very low water with him. This modern life hardens our hearts more than it should.'"[4] The incident is characteristic. For the "Devil's elect" as such Carlyle had no enmity—pity, rather, and a brotherly feeling. It might even be said, perhaps, that a large part of his literary work was devoted to interpreting to his fellow-countrymen the duty of sympathy with those whom they lightly classed as "Devil's elect"—revolutionists, English and French, terrorists, tyrants, working-men, and the great names of German literature.

"Oh, my dear Jeannie," Carlyle wrote to his wife in September 1831, "do help me to be a little softer, to be a little merciful to *all* men, even gigmen. Why should a man, though bilious, never so 'nervous,' impoverished, bugbitten, and bedevilled, let Satan have dominion over

---

[1] *Heroes*, iv.
[2] *Reminiscences*, ii. 173 (Froude).
[3] *Sartor*, ii. 6.
[4] *Life in London*, ch. 17.

him?" Again and again, he lays stress on the fact that "the real quantity of our insight,—how justly and thoroughly we shall comprehend the nature of a thing, especially of a human thing,—depends on our patience, our fairness, lovingness, what strength soever we have: intellect comes from the whole man, as it is the light that enlightens the whole man."[1] "A loving heart is the beginning of all knowledge."[2] Nearly all the men he admires have this quality—Werner, Burns, Boswell, Johnson, Mirabeau, even Voltaire "had a true kindness of heart."

Sarcasm, Teufelsdröckh discovers, is "in general the language of the devil,"[3] and this is the only thing some people see in his creator. "Alas! it is so much easier," he owns, "to love men while they exist only on paper, or quite flexible and compliant in your imagination than to love Jack and Kit who stand there in the body, hungry untoward, jostling you, barring you, with angular elbows, with appetites, irascibilities, and a stupid will of their own! There is no doubt but old Marquis Mirabeau found it extremely difficult to get on with his brethren of mankind: and proved a crabbed, sulphurous, choleric old gentleman many a sad time."[4] The man who wrote these words was not wanting in humour or self-criticism, and no doubt thought of another to whom they might apply, as perhaps he did when he wrote of Dante : "I fancy the rigorous earnest man, with his keen excitabilities, was not altogether easy to make happy."[5]

Once, while he was working at the *French Revolution* Carlyle met a famous humorist of the day. "I had been at Mrs Austin's, heard Sydney Smith for the first time guffawing, other persons prating, jargoning. To me through these thin cobwebs Death and Eternity sate glaring. Coming homewards along Regent Street, through street-walkers, through— *Ach Gott!* unspeakable pity swallowed up unspeakable abhorrence of it and of myself.

[1] *Mirabeau.*   [2] *Biography.*   [3] Sartor, II. iv.
[4] *Mirabeau.*   [5] *Heroes*, lect. iii.

The moon and the serene nightly sky in Sloane Street consoled me a little. Smith, a mass of fat and muscularity, with massive Roman nose, piercing hazel eyes, huge cheeks, shrewdness and fun, not humour or even wit, seemingly without soul altogether."[1]

Carlyle had another idea of humour than this. "The essence of humour," he says, "is sensibility: warm, tender, fellow-feeling with all forms of existence.... True humour springs not more from the head than from the heart; it is not contempt, its essence is love; it issues not in laughter, but in smiles which lie far deeper.... It is, in fact, the bloom and perfume, the purest effluence of a deep, fine and loving nature; a nature in harmony with itself, reconciled to the world and its stintedness and contradiction, nay, finding in this very contradiction new elements of beauty as well as goodness."[2]

But, in discussing Carlyle's attitude to humour, we have touched one of the central motives of his character—and, in his case above all, character and life-work are almost interchangeable terms. "How will this look in the Universe, and before the Creator of Man?"[3] So he wrote in 1828. Decades later, someone tried to trip him in discussion by asking who was to be the judge, and he answered, fiercely enough, "Hell-fire will be the judge. God Almighty will be the judge, now and always."[4] Such words sound strangely in the nineteenth century, but in all their literalness they had once represented the mind of serious men.

> *Tuba mirum spargens sonum*
> *Per sepulcra regionum*
> *Cogit omnes ante thronum.*

And for Carlyle the words had still an awful truth, deeper and more awful than the literal. "Prepare us for those solemn events, death, judgment and eternity," James Carlyle had daily prayed, and so, in his own way, prayed

---

[1] *Life in London,* i. 56, 57.
[2] *Richter* (first essay).
[3] *Goethe.*
[4] *Life in London,* ii. 487.

CARLYLE

his son. He wrote of Sterling: "Looking steadfastly into the silent continents of Death and Eternity, a brave man's judgments about his own sorry work in the field of Time are not apt to be too lenient."[1] Of the dying Cromwell it was recorded, as Carlyle reminds us, that "he spake some exceeding self-debasing words, annihilating and judging himself."[2] It is the testimony of those who knew Carlyle that he was singularly free from the vanity of authors,[3]—and here was the reason. Like the old Scottish Calvinists, of whom he came, he worked and thought in the consciousness of the ultimate background.

"You are so dreadfully in earnest!" Jeffrey said to him in early days.[4] "What an earnest man he is!" said Goethe to Eckermann.[5] "One thing in the middle of this chaos," he wrote to his wife (2 Nov. 1835), "I can more and more determine to adhere to—it is now almost my sole rule of life—to clear myself of cants and formulas as of poisonous Nessus shirts; to strip them off me, by what name soever called, and follow, were it down to Hades, what I myself know and see. Pray God only that sight be given me, freedom of eyes to see with. I fear nothing then, nay, hope infinite things."[6] A month later his mother wrote to him: "Let us not be careful what the world thinks of us, if we can say with a good conscience with Toplady:

> Careless, myself a dying man,
>   Of dying men's esteem;
> Happy, oh Lord, if Thou approve,
>   Though all beside condemn.

You will say, 'I know all these things.' But they are sooner said than done. Be of courage, my dear son, and seek God for your guide."[7] So, helped by the memory of

---
[1] *Sterling*, p. 1.
[2] *Cromwell*, vol. iii. p. 218 (Lomas edition).
[3] *Cf.* Edward Fitzgerald, letter of 1 September 1882.
[4] *Reminiscences*, ii. 40. [5] *Conversations of Goethe*, 11 Oct. 1828.
[6] *Life in London*, i. 63. [7] *Life in London*, i. 67.

his father and backed by his mother's letters, he went on, "frightened at no Reviewer's shadow; having, in his time, looked substances enough, in the face, and remained unfrightened." [1]

He is always emphasizing the thought of keeping in touch with Realities, with Verities. He loves Mirabeau for his " swallowing Formulas, getting endless acquaintance with the Realities of things and men;" [2] because, "there lay verily in him, as the basis of all, a Sincerity, a great free Earnestness; nay, call it Honesty, for the man did before all things see, with that clear flashing vision, into what *was*, into what existed as fact; and did, with his wild heart, follow that and no other. Whereby on what ways soever he travels and struggles," continues Carlyle, "often enough falling, he is still a brother man. Hate him not; thou canst not hate him." [3] Danton too he can like, as "a man that went honestly to work with himself." [4] He quotes with zest Mirabeau's prophecy of Robespierre—"This man will do somewhat: he believes every word he says." [5] In the early nineteenth century heroes of this order were still suspect. It was a new thing to try to understand them by means of sympathy and without conventions.

The real is for Carlyle the basis of everything. Taste is "a general sensibility to truth and nobleness." [6] "Poetry, it will more and more come to be understood, is nothing but higher Knowledge; and the only genuine Romance (for grown persons) Reality." [7] In the lecture on *The Hero as Poet*, Carlyle develops this. "If your delineation be authentically *musical*, musical not in word only, but in heart and substance, in all the thoughts and utterances of it, then it will be poetical; if not, not. Musical: how much lies in that! A *musical* thought is one spoken by a mind that has penetrated into the inmost heart of the thing;

---

[1] *Corn-law Rhymes.*
[2] *Mirabeau.*
[3] *French Revolution*, vol. ii., bk iii. ch. 7.
[4] *Mirabeau.*
[5] *French Revolution*, vol. i. bk. vi. ch. 2.
[6] *State of German Literature.*
[7] *Diderot.*

detected the inmost mystery of it, namely the *melody* that lies hidden in it; the inward harmony of coherence which is its soul, whereby it exists and has a right to be, here in this world. All inmost things, we may say, are melodious; naturally utter themselves in Song. The meaning of Song goes deep. . . . All deep things are Song. It seems somehow the very central essence of us, Song; as if all the rest of us were but wrappages and hulls. The primal element of us; of us and of all things. . . . Poetry, therefore, we will call *musical Thought*. . . . See deep enough, and you see musically; the heart of Nature *being* everywhere music, if you can only reach it." This is so because Nature is "what the Earth-Spirit in *Faust* names it, *The living visible Garment of God*."[1]

Hence the value of "the eye that flashes direct into the heart of things," of "the power to escape out of hearsays." What is, has meaning; and similarly "whatsoever has existed has had its value: without some truth and worth lying in it, the thing could not have hung together, and been the organ and sustenance, and method of action, for men that reasoned and were alive."[2] Carlyle's quarrel with History and Historians is that they do not show him this—they tell him an infinite number of things and illuminate nothing—to say nothing of their "writing in hysterics." The Past "was a Reality, and it is one. The garment only of it is dead; the essence of it lives through all Time and all Eternity."[3] "The Old never dies till this happens, Till all the soul of good that was in it have got itself transfused into the practical New."[4] And then, the sooner it dies and is buried the better.

It is in the light of this faith of his that we must interpret his much-questioned equation of Rights and Mights and not less his angry denunciation of the political men and methods of his day. The peasant's son knew the facts

---

[1] *Sartor*, bk. i. ch. 8; *Faust*, part i. 1st scene, der Gottheit lebendiges Kleid. [2] *Boswell*.
[3] *Past and Present*, bk. ii. ch. 15. [4] *Heroes*, lect. iv.

of life. Scottish Presbyterianism is essentially democratic —not least that branch of which he sprang. He came of a stock, too, that had worked for bread and had hungered. The story of the Carlyles is written not faintly in his essay on Burns. "Poor Lackalls, all betoiled, besoiled, encrusted into dim defacement;—into whom nevertheless the breath of the Almighty has breathed a living soul! To them it is clear only that eleutheromaniac Philosophism has yet baked no bread."[1] So he wrote of France during the Revolution, and thought of England as he wrote. Little Louis XVII. "lies perishing . . . amid squalor and darkness, lamentably,—so as none but poor factory children and the like are wont to perish, and *not* be lamented."[2] "Sad to look upon," he says elsewhere, "in the highest stage of civilization, nine tenths of mankind have to struggle in the lowest battle of savage or even animal man, the battle against Famine. Countries are rich, prosperous in all manner of increase, beyond example: but the Men of those countries are poor, needier than ever of all sustenance outward and inward; of Belief, of Knowledge, of Money, of Food."[3] "My reviewer in the *Edinburgh*," he wrote in 1840, "writes down this doctrine, That '*hunger*' is perennial, irremediable among the lower classes of men, here, everywhere and at all times,—the horse that will work is fed and lodged, but the man cannot be so; and all 'liberal government,' what does it mean but a joining together of those who have some money to keep those who have none quiet—in their hunger? The pigs have all to die, *no* help for that; but by God's blessing we will keep down their *squealing!* It struck me I had never seen in writing so damnable a statement."[4]

The *facts* of English life as Carlyle saw them were ignorance, enforced idleness, starvation, and "the back-

[1] *French Revolution*, vol. i. book iv. ch. 3.
[2] *Ib.*, vol. iii. bk. vi. ch. 3. [3] *Characteristics*.
[4] *New Letters*, vol. i. p. 216. The reviewer was Herman Merivale, Professor of Political Economy at Oxford. Perhaps Carlyle's view of "the dismal science" had such utterances to support it.

scene and bottom-decoration of it all, no other than a Workhouse"; and meanwhile the statesmen were some of them battling for "the Divine Right of Squires" and "preserving their game,"[1] and others "motive-grinding" and talking about ballot-boxes. If his criticism of Democracy is insufficient, if he does not realize how a nation can be educated even in the most difficult matters, if time be allowed,[2] it is partly the fault of his temperament—"I believe I have a natural *talent for being in a hurry;*" he says, "which is a very bad talent"[3]—and partly it is due to his sense of the fact that men "into whom the breath of the Almighty has breathed a living soul," are dying of starvation and hardly a thought given to them by the rulers. Sympathy enough for Louis XVI. and his Queen and his son; and yet "miserablest mortals, doomed for picking pockets, have a whole five-act Tragedy in them, in that dumb pain, as they go to the gallows unregarded; they consume the cup of trembling down to the lees. For Kings and for Beggars, for the justly doomed and the unjustly, it is a hard thing to die."[4]

"Needier than ever of inward sustenance, of Belief" Carlyle finds the men of his day. Was Belief still possible? Belief in the Christain religion? It was recognized that Christian belief had a value and should be maintained—"if not Religion, and a devout Christian heart, yet Orthodoxy, and a cleanly Shovel-hatted look" (as in Mr Croker's *Boswell*), "which, as compared with flat Nothing, is something very considerable."[5] Others again, more serious and more honest, looked to Coleridge, as he "sat on the brow of Highgate Hill, in those years." "He was thought to hold, he alone in England, the key of German and other Transcendentalisms; knew the sublime secret of believing by 'the reason' what 'the understand-

---

[1] *Sartor*, bk. iii. ch. 4 (Helotage).
[2] So Dr Johnson held: "About things on which the public thinks long it commonly attains to think right."
[3] *New Letters*, ii. 15.   [4] *French Revolution*, vol. iii. bk. ii. ch. 8.
[5] *Boswell*.

ing'[1] had been obliged to fling out as incredible; and could still, after Hume and Voltaire had done their best and worst with him, profess himself an orthodox Christian, and say and print to the Church of England, with its singular old rubrics and surplices at Allhallowtide, *Esto perpetua*."[2]

Carlyle was taken to see Coleridge, and he has left a vivid account of their meeting. The chapter in the *Life of Sterling* which deals with the "sublime man" is one of his most characteristic—keen in its criticism, and not without a vein of humour. Yet trait after trait is confirmed by the evidence of others less critical. In Cottle's *Reminiscences of Coleridge and Southey* and other records we find—at once in the letters of the young poet himself and in the memories of his intimates—a remarkably close likeness to the old philosopher, whom Carlyle studied so shrewdly as he shambled about Dr Gilman's garden and talked of "sum-m-ject and om-m-ject." There is the same stream of incomparable monologue, unbroken hour after hour, the same vast literary projects never executed, the same fancy for strange voyaging "among the lovely shades of things."

Carlyle's criticism illuminates his own mind. "The truth is, I now see, Coleridge's talk and speculation was the emblem of himself: in it as in him, a ray of heavenly inspiration struggled, in a tragically ineffectual degree, with the weakness of flesh and blood. He says once, he 'had skirted the howling deserts of Infidelity;'[3] this was evident enough: but he had not had the courage, in defiance of pain and terror, to press resolutely across said deserts to the new firm lands of Faith beyond; he preferred to create logical fatamorganas for himself on

---

[1] Cf. *Biographia Literaria*, ch. 10, where these terms, as well as "subjective" and "objective" are cited with some genial self-approval.

[2] *Biographia Literaria*, ch. 10.

[3] In *Biographia Literaria*, ch. 9, Coleridge says that George Fox, Behmen and Law "enabled me to skirt, without crossing, the sandy deserts of utter unbelief."

this hither side, and laboriously solace himself with these. . . .

"Strange enough: here once more was a kind of Heaven-scaling Ixion; and to him, as to the old one, the just gods were very stern! The ever revolving, never-advancing Wheel (of a kind) was his, through life; and from his Cloud Juno did not he too procreate strange Centaurs, spectral Puseyisms, monstrous illusory Hybrids, and ecclesiastical Chimeras,—which now roam the earth in a very lamentable manner!"

On " bottled moonshine" Carlyle could not live, and at times it seemed as if the age had nothing else to offer. "Voltaire's *Écrasez l'Infame*," he once said to Milnes, " had more religious earnestness in it than all the religions of nowadays put together."[1] " It is not now known, what never needed proof or statement before, that Religion is not a doubt; that it is a certainty,—or else a mockery and a horror. That none or all of the many things we are in doubt about, and need to have demonstrated and rendered probable, can by any alchemy be made a 'Religion' for us."[2]

Carlyle's view was quite definite. " The thing a man does practically believe (and this is often enough *without* asserting it even to himself, much less to others); the thing a man does practically lay to heart, and know for certain, concerning his vital relations to this mysterious Universe, and his duty and destiny there, that is in all cases the primary thing for him and creatively determines the rest. That is his *religion;* or, it may be, his mere scepticism and *no-religion*: the manner it is in which he feels himself to be spiritually related to the Unseen World or No-world; and I say, if you tell me what that is, you tell me to a very great extent what the man is, what the kind of things he will do is."[3]

[1] Wemyss Reid's *Lord Houghton*, i, p. 435. Jowett's obiter dictum that Voltaire "had done more good than all the Fathers of the Church put together," is quoted in his *Life*, vol. ii. 293.
[2] *Sterling*, part i. ch. 15.   [3] *Heroes*, lect. i.

Some belief, some truth Carlyle found in all religions by which men have striven to walk; quackeries have abounded in religions in their decaying stages, but have not given birth to them. "Quackery gives birth to nothing; gives death to all. . . . Man everywhere is the born enemy of lies."[1] "Men, I say, never did believe idle songs, never risked their soul's life on allegories: men, in all times, especially in early earnest times, have had an instinct for detecting quacks, for detesting quacks."[2] All religions have "a kind of fact at the heart of them."

It falls then to a man to-day to find "the kind of fact at the heart" of Christianity, and nothing but a fact will content him. In Teufelsdröckh's progress from the Universal No through the Centre of Indifference to the Universal Yea, Carlyle pictures such a voyage of discovery, with a strong suggestion of autobiography. Every book with anything in it is an autobiography in some degree, and great books most of all. The main thing, he holds, is courage to go forward, resolved not to find Peace by "a surrender to Necessity or any compact with Delusion: a seeming blessing, such as years and dispiritment will of themselves bring to most men, and which is indeed no blessing, since even continued battle is better than destruction or captivity."[3] Thus Goethe became a believer "not by denying his unbelief, but by following it out."[4] "A region of Doubt hovers forever in the background; in Action alone can we have certainty. Nay, properly Doubt is the indispensable material whereon Action works, which Action has to fashion into Certainty and Reality; only on a canvas of Darkness, such is man's way of being, could the many-coloured picture of our Life paint itself and shine."[5] Doubt then will follow us all the way as it did Christian in the *Pilgrim's Progress*. But the easy acceptance of Doubt, the attempt to base religion upon

---

[1] *Heroes*, lect. i. [2] *Ib.* [3] *Goethe.*
[4] *Ib.* [5] *Characteristics.*

CARLYLE

the impossibility of knowledge, was not Carlyle's way, and he disliked compromises in this region.[1] The writers of the *Essays and Reviews*, he thought, were playing tricks with their consciences. As to such views as that once expressed by Canon Ainger, when he said that clergymen do best to go in blinkers—a view humorously phrased, but seriously held, Carlyle was definite enough. "What is incredible to thee, thou shalt not, at thy soul's peril, attempt to believe!—Elsewhither for a refuge or die here. Go to Perdition if thou must,—but not with a lie in thy mouth; by the Eternal Maker, no!"[2] "Falsehood is the essence of all sin."[3]

What then did he find in his search for truth? On what facts did he rest? In a fine passage in the first chapter of *The Diamond Necklace*, he speaks of the realities which he has seen—overhead the infinite Deep, under him the wonderfulest Earth, Eternity behind him and before him, the all-encircling mysterious tide of FORCE, from which rose and vanished, in perpetual change, the lordliest Real Phantasmagory, which men name Being;—"a sight for angels, and archangels; for, indeed, God Himself had made it wholly." The withered leaf tells him the same story; "rightly viewed no meanest object is insignificant; all objects are windows, through which the philosophic eye looks into Infinitude itself."[4] In his diary in 1868 he wrote; "The *fool* hath said in his heart there is no God. From the beginning it has been so, is now and to the end will be so. The *fool* hath said it,—he and nobody else; and with dismal results in our days,—as in all days." "Of final causes, man by the nature of the case, can *prove* nothing; knows them, if he knows anything of them, not by glimmering flint-sparks of Logic, but by an infinitely

---

[1] *Life in London*, ii. 283. "I am astonished at the carelessness about truth which there is in the Church of England. If it goes on, it will lead to utter unbelief among intellectual men," writes Jowett, Letter of 22 January 1861 (in *Life of Jowett*, vol. i. p. 322).

[2] *Sterling*, pt. ii. ch. 2.   [3] *Sartor*, bk. iii. ch. 6.

[4] *Sartor*, bk. i. ch. 11. Compare a similar passage in the essay on Schiller.

higher light of intuition; never long, by Heaven's mercy, wholly eclipsed in the human soul; and (under the name of Faith, as regards this matter) familiar to us now, historically or in conscious possession, for upwards of four thousand years."[1]

Witness to God he finds in man's nature—"Man's life is the genuine work of God; wherever there is a Man, a God also is revealed and all that is Godlike; a whole epitome of the Infinite, with its meanings, lies enfolded in the Life of every man"[2]— in the life of a city and a community, every one of them with "a spiritual principle"—in man's instinct for truth—in work—"all *work* properly so called is an appeal from the Seen to the *Unseen*—a devout calling upon Higher Powers"[3]—in duty—"is what we call Duty no divine Messenger and Guide?"[4]—in justice and retribution—in man's craving for the infinite.[5]—"Often in my life . . . looking before and after, [I] have felt though reluctant enough to believe in the importance or significance of so infinitesimally small an atom as myself, that the doctrine of a special providence is in some sort natural to man."[6]

Sir William Harcourt once said that Carlyle's religion was "Calvinism without Christianity."[7] What Carlyle might have said in reply, we can guess. "It is mere Pantheism, that!" said John Sterling once, and got the answer: "And suppose it were Pot-theism? if the thing is true."[8] Men of Carlyle's type are apt to "re-mint the currency," to sum up a matter under one aspect, the aspect that appeals most to themselves, and to allow all others a secondary place as consequents, not asserting, but not denying. Carlyle used no names, though he had a tender feeling for Calvinism—which, he said, had made all the Heroes. To him, as to Calvin and his followers, God was

---

[1] *Diderot.*
[2] *Biography.*
[3] Letter to Erskine, 22 Oct. 1842.
[4] *Sartor*, bk. ii. ch. 7.
[5] *Sartor*, bk. ii. ch. 9.
[6] *Reminiscences*, ii. p. 31.
[7] Wemyss Reid's *Lord Houghton*, ii. 478.
[8] *Sterling*, part ii. ch. 3.
[9] *Reminiscences*, ii. p. 13.

CARLYLE

the final Reality—Truth, manifested in all being. If it is said that this obscures other aspects of God, it is just to remember that before we can be clear how much a man's silences mean, we must fathom his affirmations—how much does what he says mean for himself? For Carlyle Reality carried everything with it.

To Carlyle everything real is significant. In his "battles with Dulness and Darkness" he has only to go back to facts—" Antæus-like, his strength is got by *touching the Earth* his Mother; lift him up from the Earth, lift him up into Hypocrisy, Inanity, his strength is gone."[1] Metaphysics and Theologies tend to take him from that kindly touch. "Theologies, rubrics, surplices, church-articles, and this enormous ever-repeated thrashing of the straw? A world of rotten straw; thrashed all into powder; filling the Universe and blotting out the stars and worlds:—Heaven pity you!"[2] So he reflects on the experience of John Sterling, "involved in the shadows of the surplice."

There are things more real than tradition and dogma and Ecclesiastical antiquities. "*We* are the miracle of miracles,—the inscrutable mystery of God."[3] So he says, writing of Novalis, and the belief lies at the very centre of his thoughts and gives its significance to all his work, though it receives more emphasis in the early period.[4] "Man is what we call a miraculous creature, with miraculous power over men; and, on the whole, with such a Life in him, and such a World round him, as victorious Analysis, with her Physiologies, Nerve-systems, Physic and Metaphysic, will never completely *name*, to say nothing of explaining."[5] His fierce denunciation of "Benthamee" philosophy, of profit and loss calculations, of motive-grinding, are all inspired by his faith in the essentially

---

[1] *Heroes*, lect. vi. Cf. *Past and Present*, bk. iii. ch. 12. "Antæus-like, their foot on Mother fact."
[2] *Sterling*, pt. ii. ch. 4.   [3] *Heroes*, lect. i
[4] Cf. *Sartor*, bk. iii. ch. 3.
[5] *French Revolution*, vol. i. bk. ii. ch. 6.

spiritual nature of man. "That mysterious Self-impulse of the whole man, heaven-inspired, and in all senses partaking of the Infinite, being captiously questioned in a finite dialect, and answering, as it needs must, by silence —is conceived as non-extant, and only the outward Mechanism of it remains acknowledged."[1] So he sums up the view of the other school, but to himself it is clear from history that man is by nature an idealist, that he "never yields himself wholly to brute force, but always to Moral Greatness,"[2] that he "has transcendentalisms in him,"[3] that he will respond to nothing so readily as a spiritual appeal, but this, to be effective, must be embodied in another man—"Thought kindling itself at the fire of Living Thought,"[4] and the Godlike in man leaping forth at the call of God through the lips of another.

The "Hero" is the central fact of every experience. If there is any truth in the French proverb that no man is a Hero to his valet-de-chambre, it is not that Heroes do not really exist, but that the valet's soul is "a mean valet-soul," that he does not know a hero when he sees him.[5] The valet, of course, may be a historian by profession, but it remains true that quite common men are capable of divining manhood when they meet it. No, "let a man but speak forth with genuine earnestness the thought, the emotion, the actual condition of his own heart; and other men, so strangely are we all knit together by the tie of sympathy, must and will give heed to him. In culture, in extent of view, we may stand above the speaker or below him; but in either case, his words, if they are earnest and sincere, will find some response within us; for in spite of all casual varieties in outward rank or inward, as face answers to face, so does the heart of man to man."[6]

Men are apt to overdrive their ideas, and Carlyle

---

[1] *Characteristics.*   [2] *Ib.*   [3] *French Revolution*, vol. iii. bk. i. ch. 6.
[4] *Sartor*, bk. ii. ch. 3.   [5] *Heroes*, lect. v.   [6] *Burns*.

obviously pushed his conception of the hero too far. His "natural talent for being in a hurry" betrayed him. As a man of letters he could have little knowledge of the difficulties of action in the immense complexity of life. It is so easy to see what should not be—so much easier than to bring what should be out of what is. With years he grew impatient with the slowness of ordinary men, and he fell into a habit of undervaluing them—they did not respond quickly enough to the truth so evident in facts and in heroes. "We will say, with the poor Frenchman at the Bar of the Convention, though in a wiser style than he, and 'for the space' not 'of an hour' but of a lifetime: '*Je demande l'arrestation des coquins et des lâches.*' 'Arrestment of the knaves and dastards': ah, we know what a work that is; how long it will be before *they* are all or mostly got arrested."[1] We know how long it will be; yet his tone at times suggests that he has forgotten how long.

In despair of getting things done quickly—and we must not forget that all the while he saw men and women and children starving and dying, body and soul—he began to look to a particular type of hero, the drastic effective man, who does the thing that has to be done, without waiting to convince his fellow-men beforehand and to take them with him, secure that by-and-by they will accept his work when done and understood. There was always a grotesque element in Carlyle's speech, which became more conspicuous when he thus overstated the real truth that underlies his conception of the value of the Hero. Over-statement is a sure means to give oneself the lie; and critics asked whether Frederick and Dr Francia and Governor Eyre were in truth such heroic superiorities as to leave mankind no further function but to give God thanks and obey them. To adjust the balance, Carlyle's critics developed the view, not essentially a false one at all, that heroes are representative. So much is almost

[1] *Past and Present*, bk. i. ch. 6, p. 47

implied by Carlyle himself when he speaks quietly. But they also overstated their side by dwarfing the heroes into being merely representative. Mankind advances, they said, gradually, by general movements made in common in response to instincts and intuitions shared and communicated they know not how. Yes, but, Carlyle would reply, in all such movements some one lifted his foot first—the Hero of the moment, not less Heroic if there were half a dozen of him, though Nature is not often so prodigal.

One of the cardinal moments in the French Revolution, on which Carlyle loved to dwell,—perhaps the most crucial moment—was when Mirabeau, "the Swallower of Formulas," told de Brézé: "Go, Monsieur, tell those who sent you that we are here by the will of the People, and that nothing but the force of bayonets shall send us hence."[1] Of late years we have seen two Russian Dumas dissolved—bodies without a Mirabeau, and the question rises whether, if there had been a Russian Mirabeau capable of saying what the French one said, capable too of waiting to be bayoneted, the course of Russian history might not have been very different. It is again very hard to think with the orthodox historians that the Hero is more product than producer.

"Speak to any small man," says Carlyle, "of a high, majestic Reformation, of a high majestic Luther; and forthwith he sets about 'accounting' for it; how the 'circumstances of the time' called for such a character, and found him, we suppose, standing girt and road-ready to do its errand; how the 'circumstances of the time' created, fashioned, floated him quietly along into the result; how, in short, this small man, had he been there, could have performed the like himself!"[2] Of late, historians have improved on this and we learn that the circumstances of the time pointed all the other way—there were hardly any

---

[1] *French Revolution*, vol. i. bk. v. ch. 2; and Essay on *Mirabeau*.
[2] *Signs of the Times*.

abuses that a student of history can feel or notice, hardly anything to reform, hardly anybody that wished any reform to be made—and somehow a Reformation gratuitously occurred without circumstances and without the faintest shred of a hero. This comes perhaps from relying too exclusively upon State papers. Official knowledge, it has been said, has always a peculiar cast. Carlyle sees that to understand great things a man must have greatness. Jeffrey, he says, "was not deep enough, pious or reverent enough, to have been great in literature." That is where Jeffrey failed as a critic of literature, where others fail as historians.

Carlyle does not deny the "circumstances of the time." On the contrary, it is because the Hero, the "true Son of Nature and Fact," realizes the circumstances of the time and of all time—"holds on to Truth and Fact"—is "open to the divine significance of life" and "stands upon things and not shows of things"—it is because he sees and knows better than the rest of us, and is less afraid, that the Hero does his work. He does it, too, in virtue of our being "potential heroes"[1] in our turn, for "the real Force which in this World all things must obey is Insight, Spiritual Vision and Determination."[2] As long as man is "the born enemy of all lies," even in the most "beggarly ages" men will follow such Heroes. The "indestructibility of Hero-worship" is "the everlasting adamant lower than which the confused wreck of revolutionary things cannot fall."[3]

The life-work of Carlyle was above all the reassertion of this fundamental fact in human history and human life, chiefly by the interpretation of heroic character. It was no easy work. The "stringing of facts," or "agglomeration," avails little, as he said, in literature—or anywhere else. It is only the beginning. Carlyle makes no secret of his method. "I go into the business with all the intelligence, patience, silence and other gifts and virtues that I

---

[1] *Past and Present*, bk. iii. ch. 12. "Is not every man, God be thanked, a potential hero?" [2] *Death of Goethe*. [3] *Heroes*, lect. i.

have; find that ten times or a hundred times as many could be profitably expended there and prove insufficient... Only what you at last *have living* in your own memory and heart is worth putting down to be printed; this alone has much chance to get into the living heart and memory of other men."[1] He would read very widely about the man who was to be his subject, keeping, if he could get one, a picture of him before his eyes, and accumulating notes which he held together with a clothes-peg.[2] He was eager for "the smallest historical fact that would help him to realize the man"—as, for instance, the "old pair of shoes" which the rustic gave to Charles II. in his flight after Worcester.[3] "'Stern Accuracy in inquiring, bold Imagination in expounding and filling up; these,' says friend Sauerteig, 'are the two pinions on which History soars,'— or flutters and wabbles."[4] Lastly, "a true work of art requires to be *fused* in the mind of its creator, and, as it were, poured forth (from his imagination though not from his pen) at one simultaneous gush."[5]

Such fusing is only done at great cost. "My work," he wrote, "needs all to be done with my nerves in a kind of blaze; such a state of soul and body as would soon *kill* me, if not intermitted."[6] How true this is no one knows who has not made some such experiment, and it would be a curious thing to learn how many critics who have pronounced upon Carlyle's relations with his wife have any real knowledge from experience of the kind of life he necessarily lived.

No one who writes of Carlyle can well avoid the question of his relations with his wife, but here it shall be touched only in parenthesis. That he loved her intensely and proudly, is manifest in his letters and journals,— irritably, too, it is clear. But if the lady accused him of self-pity, she herself was not free from it. There was an

---

[1] New Letters, ii. pp. 10, 11.
[2] Gavan Duffy, *Conversations with Carlyle*, p. 92.   [3] *Biography.*
[4] *Count Cagliostro.*   [5] *Jean Paul Friedrich Richter.*
[6] Journal, 16 November 1849.

edge to her tongue, "that Scots strength of sarcasm which is peculiar to a North Briton,"[1] and after "the long day's work" he was not always equal to bearing it in patience. Robert Browning "always thought her a hard unlovable woman," and did not like her, nor she him. There was an element of the Scottish in Carlyle's speech too. The native accent in tone and phrase is liable to be misunderstood south of the border. His style was not peculiar to his writing, he thought and spoke so; in playful talk he "laughed at his own exaggerations," and when he spoke in irritation, he probably said a great deal more than he meant. Self-parody, especially when it takes the form of a rivalry in hyperbole between husband and wife, is dangerous, and betrays one at unhappy moments. The knowledge that Jane Welsh, a Scotswoman herself, had of his ways of speech, must have softened the impression of some of his words, but they would still hurt. It remains, however, that he never wrote an unkind word to her or of her, that he bitterly repented his hard sayings and very quickly, and that she replied to one letter of apology he wrote her by saying that it was "written for his biographer."[2] What it cost him to read this may be dimly imagined. If, as time went on, his published writings show tendencies to reckless statement and exaggeration, less and less controlled, one need hardly be a psychologist to attribute something of it to Jane Welsh and the wounds she dealt to the man who loved her.

At such cost Carlyle drew his heroes and wrote his histories. Faults are found in his work. His friends criticized his style. He printed one such criticism at some length in his *Life of Sterling*—a long and searching letter, which a smaller man would never have given to the world. But it was characteristic of the "true Son of Fact" to print it, as it was to allow much else to be printed after his death. There are many sayings, too,

---

[1] Boswell's phrase; letter to Temple: 9 Sept. 1767.
[2] Nichol, *Carlyle*, p. 129.

scattered about his works, which suggest self-criticism—as when he praised Goethe for "his entire freedom from Mannerism,"[1] when he criticized Richter's style,[2] and when in *Sartor* he asked whether he had not in "working over Teufelsdröckh's German, lost much of his own English purity?"[3] But, as he said, a style is more like a skin than a coat. He never "played the sedulous ape" to other writers.[4] "How nearly does this manner of writing represent his real manner of thinking and existing?"[5] he asked. In his Journal (15 July 1835) he records his doubts of himself—"I seldom read in any dud of a book, novel, or the like, where the writing seems to flow along like talk . . . without a certain pain, a certain envy . . . . What to do? To write on *the best one can*, get the free'st, sincerest possible utterance." This he did, and on 12 January 1837, when he had finished the *French Revolution*, he told his wife he did not know whether the book was worth anything, or what the world would do with it, but that he could say to the world: "You have not had for a hundred years any book that comes more direct and flamingly from the heart of a living man. Do what you like with it, you ——"[6] We may take the world's opinion of this book as typical of what it thought of the rest of the histories.[7]

The *French Revolution*, as Thackeray wrote two months after its appearance,[8] "raised among the critics and the reading public a strange storm of applause and discontent." He himself makes some apology for the style so much attacked. Citing the passage that tells of the Taking of the Bastile, he asks: "Could sober prose have described the incident in briefer words, more emphatically, or more sensibly?" Adverse criticism continued and it is still

[1] *Goethe.*   [2] *Jean Paul Friedrich Richter.*
[3] *Sartor*, bk. iii. ch. 12.
[4] G. Balfour, *Life of R. L. Stevenson*, p. 100, the confession of Stevenson himself.
[5] *J. P. F. Richter.*   [6] *Life in London*, i. p. 89.
[7] See Firth's Introduction to Carlyle's *Cromwell* (1904), p. xxxiv.
[8] Review of the book.

CARLYLE

heard. Lowell, in 1871, complained that Carlyle's history was "history seen by flashes of lightning." Lord Acton wrote to Miss Gladstone that Carlyle was, in his opinion, "the most detestable of all historians," with the single exception of Froude. E. A. Freeman disliked him along with Plato, Ruskin and Virgil—an interesting group.[1] "Do what you like with it!"

The book has held its own for seventy years, and a good many historians have risen and become obsolete in the meantime. It all depends on what the reader really wants, whether he praise or blame, and here it seems as if something in Carlyle's historical work actually does appeal to thoughtful people, for his histories are not for the lazy. Lowell admits that Carlyle's criticism of men in his essays is one "based on wide and various study, which, careless of tradition, applied its standard to the real and not the contemporary worth," that he has "an unerring eye for that fleeting expression of the moral features of character, a perception of which alone makes the drawing of a coherent likeness possible." And here perhaps lies his greatest value as a historian. His sympathy with men, his insight, turns him into an eye-witness—and, more than that, into a participant in every action. When Lowell says that he "teaches us comparatively little," he probably means that it is sometimes hard to realize from Carlyle the exact position of affairs at the moment, and so it is. That is the difficulty of the eye-witness. Carlyle brings the Revolution and its men and women into our life—together they form an experience we can never outlive. The reader can say with emotion *Et quorum pars magna fui*. This may be a "detestable" way of writing history—the critic who so judged never got his history written at all. There are many ways in which history may be written. Some of the most admired lead to history of a kind no human being can read. Is it history if it is dead?

Carlyle's men and women live, and that in no conven-

[1] Bryce, *Contemporary Biography*, p. 269.

tional sense of the word.[1] They are not "people in books." We see into them too well, and see out of them—"see the world with their eyes, feel as they felt, judge as they judged." Not one is an abstraction or an allegory—not even "the poor sea-green Formula." Robespierre is, like Shylock, a possibility within every one of us. "Wert thou worse than other advocates? Stricter man, according to his Formula, to his Credo and his Cant, of probities, benevolences, pleasures-of-virtue, and such like, lived not in that age. A man fitted, in some luckier settled age, to have become one of those incorruptible barren Pattern-Figures and have marble-tablets and funeral-sermons." He might have been a historian of the most accurate type; but to continue: "His poor landlord, the Cabinet-maker in the Rue Saint-Honoré, loved him; his Brother died for him. May God be merciful to him and to us!"

Various criticisms have been passed upon Carlyle's *Cromwell*. We are told by some critics to remember that Cromwell was human—a man of like passions with ourselves. But this is really a tribute to Carlyle, for before he wrote there was little disposition to admit so much. Right or wrong in this or that matter or in his general conception, he forced Englishmen to re-study Cromwell without "hysterics." More than this Cromwell himself would not have asked. It is the verdict of Professor Firth that Carlyle "triumphantly achieved" his main purposes, which were to show that Cromwell was "not a man of falsehoods but a man of truths" and to make "the heart of that grand Puritan business once again visible."

When we are reminded that there are inaccuracies in Carlyle's books, we may remember that much[2] that is accessible to his critics was not in print in his day, and then we may own at once that he made slips, that he

---

[1] "It is a superb prose epic, not a history . . . . On the other hand he excels in portraits, and the King, the Queen, Lafayette, Mirabeau, Danton, Robespierre, are still what he left them." G. P. Gooch, in *Cambridge Modern History*, xii. 838.

[2] E.g. the *Clarke Papers*, Gooch loc. cit.

misconceived and grew tired. If his History "fluttered or wabbled" sometimes, it was still his aim to trust only to the two wings named by Sauerteig—to "stern Accuracy in inquiring" as much as to "bold Imagination in expounding." His *Frederick* was at once translated into German, and was long used in the German military schools, as an authority on Frederick's campaigns. This at least suggests that criticisms of Carlyle on the score of inaccuracy may themselves need to be weighed.

"Do what you like with it,"—his work was done, and there followed a long period of waiting—" looking steadfastly into the silent continents."

On February the 4th, 1881, he died, and a few days later he was buried in the snow-clad graveyard at Ecclefechan, reunited, as he wished to be, in death with those who in life had been most to him. Of the world's judgments upon him he thought little. He took the Prussian "Order of Merit," because he could not well refuse it. Disraeli's offer of a title and a pension he declined. It was not for these things that he had worked. "How will this look in the Universe and before the Creator of Man?"

That question few of us will care to try to resolve, but in the meantime a tentative answer may be gathered from movements of contemporary thought. Thirty years have passed since Carlyle's death, and we can begin to take note of the correspondence or dissonance of his thoughts with those that most live among men, " born enemies of lies " as they are.

To begin ; the cult of the strong man, proclaimed in every work of a popular writer of our day, bears a strong likeness to Carlyle's "hero-worship." It is unhappy that, on the whole, the preference is given to the hero of the Francia type—the drastic administrator, who "takes up the white man's burden," and rules the black man with a rod of iron. It is a pity, too, that the Francias of contemporary literature and contemporary politics have not all the South American's ideas; they seem more materialistic. The story of the shoemaker and the gallows shows where Carlyle found Francia's excellence —he would make men honest by act of autocrat. Physical well-being and political obedience are all the strong man seems to care about to-day; the spiritual and moral development of his charge, "half devil and half child," seems to be a remoter interest. Some day, perhaps, our generation, or another, may move on toward a hero of higher quality—the spiritual hero, whom Carlyle himself preferred, who shall stand to some of our heroes, in and out of our books, as Cromwell and Luther stood to Dr Francia,—and feel again, as Carlyle felt, the spiritual dignities and powers of Man.

Meanwhile, in the second place, along another line of thought and action, Carlyle's teaching is being fulfilled, and that so vigorously that it becomes yearly harder to understand what a pioneer Carlyle was. All he taught of work and poverty—new and strange as it was to the cultured and well-to-do of his day—is now finding fuller expression in action, individual, social and national. As men and as nations, we are realizing more and more fully the duties and responsibilities of wealth and culture and the sufferings and the needs of poverty. Legislation is more and more directed to bring within the reach of the poorest the possibilities of decent living, of constant work, of an old age with some other background than the workhouse. Not these alone, but the other needs of men, which Carlyle felt more keenly than some of his critics,—the needs of inward sustenance, of training for mind and soul, of education in the largest sense, these too fall within our outlook to-day, and more and more is done to meet them; and here too, if others were with him, Carlyle gave utterance to the craving as did no other man of letters of his century.

Finally, when we turn to the inmost things in man, do men re-affirm Carlyle's conviction of man's spiritual

CARLYLE

nature, of the supreme value of belief, the imperative claims of duty, the significance of the Hero and of the Facts? Is there less thrashing of powdered straw? Are there signs of " a spiritual return to the open air?"

"The Highest Gospel was a biography,"[1] wrote Carlyle. "The Old World knew nothing of Conversion: instead of an *Ecce Homo*, they had only some *Choice of Hercules*. It was a new-attained progress in the Moral Development of man: hereby has the Highest come home to the bosoms of the most Limited; what to Plato was but a hallucination, and to Socrates a chimera, is now clear and certain to your Zinzendorfs, your Wesleys, and the poorest of their Pietists and Methodists."[2] "Look on our divinest Symbol: on Jesus of Nazareth, and his Life, and his Biography, and what followed therefrom. Higher has human Thought not yet reached: this is Christianity and Christendom; a Symbol of quite perennial, infinite character; whose significance will ever demand to be anew inquired into, and anew made manifest."[3] What does the Symbol mean? Here is a passage from a letter to his brother: "'Be of good cheer, I have *overcome* the world': so said the wisest man, when what was his overcoming? Poverty, despite, forsakenness, and the near prospect of an accursed Cross. 'Be of good cheer; I have overcome the world.' These words on the streets of Edinburgh last winter almost brought tears into my eyes."[4]

Duty and the Hero are his two fixed points, and to them Christian thought seems to be returning. In a well-known work, which represents perhaps the strongest school of Christian thinkers to-day, the return to these great facts of experience as the basis of all Christian thinking and living is emphasized and developed as of fundamental significance. "The Christian's consciousness that God communes with him rests on two objective facts, the first

---

[1] *Boswell*.
[2] *Sartor*, bk. ii. ch. 10.
[3] *Sartor*, bk. iii. ch. 3.
[4] *Early Life*, ii. 378.

of which is the historical fact of the Person of Jesus. ... The second objective ground is that we hear within ourselves the demand of the moral law."[1] These are the words of Wilhelm Herrmann, of Marburg. Are the thoughts not familiar to the reader of Carlyle in every variety of emphatic language?

But the man is more than his words, more than any thought that he can put into words. With all his mistakes in history and criticism (and they are not as many as might be supposed from the tone of certain writers)—with all his mistakes in life and character, he remains a great and helpful Man in virtue of his open eye and heart, his sincerity, his conviction of "the divine and awful nature of God's truth "—

> Im Ganzen, Guten, Wahren,
> Resolut zu leben.[2]

[1] Herrmann, *Communion with God* (tr. 2nd ed. p. 103.)
[2] It is perhaps significant that Carlyle at least twice misquotes this passage as above. In Goethe's *Generalbeichte*, the passage runs:

> Uns vom Halben zu entwöhnen,
> Und im Ganzen, Guten, Schönen,
> Resolut zu leben.

INDEX

"Aaron's old wardrobe," 40.
Acrasia, 26, 27.
Acton, Lord, 309.
Aldeburgh, 214, 224, 225.
Algebra, the first English, 5.
Allegory, 17, 18, 21, 126, 128.
America, 9, 10, 19, 77, 105, 163, 201, 206-207, 211, 278.
Animal lore in 16th century, 20.
Aristotle, 126, 130, 287.
Armada, 8, 11.
Arthur, King, 17, 18.
Ashford, Isaac, 231, 232.
Augustine, St., 118, 129.
Austen, Jane, 229.
Austen, Lady, 157-158.

Barbados, 109.
Bastile, fall of, 257, 308.
Beaupuy, Michel, 254, 255.
Bellay, du, 5, 14.
Birmingham, 167.
Blair, Dr Hugh, 187.
Boswell, James, his character, 178, 185, 196, 197, 201-202, 208.
    his father, 177, 197, 202, 203.
    education, 175.
    his "facility of manners," 175, 191.
    his charm, 184, 185.
    ridiculous, 185, 186.
    "longer a boy," 193.
    cultivation of the great, 176, 187.
    frequently in love, 176, 188, 196.

Boswell, James—*continued*.
    wishes to enter army, 177
    his Greek and Latin, 177, 195.
    his interest in literature, 177, 179.
    contemplation of himself, 191, 196, 209.
    "naturally somewhat singular," 197.
    "luxury of noble sentiment," 192.
    drink, 177, 196, 197, 199, 200.
    introduction to Johnson, 175, 179, 180-182
    friendship with Johnson, 183, 184.
    views on religion, 176, 183, 201, 203, 204.
    on morals, 189-190, 197.
    "*encore* the cow," 187.
    in Holland, 188.
    Corsica, 189-195.
    friendship with Paoli, 190-194.
    journey to Hebrides, 188, 197-203.
    views on Scotland, 189.
    marriage, 196, 197, 203, 208.
    "*gust* for London," 177, 179, 197, 203.
    his writings, 177.
        Corsica, 193-194.
        Life of Johnson, 207, 209, 210.
    fidelity to fact, 205, 209.
    his verses, 177, 185.
    his letters, 196, 204, 207.
Bourne, Vincent, 146.
Brandes, G., 285.
Bristol, 87-88, 104-106, 272, 284.

Britomart, 24, 27.
Broadmead Records, 104, 106, 109.
Browne, Sir Richard, 84-85, 95.
Browne, Sir Thomas, 74, 82, 100, 118.
Browning, Robert, 68, 307.
Bull, William, 155, 167-169.
Bunyan, John—
  birth, 115.
  education, 107, 140.
  temperament, 122-124, 128-129.
  appearance, 142.
  the books he read, 115, 133.
  soldiering, 118.
  story of his conversion, 117-124, 128.
  consciousness of Christian past, 115.
  minister in Bedford, 106-107.
  first imprisonments, 107-114.
  last imprisonment, 114, 124.
  first wife, 115, 118.
  second wife and children, 110.
  his sound sense, 124.
  value of his books, 114-115.
  the happiness in them, 116-117.
  the plain style, 117.
  written out of his experience, 117, 128-129, 133, 134.
  mastery of language, 117.
  imagination, 123, 137.
  his enjoyment in writing, 124-125
  his humour, 125-126, 134.
  originality, 126.
  nobility of his theme, 127-128.
  preconceptions, 130.
  character-drawing, 130-134, 137.
  self-revelation of his characters, 130.

Bunyan, John—*continued*.
  gift of narrative. 135.
  dialogue, 134, 139.
  effect of his books, 142.
  their popularity, 142.
  his verses, 112, 113, 136, 140, 141.
  his books—
    Grace Abounding, 114, 117-124.
    Pilgrim's Progress, Part I., 114-116, 124-135.
    Holy War, 135-137.
    Pilgrim's Progress, Part II., 138.
Burke, Edmund, 187, 211.
Burleigh, Lord, 8.
Burnet, Gilbert, 87.
Burns, Robert, 208, 235-239, 241.
Burton, 14, 78.
Byron, Lord, 232, 283, 284.

CAMBRIDGE, 80, 99.
  Spenser, 5.
  Milton, 38-41.
  Evelyn, 88.
  Cowper's brother, 145, 147.
  Gray, 177, 225.
  Wordsworth, 250-253.
  studies and interests in 16th century, 6.
  in 17th century, 38-41.
  in 18th century, 250-252.
Camden, 40.
Carlyle, Jane W., 288, 306-307.
Carlyle, Thomas—
  his parents, 280-282, 291.
  birth, 280.
  upbringing, 281, 286, 291, 294.
  neat-handedness, 287.
  dyspepsia, 287, 288.
  his seriousness, 290-291.
  sincerity, 292, 299.

INDEX

Carlyle, Thomas—*continued*.
  instinct for reality, 292-293, 296-298, 301.
  religion, 295-302, 313-314.
  principles in writing, 305-306.
  his style, 307-309.
  character-drawing, 288, 310.
  on order, 287.
  on belief, 286.
  on how to criticize, 280, 289.
  on humour, 290.
  on musical thought, 292-293.
  on history, 293, 306.
  on hunger, 294.
  on heroes, 302-305, 311, 313.
  his writings—
    French Revolution, 308-309.
    Cromwell, 310.
    Frederick, 311.
  his great vogue, 279.
  his work and its effects, 311-314.
  Carlyle on Spenser, 24.
  on Burns, 240.
  on Wordsworth, 262.
  on Coleridge, 295-297.
Cartwright, Thomas, 6.
Cervantes, 22, 23, 35, 127, 137.
Charles I., 81, 85, 165.
Charles II., 60, 85, 87, 90-96, 104.
Chaucer, Geoffrey, 12, 13, 14.
Church, R. W., 1, 5, 6, 26.
Civil War, 50, 56, 82.
Clarendon, Lord, 91, 92, 94.
Clarendon Code, 92-93, 104-105.
Classics, study of, 14, 43, 80, 102, 146, 172, 177, 195, 223.
Coleridge, S. T., 127, 155, 242, 245, 265, 270-272, 295-297.
Comets, 71, 74.
Conington, John, 146.
Copernicus, 48, 49.
Corsica, 189-195.

Cottle, Joseph, 272, 296.
Cowley, Abraham, 76, 89, 91, 100, 102, 103.
Cowper, William—
  the Cowper family, 144, 145.
  Whig tradition, 144, 146.
  classical training, 146.
  nine years at the Bar, 144.
  the House of Lords affair, 144-145.
  insanity, 122, 145, 172.
  Christian conviction, 145.
  humour, 144, 146, 154-155.
  at Huntingdon, 147.
  lives with the Unwins, 149.
  life at Olney, 149-150, 161-165, 169-170.
  gardening, 152.
  his hares, 152-153.
  feeling for Nature, 158-160.
  politics, 164-167.
  feeling for poverty, 162-163.
  Sunday School, 163.
  friendships, 147, 148, 150, 155, 157, 167, 169.
  his dress, 170-171.
  diet, 169-170.
  removal to Weston Underwood, 171.
  translates Homer, 172.
  portraits, 171.
  his letters, 146, 160-161, 173-174.
    Wordsworth on them, 161.
    "talking letters," 160.
  his poetry—
    ease of his metre, 146.
    Olney Hymns, 151.
    Progress of Error, 153.
    his first volume, 153-156.
    John Gilpin, 158.
    The Task, 158-160.
    likeness to Wordsworth, 153, 159, 160.
    The Castaway, 173.
Cowper and Milton, 62.

Cowper, W.—*continued*.
   Cowper and Johnson, "his old jacket," 62.
   Cowper and Bunyan, 122.
Crabbe, George—
   parents, 214, 215.
   birth, 214.
   early surroundings, 212, 214, 218
   education, 215.
   goes to London, 221.
   relations with Burke, 211-214.
   his wife, 215, 221-222.
   his sons, 216, 228.
   interest in botany, 220
   ordination, 221.
   a Whig, 221.
   relations with Dr Johnson, 222-223.
   on marriage, 229.
   "poet of disillusion," 232.
   not "stern," 232-233.
   criticism of Gray and Goldsmith, 223-227, 233-235.
   his poems, 212, 213.
      Inebriety, 219-220.
      The Village, 222-228.
      The Newspaper, 228.
      The Parish Register, 228, 233.
      Tales of the Hall, 229.
Cromwell, Oliver, 56, 57, 60, 87, 90, 92, 110, 116, 117, 139, 202, 291, 310.

DEFOE, Daniel, 35.
Don Quixote, 22, 127, 247.
Drake, Francis, 9.
Drummond of Hawthornden, 8.
Dryden, John, 72, 97, 274.

Eikon Basilike, 52, 53, 57.
Eldon, Lord, 282, 285.
Elephant's knees, 81-82.
Elizabeth, Queen, 1, 4.

Ellwood, Thomas, 72, 105, 106, 111.
Emerson, R. W., 285.
England—
   in 16th century, 9-12.
   in 17th century, 37-40, 74, 77-79, 97, 105.
   in 18th century, 161-166, 167, 169, 216-218, 221, 223-228, 230-232, 259-260.
   in 19th century, 282-286, 294-295.
   in 20th century, 312.
Eros and Anteros, 53-54.
Erskine, Hon. Andrew, 178.
Euphues, 16.
Evelyn, John—
   his parents, 77, 79, 81.
   birth, 77.
   education, 79.
   begins to keep a diary, 79
   his miscellaneous learning, 79-80.
   false quantity, 81.
   foreign travels, 81-85.
   on Popish relics, 84.
   arts, 84.
   marriage, 84-86.
   his character, 75.
   typically English, 75.
   settles at Sayes Court, 87.
   travels in England, 87-88.
   Church of England, 77, 79, 81, 93-94, 102.
   little interest in liberty, 81.
   relations with the Kings, 82, 85, 87, 91, 94, 97
   tendency to moralize, 75, 81, 91, 92, 96, 98.
   the Royal Society, 75, 100.
   friendship with Pepys, 98-99.
   garden 90.
   his death, 102.
   his writings, 76, 86, 88, 89, 90, 94, 100-102.
   on comets, 74.

INDEX

Evelyn, John—*continued*.
  on Milton, 76.
  on Sectaries, 88-89.
Evelyn, Mrs, 85.

FAIRYLAND, 18-22.
Feeblemind, 125.
Fenwick, Isabella, 246.
Firth, C. H., **87**, 310.
Fitzgerald, Edward, 150, 229, 279, 291.
Fox, Charles James, 195, 213, 260.
Fox, George, 79, 92, 106, 108, 109, 110, 115.
Foxe, Martyrologist, 13.
Francia, Dr, 287, 303, 311, 312.
Franklin, Benjamin, 153.
Freeman, E. A., 205, 309.
French Revolution, 233, 282.
  Cowper, 166.
  Wordsworth, 233, 244, 253-262.
  Carlyle, 294.
Froude, J. A., 124, 279, 288, 309.

GALILEO, 47, 48, 56.
Garrick, David, 182, 186.
Gauden, 52.
Geography, 9.
George III., Cowper on, 165-166.
Gibbon, Edward, 185.
Glasgow, 234, 284.
Glover, Robert, 115.
Godwin, William, 256-258, 261.
Goethe, 62, 257, 291, 298, 308, 314.
Goldsmith, Oliver, 174, 179, 186, 199, 223, 225, 227, 233-235.
Gray, Thomas, 177, 185, 194, 223, 225, 226.
Green, T. H., 275, 279.
Grenville, W. W., 164-165.

Gunning, Henry, 250.
Guyon, Madame, 168-169.
Guyon, Sir, 25-27.

HAKLUYT, 10.
Harcourt, Sir William, 300.
Harvey, Gabriel, 6, 15.
Hayley, 172.
Hebrides, 197-202.
Heine, Heinrich, 126, 285.
Herodotus, 186.
Herrick, 26.
Herrmann, W., 313-314.
Hesketh, Lady, 149, 160.
Hexameter, English, 15.
Homer, 172.
Horace, 154, 187, 221.
  compared with Cowper by Conington, 146.
Hume, David, 176, 194.
Hunt, Leigh, 287.
Huxley, T. H., 279.

IGNATIUS' Epistles, 52.
Iliad, 112.
Ireland—
  in 17th century, 7.
  Goldsmith, 233.

JAMES II., 97.
Jeffrey, Lord, 291, 305.
Jeffreys, Judge, 97.
Jews, 82.
Johnson, Johnny, 160, 172.
Johnson, Joseph, 153, 256.
Johnson, Samuel—
  references, 41, 50, 51, 53, 60, 62, 72, 147, 211, 287, 295.
  on Whigs, 51, 175, 202.
  "That great CHAM," 179.
  Horace Walpole on Johnson, 179.
  his appearance, 180-181, 182-183.
  on Scots and Scotland, 182, 188, 189, 200.

Johnson, Samuel—*continued*.
  on "the young dogs," 183.
  shelters the helpless, 183, 204.
  corrects Crabbe's poems, 222-223.
  journey to Hebrides, 188, 197-203.
  shortens his friends' names, 199.
  religion, 204.
  never querulous, 205.
  "clear your *mind* of cant," 205.
  his gift for nonsense, 205-206.
  on America, 206-207.
Jonson, Ben, 1, 8, 77.
Jowett, Benjamin, 209, 288, 297, 299.

K, the letter, 188.
Kant, 127.
Keats, John, on Spenser, 43.
  on Milton, 45.
  in Scotland, 237.

LAMB, Charles, 58-59, 146, 161, 172, 210, 242, 246.
Lamb, Mary, 88.
Latimer, Bp., 108.
Latin, 107, 108, 140.
Laud, Abp., 38, 39, 79, 105.
Legouis, E., 245, 254, 255, 285.
Leland, C. G., 279.
Lepanto, battle in 1571, 6.
l'Estrange, Roger, 60.
Lincoln, Abraham, 191.
Lockhart, J. G., 174, 213.
London, 4, 5, 11, 91, 161, 253.
  its smoke, 101.
Longinus, 276.
Lonsdale, Lord, 208, 246.
Lords, House of, "wise and independent," 207.
Lowell, J. R., 309.
Lucan, 63.
Lucian, *Hermotimus*, 131, 132.

Luther, Martin, 39, 115, 280, 286, 288, 304.

MACAULAY, Lord, 124, 185.
Marvell, Andrew, 61.
Mary, Queen, 4, 115.
Merivale, Herman, 294.
Mill, J. S., 242, 243.
Milnes, R. M., 287, 297.
Milton, Christopher, 77.
Milton, John—
  his parents, 35.
  birth, 35.
  education, 35-40.
  the classics, 43.
  Protestantism, 35.
  England in his day, 37, 39, 40.
  views on church government, 41, 51, 52.
  years of retirement, 42, 43.
  his preparation, 44.
  slow choice of subject, 35, 61.
  foreign travel, 46.
  return home, 50.
  marriage, 53-57.
  Latin secretary, 57.
  blindness, 57-59.
  at the Restoration, 60, 61.
  his old age, 72.
  death, 73.
  his style, 62-65.
  his seriousness, 36.
  his sense of truth, 56.
  his progressive mind, 39, 53, 69.
  his imagination, 66.
  his sense for freedom, 39-41, 46-47, 50, 56.
  his sense of a call, 41.
  his early poetic gifts, 42.
  his interest in stars, 45, 47-50, 66.
  appeal of sound, 45.
  his controversies, 51, 58.
  views on marriage, 53-55.
  on civil government, 57-58, 74.

INDEX

Milton, John—*continued.*
  on poetry, 62, 65.
  on sin, 67-68.
  on Providence, 68, 69.
  his use of symbol, 65, 68, 70.
  his writings—
    Psalm cxxxvi., 42.
    Ode on Nativity, 43.
    L'Allegro, 44, 45.
    Il Penseroso, 44-46.
    Areopagitica, 56, 66-67, 71.
    Paradise Lost, 62-71.
    Paradise Regained, 72
  Milton on Spenser, 13, 17, 25, 26, 43.
  Evelyn on Milton, 76.
  Wordsworth on Milton, 35, 38, 39.
  Cowper on Milton, 62.
Mirabeau, 289, 304.
Mittimus, 107, 109.
Montaigne, vii., 14, 19.
More, Hannah, 41, 209.
Morley, Lord, 57, 245, 267.
Moseley, Humphrey, 34.

NAPOLEON, 189, 258.
Negroes, 207.
Newton, John, 150-151.
Nietzsche, 230.
North's *Plutarch*, 7.
Novalis, 280.
Nowell accounts, 5.

OLNEY, life at, 149-152, 155-156, 157, 161-165, 169.
Olney Hymns, 151-154.
Oxford, 51, 79, 82.

PAOLI, Pascal, 190-194, 196.
Paris, 84, 86.
Penn, William, 74, 105.
Pepys, Samuel, 48, 76, 91, 92, 93, 98-99, 105, 133.
Petrarch, 5, 14.

Plato, 2, 6, 17, 22, 27, 40, 127, 154, 287, 309.
Powell, Mary, and her family, 53-56
Priestley, 167.
Prisons, 110-112.
Protestantism, 4, 11
Puritanism, 6, 11, 16, 27, 37-38.

RABELAIS, 4, 14
Raleigh, Sir Walter, 8, 10, 17, 77.
Red Cross Knight, 4, 18, 21, 29.
Reformation, 9, 11, 35-36, 37.
Religious toleration, etc., 46-47, 60, 90, 93, 104-106, 166, 167, 285.
Renaissance, 9.
Restoration of Charles II., 60-61, 90-91.
Reynolds, Sir Joshua, 183, 186, 187, 209, 213.
Robespierre, M., 292, 310.
Robinson Crusoe, 127.
Romney, George, 171.
Rousseau, J. J., 57, 187, 188, 189, 257.

SCIENCE—
  popular notions, 69, 70, 127.
Scotland in 18th century, 197, 198.
Scott, Sir Walter, 229.
Sects in England, 38, 78-79, 88-89, 105, 109, 115, 167, 285.
Selden, John, 89.
Sidney, Sir Philip, 7, 8, 15, 17, 20, 52
"Simple, sensuous, and passionate," 65.
Slavery, 207.
Smerwick, 7.
Smith, Adam, 175, 180.

21

Smith, Sydney, 289.
Snuff-boxes, 167.
Spenser, Edmund—
  birth, 4.
  education, 5.
  "Rosalind," 7.
  at court, 7, 8.
  in Ireland, 7, 8, 9.
  marriage, 8.
  death, 8-9.
  his contact with his age, 9-12.
  literary interests, 5, 12-15, 16, 20.
  poetic theory, 15, 16.
  metre, 24, 25.
  feeling for beauty, 2-3, 27, 28, 30, 32, 269.
  feeling for truth, 4, 29, 30.
  religion, 29-32.
  Platonism, 6, 17, 22, 27.
  Puritanism, 6, 11, 16, 27.
  sincerity, 3.
  humour, 15, 17.
  his picture of hero, 17, 23.
  Protestantism, 4.
  on Incarnation, 31.
  mutability, 32-33.
  defects, 1.
  his poems—
    Shepheard's Calender, 7, 16, 17.
    Faerie Queene, 17.
    Hymne in Honour of Beautie, 2.
    Hymne of Heavenlie Love, 30-32.
Spenser and later poets, 13, 17, 25, 26, 43.
  did Bunyan read *Faerie Queene*? 126, 133.
Sterling, John, 285, 300.
Sunday School, 163.

TALUS, the iron man, 7, 12, 14.
Tasso, 14, 25.

Taylor, Sir Henry, 246, 278.
Taylor, Jeremy, 99-100.
Teedons, Samuel, 122, 155-157
Telescope—
  in Milton, 47-48.
Temple, W. J., 175, 177, 196.
Tennyson, Alfred, 64, 287.
Terrill, Edward, 104, 109, 116.
Throckmorton, Sir John and Lady, 155, 171.
Thurlow, Lord, 213.
Tobacco, 10, 167.
Tompkyns, T., licenser, 71.
Tortoises, 85.
Tovell family circle, 216-218.
Transportation of dissenters, 109.
Turks, 6, 83.

UNA, 24, 29.
Unwins, the, 148-150.
Ussher, 52.

VIRGIL, 15, 16, 25, 151, 154, 190, 195, 223, 227, 309.
Voltaire, 188, 289, 297.

WALLER, Edmund, 76.
Walpole, Horace, 179-180, 185, 187, 209.
Walton, Izaak, 89.
Wesley, John, 194, 227, 257.
Wiclif, 14, 37.
"Wiggle-waggle," 204.
Wordsworth, Dorothy, 247, 251, 263-266, 271.
Wordsworth, William—
  environment, 244.
  training, 247.
  character and temperament, 233, 244, 246.
  "impulses," 247, 249, 253, 267.
  autobiography, 245-246.
  birth, 246.
  at Cambridge, 250-253.

INDEX

Wordsworth, William—*contd.*
  in Switzerland, 253.
  in France, 253-256.
  French Revolution, 233, 244, 254-262.
  Nature, 247, 248, 264-270.
  imagination, 249.
  studies Godwin, 256-258, 261-263.
  and French war, 259-260.
  "jaws like a crocodile," 262.
  life with his sister, 263.
  marriage, 263-264, 278.
  restoration, 264-272.
  feeling on beauty, 267-269, 275.
  his canons of poetry, 3, 272-276.
  truth to fact, 273, 274.

Wordsworth, William—*contd.*
  language, 274, 276.
  his poems—
    Prelude, 245-272 *passim.*
    Evening Walk, 256.
    The Echo, 269.
    Excursion, 270.
    Tintern Abbey, 240, 271, 277.
    Lyrical Ballads, 272.
    their effect, 242-243.
  on Spenser, 25, 252.
  on Milton, 35, 42, 72.
  on Cowper, 161.
  on Burns, 239-240.
  quoted, 3, 26, 123, 233.
Worldly Wiseman, 130-131.

XENOPHON, 6, 17, 18.

For Product Safety Concerns and Information please contact our EU
representative GPSR@taylorandfrancis.com
Taylor & Francis Verlag GmbH, Kaufingerstraße 24, 80331 München, Germany

www.ingramcontent.com/pod-product-compliance
Lightning Source LLC
Chambersburg PA
CBHW071801300426
44116CB00009B/1164